Hot & Spicy

This is a Parragon Publishing Book
This edition published in 2004

Parragon Publishing
Queen Street House
4 Queen Street
Bath BA1 1HE, UK

ISBN: 1-40544-384-7

Printed in China

Produced by the Bridgewater Book Company Ltd.

NOTE

This book uses imperial, metric, and US cup measurements. Follow the
same units of measurement throughout; do not mix imperial and metric.
All spoon measurements are level: teaspoons are assumed to be 5 ml,
and tablespoons are assumed to be 15 ml. Unless otherwise stated,
milk is assumed to be whole, eggs and individual vegetables such as
potatoes are medium, and pepper is freshly ground black pepper.

The times given for each recipe are an approximate guide
only because the cooking times may vary as a result of the
types of oven and other equipment used.

Recipes using raw or very lightly cooked eggs should be
avoided by infants, the elderly, pregnant women, convalescents, and
anyone suffering from an illness. Pregnant and breast-feeding women
are advised to avoid eating peanuts and peanut products.

Hot & Spicy

p

Contents-Indian

Contents-Thai

Indian

Introduction

Indian cuisine is among the most diverse and versatile in the world, employing a wide range of cooking techniques and a vast array of ingredients and flavors. This is hardly surprising given the sheer size of the country and its long and eventful history. The story of Indian food is, indeed, one of geography and history, but it is also profoundly influenced by religion, and these three elements are closely interwoven with one another.

Each region of India has its own specialties and characteristic dishes. For example, Mumbai, formerly Bombay, is famous for its pork curries, while Bengali cuisine features fish and Madras is well known for its superb vegetarian food. Nevertheless, in broad culinary terms the country can be divided into the north and south. The dishes of the north bear witness to a succession of invasions throughout the centuries, whereas foreign influences are less pronounced in the south.

The Moguls left a heritage of finely prepared, creamy, and rich-tasting dishes, while India is indebted to the Persians for pilafs and many other rice dishes, and to the Portuguese for the introduction of vinegar, the defining ingredient of vindaloo curries. Portuguese and Spanish explorers were also responsible for introducing the chili to Asia from its native South America.

Only the British, it seems, had little effect on the country's cooking. However, so enamored were they of Indian

seasonings and chutneys that they did much to spread the word of this delicious cuisine.

An abundance of fruit and vegetables grows in the south and, together with lentils and rice, features in the staple dishes of the region. The north is a wheat-growing area and a wide variety of different bread is produced. The main religion in southern India is Hinduism and so the majority of the population is vegetarian. There are many Hindus in the north too, but observance of a vegetarian diet is often less strict. Meat, mainly lamb and chicken, does feature in traditional dishes, although no Hindu would eat beef, because the cow is regarded as a sacred animal. In coastal areas, many Hindus eat fish, not classifying it as meat. Muslim communities eat all kinds of meat, apart from pork or products derived from pigs, which are thought to be unclean. Other groups who practise other religions are scattered throughout the country, whether Christians in the former Portuguese colony of Goa, Middle Eastern Jews, or Parsees, all of whom have their own dietary regulations and traditional foods.

Cooking techniques and equipment

One of the great things about Indian cooking is that it rarely requires much last-minute attention. It also needs little in the way of special equipment. Most Western kitchens will already include virtually everything you need to prepare the recipes in this book.

The proper blending of spices is an essential part of Indian cooking. Indian cooks grind fresh spices for each dish, using a stone rolling pin and flat stone called a sil and batta, or a heavy stone or cast-iron mortar and pestle called a hamal-dista. These are available from specialty shops, but you can use an ordinary mortar and pestle or spice grinder instead.

A heavy-bottom skillet is essential and, if you are keen on Balti dishes, you might want to invest in a karahi or Balti pan. Resembling a wok, this has a round base and two handles. A tava or tawa is a kind of grill pan used by Indian cooks for roasting spices and cooking chapatis and other flat breads. However, neither is essential if you have a good quality skillet.

Other specialty equipment includes a coconut grater, called a narial kas, and a fine strainer called a chalni. While it is fun to use authentic tools, an ordinary grater and strainer will serve the purpose.

The one piece of specialty equipment for which there is no Western equivalent is the tandoor, a clay or brick oven, which is popular in parts of northern India. Several tandoori recipes that have been adapted for cooking in a Western-style oven are included in this book.

Special ingredients
Asafetida

This is a pungent spice; its foul smell disappears on cooking and it adds a pleasant flavor to dishes. It is best bought ground and stored in an airtight container.

Ata flour

Also known as chapati flour, this is a whole-wheat flour widely used for making breads. Well sifted whole-wheat flour can be used instead.

Besan

Also known as gram flour, this is made from chickpeas. It is used to flavor and thicken curries and for making pakoras and bhajias.

Paneer

This smooth, white cheese with a delicate flavor is used throughout India by both vegetarians and meat eaters—it is often combined with meat. Ricotta cheese may be used instead.

Chana dal

A split yellow lentil with a slightly sweet taste, chana dal are used in a variety of vegetable dishes and as a binding agent.

Fenugreek

The fresh herb is used in a number of vegetable dishes and in some meat dishes. Always discard the stalks, which taste unpleasantly bitter, and use only the small leaves. Fenugreek seeds give curry spice mixes their strong aroma.

Ghee

Clarified butter or ghee used to be the standard cooking fat throughout India. Nowadays, vegetable ghee, often corn oil, is more popular because it contains less saturated fat.

Kalonji

Also known as nigella, these tiny black seeds have a slight peppery flavor and are used mainly in vegetable dishes.

Masoor dal

These split red lentils are widely available and are used in many dishes. They are actually orange in color and become much paler when they are cooked.

Moong dal

This split yellow lentil is quite similar to chana dal, but smaller.

Panch phoran

This is an Indian mix of five spices—cumin seeds, onion seeds, mustard seeds, fenugreek seeds, and anise.

Tamarind

Sour tasting and strongly flavored, this is the sticky, dried, dark brown pod of the tamarind plant. It has to be soaked in hot water, then strained before use. Tamarind paste is more convenient to use and is available in jars from Asian food stores. If unavailable, you can use lemon juice as a substitute.

Toor dal

This split lentil is similar to chana dal.

Urid dal

This lentil is available with its hull, which is black, and may be called black gram, or hulled, when it is creamy white. It takes quite a long time to cook.

Basic Recipes

curry paste

4 tbsp coriander seeds

2 tbsp cumin seeds

1 tbsp fenugreek seeds

1 tbsp fennel seeds

2 curry leaves

2 dried red chilies

2 tsp ground turmeric

2 tsp chili powder

5 tbsp white wine vinegar

2 tbsp water

½ cup vegetable oil, plus extra
   for sealing

1 Grind the coriander, cumin, fenugreek, and fennel seeds, curry leaves, and dried red chilies in a spice grinder or with a mortar and pestle. Transfer to a bowl and stir in the turmeric, chili powder, vinegar, and water to make a smooth paste.

2 Heat the vegetable oil in a large, heavy-bottom skillet, then add the paste and cook over low heat, stirring constantly, for 10 minutes, or until all the water has been absorbed and the oil rises to the surface.

3 Let cool, then spoon into a glass jar with a lid. To preserve the curry paste, heat a little more oil in a clean pan and pour it over the surface. Store in the refrigerator for up to 1 month.

garlic paste

4 oz/115 g garlic cloves, halved

½ cup water

1 Place the garlic cloves and water in a food processor or blender and process to make a paste. Transfer to a glass jar with a lid and store in the refrigerator for up to 1 month.

ginger paste

4 oz/115 g fresh gingerroot,
   coarsely chopped

½ cup water

1 Place the ginger and water in a food processor or blender and process to make a paste. Transfer to a glass jar with a lid and store in the refrigerator for up to 1 month.

garam masala

1 cinnamon stick

8 dried red chilies

5 tbsp coriander seeds

2 tbsp cumin seeds

2 tsp cardamom seeds

1 tsp fennel seeds

1 tsp black mustard seeds

2 tsp black peppercorns

1 tsp whole cloves

1 Dry-fry the cinnamon stick and dried red chilies in a heavy-bottom skillet over low heat, stirring constantly, for 2 minutes. Add the coriander, cumin, cardamom, fennel, and black mustard seeds, peppercorns, and cloves and dry-fry, stirring and shaking the skillet constantly, for 8 minutes, or until they give off their aroma.

2 Remove the skillet from the heat and let cool. Transfer the contents to a spice grinder and process until ground. Alternatively, use a mortar and pestle. Store in an airtight container in the refrigerator for up to 3 months.

Soups

All the soups in this chapter would make a
delicious and substantial lunchtime snack,
perhaps served with some Indian bread such as
Naan Bread, or as an imaginative start to a dinner party. They range from quite
fiercely spiced soups, such as Spinach Soup, to ones that are milder and more
subtle in flavor, like Seafood Soup. These soups are extremely easy to prepare
and most can be made ahead of time, then reheated until piping hot just
before serving.

spinach soup

serves six

2 tsp coriander seeds

2 tsp cumin seeds

1 tbsp ghee or vegetable oil

2 onions, chopped

1 tbsp Ginger Paste (see page 11)

2 tsp Garlic Paste (see page 11)

6 curry leaves, coarsely torn

2 dried red chilies, crushed

2 tsp black mustard seeds

½ tsp fenugreek seeds

1 tsp ground turmeric

1 cup masoor dal

2 potatoes, diced

5 cups vegetable stock

2 lb 4 oz/1 kg fresh spinach, tough
    stems removed, plus extra
    to garnish

2 tbsp lemon juice

1¼ cups coconut milk

salt and pepper

COOK'S TIP

You can prepare this soup the
day before and when cool, cover
and store in the refrigerator until
required. Make sure that it is
piping hot before serving.

1 Heat a heavy-bottom skillet and
dry-fry the coriander and cumin
seeds, stirring constantly, until they
give off their aroma. Tip into a mortar
and grind with a pestle. Alternatively,
grind in a spice mill or blender.

2 Heat the ghee in a large pan. Add
the onions, Ginger Paste, Garlic
Paste, curry leaves, chilies, mustard
seeds, and fenugreek seeds and cook
over low heat, stirring frequently, for
8 minutes, or until the onions are
softened and golden. Stir in the
ground, dry-fried spices and turmeric
and cook for an additional 1 minute.
Add the masoor dal, potatoes, and
stock and bring to a boil, then reduce
the heat and simmer for 15 minutes,
or until the potatoes are tender. Stir in
the spinach and cook for 2–3 minutes,
or until wilted.

3 Remove the pan from the heat
and let cool slightly. Ladle the
soup into a food processor or blender
and process until smooth. Return to
the pan and stir in the lemon juice and
coconut milk and season to taste with
salt and pepper. Reheat gently, stirring
occasionally, but do not boil. Ladle
into warmed soup bowls and garnish
with fresh spinach leaves, then serve
immediately.

seafood soup

serves four

1 cup vegetable stock

2 carrots, diced

3 garlic cloves, finely chopped

3 tbsp chopped cilantro,
     plus extra to garnish

1 tsp cumin seeds

1 tsp black peppercorns

½-inch/1-cm piece fresh gingerroot,
     chopped

1 tbsp ghee or vegetable oil

1 onion, chopped

1 fresh green chili, seeded
     and chopped

1 potato, diced

2 tsp ground coriander

7 oz/200 g cooked shrimp, peeled
     and deveined

generous ¼ cup plain yogurt

⅔ cup milk

3 tbsp dry white wine

8 scallops, shucked

salt and pepper

VARIATION

You could substitute 16 freshly
cooked, shucked mussels for the
scallops or 8 shucked oysters.

1 Pour the stock into a pan and
add the carrots, 2 of the garlic
cloves, the chopped cilantro, cumin
seeds, peppercorns, and ginger. Bring
to a boil, then cover and simmer for
20 minutes. Strain the stock into a
pitcher and make up to 3 cups with
water, if necessary.

2 Heat the ghee in a separate
pan. Add the onion, chili,
and remaining garlic and cook for
5 minutes. Add the potato and ground
coriander and cook for 2 minutes. Add
the reserved stock and bring to a boil,
then cover and simmer for 5 minutes,
or until the potato is tender.

3 Remove the pan from the heat
and let cool slightly. Ladle the
contents into a food processor, then
add half the shrimp and process until
smooth. Return the soup to the pan
and add the remaining shrimp with the
yogurt and milk. Reheat gently. Stir in
the wine and scallops, then season to
taste with salt and pepper and simmer
for 2–3 minutes, or until the scallops
are just cooked. Ladle into warmed
bowls, and garnish with chopped
cilantro, then serve.

entil soup

serves four

4 cups water

generous 1 cup toor dal or chana dal

1 tsp paprika

½ tsp chili powder

½ tsp ground turmeric

2 tbsp ghee or vegetable oil

1 fresh green chili, seeded and
    finely chopped

1 tsp cumin seeds

3 curry leaves, coarsely torn

1 tsp sugar

salt

1 tsp Garam Masala (see page 11),
    to garnish

VARIATION

For a fuller flavor, cook the
dal in vegetable stock
instead of water.

1 Bring the water to a boil in a large, heavy-bottom pan. Add the dal, then cover and simmer, stirring occasionally, for 25 minutes.

2 Stir in the paprika, chili powder, and turmeric, then re-cover and cook for an additional 10 minutes, or until the dal is tender.

3 Meanwhile, heat the ghee in a small skillet. Add the chili, cumin seeds, and curry leaves and cook, stirring constantly, for 1 minute.

4 Add the spice mixture to the dal. Stir in the sugar and season with salt to taste. Ladle into warmed soup bowls, then sprinkle with Garam Masala and serve immediately.

cauliflower soup

serves six

1 tbsp ghee or vegetable oil

1 small cauliflower, broken
   into florets

2 potatoes, diced

3 tbsp water

1 tsp Garlic Paste (see page 11)

1 tbsp Ginger Paste (see page 11)

2 tsp ground turmeric

1 tsp black mustard seeds

1 tsp cumin seeds

1 tbsp coriander seeds,
   lightly crushed

4 cups vegetable stock

salt and pepper

1¼ cups plain yogurt

1 Heat the ghee in a large, heavy bottom pan. Add the cauliflowe potatoes, and water and bring to a boil, then reduce the heat and simme covered, for 10 minutes.

2 Stir in the Garlic Paste, Ginger Paste, turmeric, mustard seeds, cumin seeds, and coriander seeds an cook, stirring frequently, for 3 minute Add the stock and season to taste wi salt and pepper. Bring to a boil, then cover and simmer for 20 minutes.

3 Remove the pan from the heat and let cool slightly. Ladle the mixture into a food processor or blender and process until smooth. Return to the pan and stir in the yogurt. Reheat gently until piping hot Taste and adjust the seasoning, if necessary, and serve immediately.

VARIATION

For a more subtle flavor and
color, you can substitute
½ teaspoon of saffron threads for
the ground turmeric.

pepper water soup

serves six

2 tbsp ghee or vegetable oil

2 dried red chilies

4 curry leaves, coarsely torn

1 tsp Garlic Paste (see page 11)

1 tsp cumin seeds

½ tsp ground turmeric

½ tsp mustard seeds

pinch of asafetida

salt and pepper

1¼ cups tomato juice

6 tbsp lemon juice

⅔ cup water

chopped cilantro, to garnish

VARIATION

Poach 2 lb/900 g diced chicken
in 2½ cups water until tender.
Proceed as in main recipe,
adding the chicken to reheat
at the last moment.

1 Heat the ghee in a large, heavy-bottom pan. Add the chilies, curry leaves, Garlic Paste, cumin seeds, turmeric, mustard seeds, asafetida, and ½ teaspoon pepper. Cook over medium heat, stirring frequently, for 5–8 minutes, or until the chilies are charred.

2 Add the tomato juice, lemon juice, and water and season with salt to taste. Bring to a boil, then reduce the heat and simmer for 10 minutes.

3 Remove the chilies, then taste and adjust the seasoning, if necessary. Ladle into warmed soup bowls and sprinkle with chopped cilantro, then serve immediately.

Meat & Poultry

From kabobs to curries and from chicken to lamb, the choice is huge. There are richly flavored stews, quick stir-fries, colorful tandoori dishes, and succulent roasts. Whether you want an easy, but tasty, dish for a midweek family supper, or something special for entertaining guests, you are sure to find exactly the right recipe here.

Lamb is undoubtedly India's favorite meat, and this chapter includes such classics as Rogan Josh and Lamb Koftas. However, both pork and beef also feature.

Chicken is also the perfect partner for subtle spices and is transformed when served, southern Indian-style, in a combination of coconut milk, lime juice, and cilantro. Favorites among the recipes here include Chicken Dhansak.

lamb koftas

serves four

1 lb/450 g fresh ground lamb

1 small onion, finely chopped

1 tsp ground cumin

1 tsp ground coriander

1 tsp chili powder

1 tsp Garam Masala (see page 11)

1 tsp Garlic Paste (see page 11)

2 tbsp chopped cilantro

salt

generous ¾ cup vegetable oil

6 scallions, chopped

1 green bell pepper, seeded
  and chopped

1½ cups fava beans, thawed
  if frozen

12 baby corn cobs, thawed if frozen

1 small cauliflower, cut into florets

3 fresh green chilies, seeded
  and chopped

1 tbsp lime juice

1 tbsp fresh mint leaves

VARIATION

You can use any mixture of
vegetables you have to hand,
such as red bell pepper, broccoli,
chopped green beans, or
snow peas.

---

1 Place the lamb, onion, cumin, ground coriander, chili powder, Garam Masala, Garlic Paste, and half the cilantro in a bowl and mix well with your hands. Season with salt to taste. Cover and let chill in the refrigerator for a few minutes.

2 Heat 3 tablespoons of the vegetable oil in a preheated wok or large skillet. Add the scallions and cook, stirring frequently, for 1 minute. Add the green bell pepper, fava beans, corn cobs, cauliflower, and chilies and cook over high heat, stirring, for 3 minutes, or until crisp-tender. Reserve.

3 Heat the remaining vegetable in a separate preheated wok o large skillet. Meanwhile, form the lamb mixture into small balls or ova between the palms of your hands. Add the koftas, in batches, to the h oil and cook, turning them frequent until golden brown. Remove with a slotted spoon and drain on paper towels. When they are all cooked, return the vegetables to the heat ar stir in the koftas. Cook over low hea stirring frequently, for 5 minutes, or until heated through. Sprinkle with lime juice and serve garnished with remaining cilantro and mint leaves.

COOK'S TIP

The lamb must be finely groun
for making koftas. If necessary,
process in a food processor fo
1 minute before mixing with th
other ingredients.

hot spicy lamb in sauce

¾ cup vegetable oil

2 lb 4 oz/1 kg lean leg of lamb,
    cut into large pieces

1 tbsp Garam Masala (see page 11)

5 onions, chopped

⅔ cup yogurt

2 tbsp tomato paste

2 tsp finely chopped fresh
    gingerroot

2 garlic cloves, crushed

1½ tsp salt

2 tsp chili powder

1 tbsp ground coriander

2 tsp ground nutmeg

3¾ cups water

1 tbsp ground fennel seeds

1 tbsp paprika

1 tbsp besan

3 bay leaves

1 tbsp all-purpose flour

2 tbsp warm water

2–3 fresh green chilies, chopped
cilantro, chopped, plus extra
    to garnish

thin slivers of fresh gingerroot,
    to garnish

1 Heat the oil in a skillet. Add the meat and half of the Garam Masala and stir-fry for 7–10 minutes, or until the meat is well coated. Using a slotted spoon, remove the meat and reserve until required.

2 Add the onions to the skillet and cook until golden brown. Return the meat to the skillet, then reduce the heat and let simmer, stirring occasionally.

3 Mix the yogurt, tomato paste, ginger, garlic, salt, chili powder, ground coriander, nutmeg, and the rest of the Garam Masala together in a separate bowl. Pour this mixture over the meat and stir-fry, mixing the spices well into the meat, for 5–7 minutes.

4 Stir in half the water, then add the fennel, paprika, and besan. Add the remaining water and the bay leaves, then reduce the heat. Cover and cook for 1 hour, stirring occasionally.

5 Mix the all-purpose flour and warm water together, then pour over the curry. Sprinkle with the chilies and chopped cilantro and cook until the meat is tender and the sauce thickens. Garnish with ginger and extra chopped cilantro and serve.

ɔroiled ground lamb

serves four

5 tbsp vegetable oil

2 onions, sliced

1 lb/450 g fresh ground lamb

2 tbsp yogurt

1 tsp chili powder

1 tsp finely chopped fresh
gingerroot

1 garlic clove, crushed

1 tsp salt

1½ tsp Garam Masala (see page 11)

½ tsp ground allspice

2 fresh green chilies

1 bunch of cilantro

TO GARNISH

1 onion, cut into rings

chopped cilantro

1 lemon, cut into wedges

TO SERVE

Naan Bread (see page 181)

salad greens

1 Preheat the broiler to medium.
Heat the oil in a pan. Add the
ions and cook until golden brown.

2 Place the ground lamb in a large
bowl. Add the yogurt, chili
wder, ginger, garlic, salt, Garam
asala, and allspice and mix well.

3 Add the lamb mixture to the
fried onions and stir-fry for
10–15 minutes. Remove the pan from
the heat and reserve.

4 Meanwhile, seed the chilies, then
place in a food processor with
half of the cilantro and process until
finely chopped. Alternatively, finely
chop the chilies and cilantro with a
sharp knife. Reserve.

5 Place the lamb mixture in a food
processor and process until
smooth. Alternatively, place in a large
bowl and mash with a fork. Mix the
lamb mixture with the reserved chilies
and cilantro and blend well.

6 Transfer the mixture to a shallow
heatproof dish. Cook under the
hot broiler for 10–15 minutes, moving
the mixture about with a fork. Watch it
carefully to prevent it burning.

7 Garnish with onion rings, cilantro,
and lemon wedges and serve
with Naan Bread and salad.

lamb keema

serves four

2 tbsp ghee (see page 168) or
  vegetable oil

1 onion, chopped

1 cinnamon stick

4 cardamom pods, lightly crushed

1 curry leaf

4 cloves

1 tsp Ginger Paste (see page 11)

1 tsp Garlic Paste (see page 11)

1 lb/450 g fresh ground lamb

2 tsp ground coriander

2 tsp ground cumin

1 tsp chili powder

⅔ cup plain yogurt

1 tbsp dried fenugreek

salt

chopped cilantro, to garnish

COOK'S TIP

In India, this dish would be
flavored with fresh fenugreek
leaves, known as *methi*. You
would need 1 bunch of fresh
leaves. Always remove and
discard the bitter stems.

1 Heat the ghee in a karahi,
preheated wok, or large, heavy-
bottom pan. Add the onion and cook
over low heat, stirring occasionally, for
5 minutes, or until softened.

2 Add the cinnamon stick,
cardamoms, curry leaf, and
cloves and cook, stirring constantly, for
1 minute, then add the Ginger Paste
and Garlic Paste and cook, stirring
constantly, for an additional 1 minute.

3 Add the ground lamb and
sprinkle over the ground
coriander, cumin, and chili powder.
Cook for 5 minutes, or until the lamb is
lightly browned, stirring and breaking
up the meat with a wooden spoon.

4 Stir in the yogurt and fenugreek
and season with salt to taste.
Cover and cook over low heat for
20–30 minutes, or until the lamb is
tender and the liquid has been
absorbed. Ladle into a warmed serving
dish and discard the curry leaf. Garnish
with chopped cilantro and serve.

VARIATION

You could add 1 cup frozen peas
10 minutes before the end of the
cooking time, if you like.

lamb curry in a thick sauce

serves six

2 lb 4 oz/1 kg lean lamb

7 tbsp plain yogurt

½ cup almonds

2 tsp Garam Masala (see page 11)

2 tsp finely chopped fresh
  gingerroot

2 garlic cloves, crushed

1½ tsp chili powder

1½ tsp salt

1¼ cups vegetable oil

3 onions, finely chopped

4 green cardamoms

2 bay leaves

3 fresh green chilies, chopped

2 tbsp lemon juice

2 cups canned tomatoes

1¼ cups water

1 small bunch of cilantro, chopped

freshly cooked rice, to serve

1 Using a sharp knife, cut the lamb into small, even-size pieces.

2 Mix the yogurt, almonds, Garam Masala, ginger, garlic, chili powder, and salt together in a large bowl. Stir until well mixed.

3 Heat the oil in a large pan. Add the onions, cardamoms, and bay leaves and stir-fry until golden brown.

4 Add the meat and yogurt mixture to the pan and stir-fry for 3–5 minutes.

5 Add 2 of the green chilies, the lemon juice, and canned tomatoes to the mixture in the pan and stir-fry for an additional 5 minutes.

6 Add the water, then cover and let simmer over low heat for 35–40 minutes.

7 Add the remaining green chili and cilantro and stir until the sauce has thickened. Remove the lid and increase the heat if the sauce is too watery.

8 Transfer the curry to warmed serving plates and serve hot with freshly cooked rice.

marinated roast lamb

serves six

¾ cups plain yogurt

½ cup lemon juice

3 tbsp malt vinegar

2 tsp chili powder

2 tsp Ginger Paste (see page 11)

2 tsp Garlic Paste (see page 11)

1 tsp brown sugar

1 tsp salt

few drops red food coloring
(optional)

5 lb 8 oz/2.5 kg leg of lamb

vegetable oil, for brushing

cilantro sprigs, to garnish

COOK'S TIP

Red food coloring gives the lamb an attractive appearance. However, some synthetic coloring agents have been associated with allergies and other effects, so you may wish to omit it.

1 Mix the yogurt, lemon juice, vinegar, chili powder, Ginger Paste, Garlic Paste, sugar, salt, and food coloring (if using) together in a bowl. Make several deep gashes all over the lamb and place in a large roasting pan. Pour over the yogurt mixture, turning to coat and pressing it well into the gashes. Cover and let chill in the refrigerator for 8 hours or overnight.

2 Preheat the oven to 375°F/190°C. Remove the lamb from the refrigerator and bring to room temperature. Roast the lamb in the preheated oven for 1¼ hours, basting occasionally with the marinade.

3 Remove the lamb from the oven and reduce the oven temperature to 325°F/160°C. Place the lamb on a large sheet of foil and brush with vegetable oil, then wrap the foil around the meat to enclose it completely. Return to the oven and roast for an additional 45–60 minutes, or until tender.

4 Let the lamb rest for 10 minutes before carving and serving, garnished with a few cilantro sprigs.

cauliflower with meat

1 Using a sharp knife, cut the cauliflower into small florets. Chop the green chilies finely.

2 Heat the oil in a large skillet. Add the onions and cook until golden brown. Reduce the heat and add the meat, stirring.

3 Add the ginger, garlic, chili powder, and salt. Stir-fry for 5 minutes, stirring to mix.

4 Add half of the green chili and half of the cilantro. Stir in the water, then cover and cook over low heat for 30 minutes.

5 Add the cauliflower and simmer for 15–20 minutes, or until the water has evaporated completely. Stir-fry the mixture for an additional 5 minutes. Remove the skillet from the heat and sprinkle over the lemon juice.

6 To make the baghaar, heat the in a small pan. Add the dried re chilies and the mixed mustard and onion seeds and cook until they turn a darker color, stirring occasionally. Remove the pan from the heat and pour the mixture over the cauliflowe

7 Garnish with the remaining gre chili and chopped cilantro. Serv immediately.

ground lamb with peas

serves four

6 tbsp vegetable oil

1 onion, sliced

2 fresh red chilies, chopped

1 bunch of cilantro, chopped

2 tomatoes, chopped

1 tsp salt

1 tsp finely chopped fresh
  gingerroot

1 garlic clove, crushed

1 tsp chili powder

1 lb/450 g fresh lean ground lamb

1 cup peas

2 fresh green chilies, to garnish

1 Heat the oil in a medium-size pan. Add the onion slices and cook until golden brown, stirring.

2 Add the red chilies, half of the chopped cilantro, and the tomatoes to the pan and reduce the heat to a simmer.

3 Add the salt, ginger, garlic, and chili powder to the mixture in the pan and stir well.

4 Add the ground lamb to the pan and stir-fry the mixture for 7–10 minutes.

5 Add the peas and cook for an additional 3–4 minutes, stirring occasionally.

6 Transfer the lamb and pea mix to warmed serving plates and garnish with green chilies and the remaining cilantro.

COOK'S TIP

The flavor of garlic varies in strength depending on how it prepared. A whole garlic clove added to a dish will give it the flavor but not the pungency of garlic; a halved clove will add little "bite"; a finely chopped garlic clove will release most of its flavor, and a crushed clove will release all of the flavor.

amb pot roast

serves four

lb 8 oz/2.5 kg leg of lamb
tsp chopped fresh gingerroot
tsp crushed garlic
tsp Garam Masala (see page 11)
tsp salt
tsp black cumin seeds
black peppercorns
cloves
tsp chili powder
tbsp lemon juice
¼ cups vegetable oil
large onion, peeled but kept whole
bout 9 cups water
O SERVE
lad greens
eshly cooked potatoes

COOK'S TIP

Traditionally, a pan called a
degchi is used for pot-roasting in
ndia. It is set over hot ashes and
contains hot coals in its lid.

1 Using a sharp knife, remove the fat from the lamb. Prick the lamb all over with a fork.

2 Mix the ginger, garlic, Garam Masala, salt, black cumin seeds, peppercorns, cloves, and chili powder together in a bowl. Stir in the lemon juice and mix well. Spoon the mixture over the leg of lamb and rub into the meat, making sure it is well coated, then reserve.

3 Heat the oil in a large pan. Add the meat and place the onion alongside the leg of lamb.

4 Add enough water to cover the meat and cook over low heat for 2½–3 hours, turning occasionally. (If the water has evaporated after a while and the meat is not tender, add a little extra water.) Once the water has completely evaporated, turn the roast over to brown it on all sides.

5 Transfer the roast to a serving dish. Cut the roast into slices or serve it whole to be carved at the table. Serve the lamb hot or cold with salad greens and potatoes.

rogan josh

serves six

1 cup plain yogurt

½ tsp cayenne pepper

¼ tsp asafetida

2 lb 4 oz/1 kg diced lamb

1 tbsp coriander seeds

1 tbsp cardamom seeds

1 tsp cumin seeds

1 tsp white poppy seeds

8 black peppercorns

4 cloves

1¼-inch/3-cm piece fresh
   gingerroot

4 garlic cloves

2 tbsp almonds

1¼ cups water

4 tbsp ghee or vegetable oil

1 onion, chopped

1 tsp ground turmeric

2 tbsp chopped cilantro

1 tsp Garam Masala (see page 11)

salt

1 Mix the yogurt, cayenne, and asafetida together in a large, shallow dish. Add the lamb and toss well to coat. Cover and reserve.

2 Preheat the oven to 275°F/140°C. Place the coriander seeds and the cardamom, cumin, and poppy seeds in a food processor or blender with the peppercorns, cloves, ginger, garlic, almonds, and 4 tablespoons of the water and process to make a paste, adding a little more water, if necessary. Reserve until required.

3 Heat the ghee in a flameproof casserole. Add the onion and cook over low heat for 10 minutes, or until golden. Stir in the spice paste and turmeric and cook, stirring, for 5 minutes. Add the lamb, with its marinade, then increase the heat to high and cook, stirring, for 10 minutes. Reduce the heat, then cover and simmer for 45 minutes.

4 Stir 4 tablespoons of the water into the casserole and cook, stirring, until it has been incorporated. Stir in another 4 tablespoons of the water and cook until incorporated. Add the remaining water, then re-cover the casserole and simmer for 15 minutes. Stir the chopped cilantro and Garam Masala into the lamb and season with salt to taste. Cover, then transfer the casserole to the oven and cook for an additional 25 minutes. Serve immediately.

meatballs in sauce

serves four

1 lb/450 g fresh ground lamb

1 tsp crushed fresh gingerroot

1 garlic clove, crushed

1 tsp Garam Masala (see page 11)

1½ tsp poppy seeds

1 tsp salt

½ tsp chili powder

1 onion, finely chopped

1 fresh green chili, finely chopped

¼ bunch of cilantro,
    finely chopped

1 tbsp besan

⅔ cup vegetable oil

SAUCE

2 tbsp vegetable oil

3 onions, finely chopped

2 small cinnamon sticks

2 large black cardamoms

1 tsp finely chopped fresh
    gingerroot

1 garlic clove, crushed

1 tsp salt

generous ¼ cup plain yogurt

⅔ cup water

TO GARNISH

finely chopped cilantro

1 fresh green chili, finely chopped

1 lemon, cut into wedges

1 Place the lamb in a large bowl. Add the ginger, garlic, Garam Masala, poppy seeds, salt, chili powder, onion, chili, cilantro, and besan and mix well with a fork.

2 With dampened hands, form the mixture into small meatballs and reserve.

3 To make the sauce, heat the oil in a skillet. Add the onions and cook until golden brown. Add the cinnamon sticks and cardamoms, then reduce the heat and stir-fry for an additional 5 minutes. Add the ginger, garlic, salt, yogurt, and water and stir to mix well.

4 Transfer to a serving bowl and garnish with the chopped cila and chili.

5 Heat the oil in a pan. Add the meatballs and cook, turning occasionally, for 8–10 minutes, or u golden brown.

6 Transfer the meatballs to warm serving plates and garnish wit lemon wedges. Serve with the sauc

potatoes cooked with meat & yogurt

serves six

3 potatoes

1¼ cups vegetable oil

3 onions, sliced

2 lb 4 oz/1 kg leg of lamb, cubed

1 tsp Garam Masala (see page 11)

1½ tsp finely chopped fresh
   gingerroot

1–2 garlic cloves, crushed

1 tsp chili powder

3 black peppercorns

3 green cardamoms

1 tsp black cumin seeds

2 cinnamon sticks

1 tsp paprika

1½ tsp salt

⅔ cup plain yogurt

2½ cups water

TO GARNISH

2 fresh green chilies, chopped

chopped cilantro

1 Peel and cut each potato into 6 pieces.

2 Heat the oil in a pan. Add the sliced onions and cook until golden brown. Remove the onions from the pan and reserve.

3 Add the meat to the pan with the Garam Masala and stir-fry for 5–7 minutes over low heat.

4 Add the onions and remove the pan from the heat.

5 Mix the ginger, garlic, chili powder, peppercorns, cardamoms, cumin seeds, cinnamon sticks, paprika, and salt together in a small bowl. Add the yogurt and mix well.

6 Return the pan to the heat and gradually add the spice and yogurt mixture. Stir-fry for 7–10 minutes. Add the water, then reduce the heat and cook, covered, for 40 minutes, stirring occasionally.

7 Add the potatoes to the pan and cook, covered, for an additional 15 minutes, gently stirring the mixture occasionally. Garnish with green chilies and cilantro and serve immediately.

39

shish kabobs

serves two

1 lb/450 g fresh lean ground lamb

1 tsp meat tenderizer

¼ bunch of cilantro

1 onion, finely chopped

2 fresh green chilies, finely chopped

2 tbsp plain yogurt

1 tsp finely chopped fresh
  gingerroot

1 garlic clove, crushed

1 tsp ground cumin

1 tsp ground coriander

½ tsp salt

1 tsp chili powder, plus extra
  to garnish

½ tsp ground allspice

1 tsp Garam Masala (see page 11)

TO SERVE

1 lemon, cut into wedges

Raita (see page 226)

1 Place the lamb in a bowl, then add the meat tenderizer and mix in well. Reserve for at least 3 hours.

2 Preheat the broiler to medium. Finely chop the cilantro. Mix the onion, green chilies, and cilantro together in a bowl.

3 Mix the yogurt, ginger, garlic, ground cumin, ground coriander, salt, chili powder, allspice, and Garam Masala together in a separate bowl. Blend with the onion mixture.

4 Add the combined mixture to the lamb and mix together. Divide the mixture into 10–12 equal portions. Roll 2 portions around each metal skewer with your fingers, pressing all around.

VARIATION

Serve in pita bread for great party food. The cooked meat can also be chopped into a salad.

5 Broil the kabobs under the hot broiler for 8–10 minutes, turning and basting occasionally with oil.

6 Sprinkle with chili powder and serve with lemon wedges and Raita of your choice.

tomatoes cooked with meat & yogurt

serves two–four

1 tsp Garam Masala (see page 11)

1 tsp finely chopped fresh
gingerroot

1 garlic clove, crushed

2 black cardamoms

1 tsp chili powder

½ tsp black cumin seeds

2 x 1-inch/2.5-cm cinnamon sticks

1 tsp salt

⅔ cup plain yogurt

1 lb 2 oz/500 g lean cubed lamb

⅔ cup vegetable oil

2 onions, sliced

2½ cups water

2 large tomatoes, cut into fourths

2 tbsp lemon juice

2 fresh green chilies, chopped,
to garnish

1 Mix the Garam Masala,
ginger, garlic, cardamoms, chili
powder, black cumin seeds, cinnamon
sticks, salt, and yogurt together in a
large bowl.

COOK'S TIP

Kormas are slowly braised
dishes, many of which are the
rich and spicy, Persian-inspired
Mogul dishes served on special
occasions. Yogurt is often
featured, both as a marinade and
as the cooking liquid.

2 Add the meat to the yogurt and
spice mixture and mix until the
meat is well coated. Reserve.

3 Heat the oil in a large skillet. Ad
the onions and cook until golde
brown.

4 Add the meat and stir-fry for
5 minutes. Reduce the heat and
add the water, then cover and simme
for 1 hour, stirring occasionally.

5 Add the tomatoes to the curry
and sprinkle with the lemon juic
Let the curry simmer for an additiona
7–10 minutes.

6 Garnish the curry with chopped
chilies and serve hot.

ean lamb cooked in spinach

serves two–four

1¼ cups oil

2 onions, sliced

¼ bunch of cilantro, chopped

3 fresh green chilies, chopped

1½ tsp finely chopped fresh
gingerroot

1–2 garlic cloves, crushed

1 tsp chili powder

½ tsp ground turmeric

1 lb/450 g lean cubed lamb

1 tsp salt

2 lb 4 oz/1 kg fresh spinach
leaves, chopped or
15 oz/425 g canned spinach

scant 3 cups water

TO GARNISH

fresh gingerroot, shredded

chopped cilantro

1 Heat the oil in a skillet. Add the
onions and cook until they turn a
ale golden color.

2 Add the cilantro and two-thirds of
the chopped green chilies to the
illet and stir-fry for 3–5 minutes.

3 Reduce the heat and add the
ginger, garlic, chili powder, and
turmeric to the mixture in the skillet.
Stir well.

4 Add the lamb and stir-fry for
5 minutes. Add the salt and the
spinach and cook, stirring occasionally,
for an additional 3–5 minutes.

5 Add the water, stirring, then cover
the skillet and cook over low heat
for 45 minutes. Remove the lid and
check the meat. If it is not tender, turn
the meat over, then increase the heat
and cook, uncovered, until the surplus
water has been absorbed. Stir-fry the
mixture for an additional 5–7 minutes.

6 Transfer the lamb and spinach
mixture to a warmed serving dish
and garnish with shredded ginger,
cilantro, and the remaining chopped
chili. Serve hot.

meat-coated eggs

serves six

1 lb/450 g fresh lean ground lamb

1 small onion, finely chopped

1 fresh green chili, finely chopped

1 tsp finely chopped fresh
   gingerroot

1 garlic clove, crushed

1 tsp ground coriander

1 tsp Garam Masala (see page 11)

1 tsp salt

1½ tbsp besan

7 eggs, 1 beaten and 6 hard-
   cooked and shelled

corn oil, for deep-frying

salad greens, to serve

TO GARNISH

tomato slices

1 lemon, cut into wedges

1 Place the lamb, onion, and chili in a bowl and mix together. Transfer the mixture to a food processor and process until well ground. Alternatively, grind by hand using a pestle and mortar.

2 Remove the mixture from the food processor and add the ginger, garlic, ground coriander, Garam Masala, salt, besan, and the beaten egg. Work the mixture together with your hands until well mixed.

3 Divide the mixture into 6 equal-size portions. Roll each portion out to form a flat circle, ¼ inch/5 mm thick. Place a hard-cooked egg in the center of each round and wrap the meat mixture around the egg to enclose it completely. When all 6 eggs have been covered, let stand in a cool place for 20–30 minutes.

VARIATION
You can serve these in a sauce.
Use the recipe for Meatballs in
Sauce (see page 38).

4 Meanwhile, heat the oil for deep frying in a deep skillet to 350°F/ 180°C, or until a cube of bread brow in 30 seconds. Gently drop the coate eggs into the oil and deep-fry for 2–4 minutes, or until golden. Using a slotted spoon, remove the eggs from the oil and transfer to paper towels to drain. Garnish with tomato slices and lemon wedges and serve with salad.

spicy lamb chops

serves four–six

2 lb 4 oz/1 kg lamb chops

2 tsp finely chopped fresh
    gingerroot

2 garlic cloves, crushed

1 tsp pepper

1 tsp Garam Masala (see page 11)

1 tsp black cumin seeds

1½ tsp salt

3¾ cups water

2 eggs

1¼ cups oil

TO GARNISH

Potato Wafers (see page 157)

tomatoes

1 lemon, cut into wedges

1 Using a sharp knife, trim away any excess fat from the lamb chops.

2 Mix the ginger, garlic, pepper, Garam Masala, cumin seeds, and salt together in a bowl and rub all over the chops.

3 Bring the water to a boil in a pan. Add the chops and spice mixture and cook for 45 minutes, stirring occasionally. Once the water has evaporated, remove from the heat and let cool.

4 Using a fork, beat the eggs together in a large bowl.

5 Heat the oil in a large pan. Dip each lamb chop into the beaten egg and cook them in the oil for 3 minutes, turning once.

6 Transfer the chops to a large, warmed serving dish and garnish with Potato Wafers, tomatoes, and lemon wedges. Serve hot.

amb & lentils

serves six

:ant ½ cup chana dal

:ant ½ cup masoor dal

:ant ½ cup moong dal

ant ½ cup urid dal

enerous ⅓ cup porridge oats

ORMA

lb 5 oz/1.5 kg cubed lamb

enerous ¾ cup plain yogurt

tsp finely chopped fresh
  gingerroot

garlic cloves, crushed

tbsp Garam Masala (see page 11)

tsp chili powder

tsp ground turmeric

green cardamoms

cinnamon sticks

tsp black cumin seeds

tsp salt

¼ cups oil

onions, sliced

ant 3 cups water

fresh green chilies

small bunch of cilantro, chopped

bunch of cilantro, chopped, to
  garnish

1 Soak the lentils and oats overnight. Drain and boil in a pan of water for 1–1 ½ hours, or until soft. Mash and reserve.

2 Place the lamb in a large bowl. Add the yogurt, ginger, garlic, Garam Masala, chili powder, turmeric, cardamoms, cinnamon sticks, cumin seeds, and salt; then mix and reserve.

3 Heat 1¼ cups of the oil in a pan. Add four-fifths of the onions and cook until golden. Add the meat and stir-fry for 7–10 minutes. Stir in the water, then reduce the heat and cook, covered, for 1 hour, stirring occasionally. If the meat is still not tender, add more water and cook for 15–20 minutes. Remove the pan from the heat.

4 Add the lentils to the meat, then stir and mix. If the mixture is too thick, add 1¼ cups water and stir, then cook for an additional 10–12 minutes. Add the chilies and cilantro. Transfer to a serving dish and keep warm.

5 Heat the remaining oil and cook the remaining onion until golden. Pour over the lamb and lentils. Garnish with chopped cilantro and serve.

stuffed tomatoes

serves six

6 large firm tomatoes

scant ¼ cup unsalted butter

5 tbsp vegetable oil

1 onion, finely chopped

1 tsp finely chopped fresh
   gingerroot

1 garlic clove, crushed

1 tsp pepper

1 tsp salt

½ tsp Garam Masala (see page 11)

1 lb/450 g fresh ground lamb

1 fresh green chili

1 small bunch of cilantro, chopped

1 lemon, cut into wedges,
   to garnish

salad greens, to serve

VARIATION

You could use the same mixture
to stuff red or green bell peppers,
if you prefer.

---

1 Preheat the oven to 350°F/180°C.
Rinse the tomatoes, then cut off
the tops and scoop out the flesh.

2 Grease an ovenproof dish with
the butter. Place the tomatoes in
the dish.

3 Heat the oil in a pan. Add the
onion and cook until golden.

4 Reduce the heat and add the
ginger, garlic, pepper, salt, and
Garam Masala. Stir-fry the mixture for
3–5 minutes.

5 Add the lamb to the pan and
cook for 10–15 minutes.

6 Add the chili and cilantro and
continue stir-frying the mixture
for 3–5 minutes.

7 Spoon the lamb mixture into th
tomatoes and replace the tops
Cook the tomatoes in the preheated
oven for 15–20 minutes.

8 Transfer the tomatoes to servir
plates, then garnish with lemo
wedges and serve with salad green

lamb with onions & dried mango powder

serves four

4 onions

1¼ cups vegetable oil

1 tsp finely chopped fresh
   gingerroot

1 garlic clove, crushed

1 tsp chili powder

pinch of ground turmeric

1 tsp salt

3 fresh green chilies, chopped

1 lb/450 g lean cubed lamb

2½ cups water

1½ tsp amchoor (dried
   mango powder)

1 small bunch of cilantro, chopped

freshly cooked rice, to serve

1 Using a sharp knife, chop 3 onions finely.

2 Heat ⅔ cup of the oil in a skillet. Add the onions and cook until golden brown. Reduce the heat and add the ginger, garlic, chili powder, turmeric, and salt. Stir-fry the mixture for 5 minutes, then add two-thirds of the chili.

3 Add the cubed lamb to the skillet and stir-fry the mixture for an additional 7 minutes.

4 Add the water, then cover and cook over low heat for 35–45 minutes, stirring occasionall• until the lamb is tender.

5 Meanwhile, slice the remainin• onion. Heat the remaining oil • a skillet. Add the onion and cook u• golden. Reserve.

6 Once the lamb is tender, add t• amchoor, the remaining green chili, and chopped cilantro and stir-• for 3–5 minutes.

7 Transfer the curry to a serving dish and pour the fried onion slices and oil along the center. Serv• hot with freshly cooked rice.

ubed lamb kabobs

serves six–eight

lb 4 oz/1 kg lean lamb, boned
  and cubed

tsp meat tenderizer

/₂ tsp finely chopped fresh
  gingerroot

–2 garlic cloves, crushed

tsp chili powder

tsp ground turmeric

tsp salt

tbsp water

tomatoes, cut in half

small pickling onions

) mushrooms

green bell pepper, cut into
  large pieces

red bell pepper, cut into
  large pieces

tbsp vegetable oil

emons, cut into wedges,
  to garnish

SERVE

shly cooked rice

ita (see page 226)

1 Place the meat in a bowl, then sprinkle over the tenderizer and rub it in, using your hands. Let stand for 3 hours at room temperature.

2 Preheat the broiler to medium. Mix the ginger, garlic, chili powder, turmeric, and salt together in a bowl. Add the water and mix to form a paste. Add the meat and mix until it is well coated with the spices.

3 Thread the meat cubes onto metal skewers, alternating with the tomatoes, pickling onions, mushrooms, and bell peppers. Brush the meat and vegetables with the oil.

4 Grill the kabobs under the hot broiler for 25–30 minutes, or until the meat is cooked through. When cooked, remove the kabobs from the broiler and transfer to a serving plate. Arrange lemon wedges on the side and serve immediately with freshly cooked rice and a Raita of your choice.

spicy lamb curry in sauce

serves four

2 tsp cumin seeds

2 tsp coriander seeds

2 tsp dry unsweetened coconut

1 tsp mixed mustard and
   onion seeds

2 tsp sesame seeds

1 tsp finely chopped fresh
   gingerroot

1 garlic clove, crushed

1 tsp chili powder

1 tsp salt

1 lb/450 g lean cubed lamb

1¼ cups vegetable oil

3 onions, sliced

3¾ cups water

2 tbsp lemon juice

4 fresh green chilies, split

TO SERVE

Onion Dal (see page 162)

freshly cooked rice

1 Dry-roast the cumin and coriander seeds, the dry unsweetened coconut, mixed mustard and onion seeds, and the sesame seeds in a heavy-bottom skillet, shaking the skillet frequently to stop the spices from burning. Grind the roasted spices using a pestle and mortar.

2 Mix the roasted ground spices, ginger, garlic, chili powder, salt, and the cubed lamb together in a bowl. Reserve.

3 Heat 1¼ cups of the oil in a pan. Add the onions and cook until golden brown.

4 Add the meat mixture to the onions and stir-fry for 5–7 minutes over low heat. Add the water and simmer for 45 minutes, stirring occasionally. When the meat is cooked through, remove the pan from the heat and sprinkle with the lemon juice.

5 Heat the remaining oil in a separate pan. Add the split gr chilies, then reduce the heat and co with a lid. Remove the pan from th heat after 30 seconds and let cool.

6 Pour the chili-oil mixture over lamb curry and serve hot with Onion Dal and freshly cooked rice.

pork with tamarind

serves six

2 oz/55 g dried tamarind, chopped

2 cups boiling water

2 fresh green chilies, seeded and
coarsely chopped

2 onions, coarsely chopped

2 garlic cloves, coarsely chopped

1 lemongrass stem, bulb end
coarsely chopped

2 tbsp ghee or vegetable oil

1 tbsp ground coriander

1 tsp ground turmeric

1 tsp ground cardamom

1 tsp chili powder

1 tsp Ginger Paste (see page 11)

1 cinnamon stick

2 lb 4 oz/1 kg diced pork fillet

1 tbsp chopped cilantro

Naan Bread (see page 181),
to serve

TO GARNISH

cilantro sprigs

sliced fresh red chilies

1 Place the dried tamarind in a small bowl, then pour in the boiling water and mix well. Let soak for 30 minutes.

2 Strain the soaking liquid into a clean bowl, pressing down the pulp with the back of a wooden spoon. Discard the pulp. Pour 1 tablespoon of the tamarind liquid into a food processor and add the green chilies, onions, garlic, and lemongrass and process until smooth.

3 Heat the ghee in a large, heavy-bottom pan. Add the ground coriander, turmeric, cardamom, chili powder, Ginger Paste, cinnamon stick, and the chili and onion paste, then cook, stirring, for 2 minutes, or until the spices give off their aroma.

4 Add the pork and cook, stirring constantly, until lightly browned and well coated in the spice mixture. Pour in the remaining tamarind liquid and bring to a boil, then reduce the heat and simmer, covered, for about 30 minutes. Remove the lid from the pan and simmer for an additional 30 minutes, or until the pork is tender. Stir in the chopped cilantro. Garnish with cilantro sprigs and sliced red chilies and serve with Naan Bread.

COOK'S TIP

Dried tamarind is usually sold in compressed blocks from large supermarkets and Asian food stores. If you can't find it, substitute 1¾ cups lemon juice, but remember that the flavor will not be the same.

pork & mushroom curry

serves four

1 lb 10 oz/750 g leg or shoulder
   of pork

3 tbsp vegetable oil

2 onions, sliced

2 garlic cloves, crushed

1-inch/2.5-cm piece fresh
   gingerroot, finely chopped

2 fresh green chilies, seeded and
   chopped, or 1–2 tsp dried
   chili flakes

1½ tbsp medium curry paste

1 tsp ground coriander

1½–2¼ cups thickly sliced
   mushrooms

3¾ cups chicken or vegetable stock

3 tomatoes, chopped

½–1 tsp salt

2 oz/55 g creamed
   coconut, chopped

2 tbsp ground almonds

freshly cooked rice, to serve

TO GARNISH

2 tbsp vegetable oil

1 green or red bell pepper, seeded
   and cut into thin strips

6 scallions, sliced

1 tsp cumin seeds

1 Cut the pork into small bite-size pieces. Heat the oil in a skillet. Add the pork, in batches, and cook until sealed, stirring frequently. Remove each batch of pork from the skillet as it is ready.

2 Add the onions, garlic, ginger, chilies, curry paste, and ground coriander to the skillet and cook gently for 2 minutes. Stir in the mushrooms, stock, and tomatoes, and season with a little salt to taste.

3 Return the pork to the skillet, then cover and simmer very gently for 1¼–1½ hours, or until the pork is tender.

4 Stir the creamed coconut and ground almonds into the curry. Cover and cook gently for 3 minute.

5 Meanwhile, make the garnish. Heat the oil in a separate skille Add the bell pepper strips and scall slices and cook gently until glistenir and tender but still crisp. Stir in the cumin seeds and cook gently for 30 seconds. Spoon the mixture ove the curry and serve immediately wit freshly cooked rice.

pork with cinnamon & fenugreek

serves four

tsp ground coriander

tsp ground cumin

tsp chili powder

tbsp dried fenugreek

tsp ground fenugreek

⅔ cup plain yogurt

lb/450 g diced pork fillet

tbsp ghee or vegetable oil

large onion, sliced

-inch/5-cm piece fresh gingerroot,
   finely chopped

garlic cloves, finely chopped

cinnamon stick

cardamom pods

whole cloves

bay leaves

¼ cup water

alt

ombay Potatoes (see page 208),
   to serve

Mix the ground coriander, cumin,
chilli powder, dried fenugreek,
und fenugreek, and yogurt together
a small bowl. Place the diced pork in
arge, shallow, nonmetallic dish and
d the spice mixture, turning well to
at. Cover and let marinate in the
igerator for 30 minutes.

2 Heat the ghee in a large, heavy-bottom pan. Add the onion and cook, stirring occasionally, for 5 minutes, or until softened. Add the ginger, garlic, cinnamon stick, cardamom, cloves, and bay leaves and cook, stirring constantly, for 2 minutes, or until the spices give off their aroma. Add the meat with its marinade and the water, and season with salt to taste. Bring to a boil, then reduce the heat and simmer, covered, for 30 minutes.

3 Transfer the meat to a preheated wok or large, heavy-bottom skillet and cook over low heat, stirring constantly, until dry and tender. If necessary, occasionally sprinkle with a little water to prevent it sticking to the wok. Serve with Bombay Potatoes.

beef dhansak

serves six

2 tbsp ghee or vegetable oil

2 onions, chopped

3 garlic cloves, finely chopped

2 tsp ground coriander

2 tsp ground cumin

2 tsp Garam Masala (see page 11)

1 tsp ground turmeric

1 lb/450 g zucchini, peeled and
   chopped, or bitter gourd or
   pumpkin, peeled, seeded,
   and chopped

1 eggplant, peeled and chopped

4 curry leaves

generous 1 cup masoor dal

4 cups water

salt

2 lb 4 oz/1 kg stewing or braising
   steak, diced

cilantro leaves, to garnish

1 Heat the ghee in a large, heavy-bottom pan. Add the onions and garlic and cook over low heat, stirring occasionally, for 8–10 minutes, or until light golden. Stir in the ground coriander, cumin, Garam Masala, and turmeric and cook, stirring constantly, for 2 minutes.

2 Add the zucchini, eggplant, curry leaves, masoor dal, and water. Bring to a boil, then reduce the heat and simmer, covered, for 30 minutes, or until the vegetables are tender. Remove the pan from the heat and let cool slightly. Transfer the mixture to a food processor, in batches if necessary, and process until smooth. Return the mixture to the pan and season with salt to taste.

3 Add the steak to the pan and bri to a boil. Reduce the heat, then cover and simmer for 1½ hours. Remc the lid and continue to simmer for an additional 30 minutes, or until the sau is thick and the steak is tender. Serve garnished with cilantro leaves.

> ### COOK'S TIP
> Bitter gourds are widely used in Indian cooking. To prepare this long, knobbly vegetable, use a sharp knife to peel the ridged skin, then scrape out and discard the seeds before chopping.

beef patties

3 tbsp chana dal

1 lb/450 g lean cubed beef

1 tsp finely chopped fresh
  gingerroot

garlic clove, crushed

1 tsp chili powder

1 ½ tsp salt

1 ½ tsp Garam Masala (see page 11)

3 fresh green chilies, chopped

bunch of cilantro

onion, chopped

¼ cups vegetable oil

¾ cups water

tbsp plain yogurt

egg

O GARNISH

small onion, sliced into rings

lemon, cut into wedges

Rinse the chana dal twice under
cold running water, removing any
nes or other impurities. Boil in a pan
water until the water has been
sorbed and the chana dal has
tened. Place in a food processor and
cess to a paste.

2 Mix the beef, ginger, garlic,
chili powder, salt, and Garam
Masala in a bowl. Add about 2 of
the green chilies, half of the cilantro,
and the onion.

3 Heat 2 tablespoons of the oil in a
pan. Add the meat mixture and
water, then cover and cook over low
heat for 45–60 minutes. Once the
meat is tender, evaporate any excess
water by removing the lid and cooking
for an additional 10–15 minutes. Place
the meat mixture in a food processor
and process to a paste.

4 Place the yogurt, egg, chana dal
paste, the remaining green chili,
and cilantro in a bowl with the meat
mixture and mix together with your
fingers. Break off small balls of the
meat paste and make 10–12 small,
flat, circular shapes between the palms
of your hands.

5 Heat the remaining oil in a skillet.
Add the patties, in batches of 3,
and cook for 5–10 minutes,
turning once.

6 Serve garnished with onion rings
and lemon wedges.

beef korma with almonds

serves six

1¼ cups vegetable oil

3 onions, finely chopped

2 lb 4 oz/1 kg lean cubed beef

1½ tsp Garam Masala (see page 11)

1½ tsp ground coriander

1½ tsp chopped fresh gingerroot

1–2 garlic cloves, crushed

1 tsp salt

⅔ cup plain yogurt

2 cloves

3 green cardamoms

4 black peppercorns

2½ cups water

pappadams, to serve

TO GARNISH

6 almonds, soaked, peeled,
   and chopped

2 fresh green chilies, chopped

chopped cilantro

1 Heat the oil in a large skillet. Add the onions and stir-fry until golden brown. Remove half of the onions from the skillet and reserve until required.

2 Add the meat to the remaining onions in the skillet and stir-fry for 5 minutes. Remove the skillet from the heat.

3 Mix the Garam Masala, ground coriander, ginger, garlic, salt, and yogurt together in a bowl. Gradually add the meat to the yogurt and spice mixture and mix until the meat is well coated. Add the meat mixture to the onions in the skillet, then return to the heat and stir for 5–7 minutes, or until the mixture is nearly brown in color.

4 Add the cloves, cardamoms, a peppercorns. Add the water, t reduce the heat and let simmer, covered, for 45–60 minutes. If the water has completely evaporated b the meat is still not tender enough, add another 1¼ cups water and co for an additional 10–15 minutes, stirring occasionally.

5 Just before serving, garnish wi the reserved onions, chopped almonds, chopped chilies, and cilan Serve with pappadams.

dry beef curry with carrot sambal

serves six

4 tbsp ghee or vegetable oil

2 fresh green chilies, seeded
and chopped

2 onions, chopped

2 lb 4 oz/1 kg stewing or braising
steak, diced

1 cup canned tomatoes, drained

salt

2 tsp ground coriander

1½ tsp Garam Masala (see page 11)

1 tsp ground cumin

3 tbsp Curry Paste (see page 11)

1¼ cups coconut milk

1 tbsp chopped cilantro,
to garnish

CARROT SAMBAL

1 tbsp ghee or vegetable oil

1½ oz/40 g shredded coconut

1 tbsp black mustard seeds

1¾ cups grated carrots

4 tbsp lemon juice

scant ½ cup golden raisins

4 tbsp chopped fresh mint

1 To make the sambal, heat the ghee in a small skillet. Add the coconut and mustard seeds and cook over low heat, stirring constantly, for 2 minutes, or until the coconut is beginning to brown. Transfer the mixture to a bowl and stir in the carrots, lemon juice, golden raisins, and mint. Mix well and reserve.

2 To make the curry, heat the ghee in a large, heavy-bottom pan. Add the chilies and onions and cook over low heat, stirring occasionally, until the onions are light golden. Add the steak and cook, stirring frequently, for 10 minutes, or until browned all over. Stir in the tomatoes and season with salt to taste.

3 Mix the ground coriander, 1 teaspoon of the Garam Masala, the cumin, Curry Paste, and coconut milk together in a bowl, then add to the pan. Stir well, then half cover and simmer over low heat for 1½ hours. Remove the lid from the pan and continue to simmer for an additional 30 minutes, or until the meat is tender and the sauce is very thick. If it dries out too much, add a little water. Transfer to a warmed serving dish, then sprinkle with the remaining Garam Masala and chopped cilantro and serve with the carrot sambal.

sliced beef with yogurt & spices

serves four

1 lb/450 g lean beef, cut into
  1-inch/2.5-cm slices

5 tbsp yogurt

1 tsp finely chopped fresh
  gingerroot

1 garlic clove, crushed

1 tsp chili powder

pinch of ground turmeric

2 tsp Garam Masala (see page 11)

1 tsp salt

2 cardamoms

1 tsp black cumin seeds

½ cup ground almonds

1 tbsp dry unsweetened coconut

1 tbsp poppy seeds

1 tbsp sesame seeds

1¼ cups vegetable oil

2 onions, finely chopped

1¼ cups water

TO GARNISH

2 fresh green chilies, cut into strips

chopped cilantro

1 Place the beef in a large bowl.
  Add the yogurt, ginger, garlic,
chili powder, turmeric, Garam Masala,
salt, cardamoms, and cumin seeds and
mix together. Reserve.

2 Dry-roast the ground almonds,
  dry unsweetened coconut, poppy
seeds, and sesame seeds in a heavy-
bottom skillet until golden, shaking the
skillet frequently to stop the spices
from burning.

3 Transfer the spice mixture to a
  food processor and process until
finely ground. Add 1 tablespoon of
water to blend if necessary. Add the
ground spices to the meat mixture and
mix well.

4 Heat a little of the oil in a
  large pan. Add the onions and
cook until golden brown. Remove
the onions from the pan. Add the
remaining oil and stir-fry the meat for
5 minutes, then return the onions to
the pan and stir-fry for an additional
5–7 minutes. Add the water and let
simmer over low heat, covered, for
25–30 minutes, stirring occasionally.
Garnish with the strips of chili and
cilantro and serve hot.

VARIATION

Substitute lamb for the beef in
this recipe, if you prefer.

eef cooked in whole spices

serves four

cups vegetable oil

onions, finely chopped

nch/2.5-cm piece fresh
gingerroot, shredded

garlic cloves, shredded

innamon sticks

green cardamoms

loves

lack peppercorns

ried red chilies

cup plain yogurt

b/450 g lean cubed beef

resh green chilies, chopped

cups water

1 Heat the oil in a skillet. Add the onions and cook, stirring, until golden brown.

2 Reduce the heat and add the ginger, garlic, cinnamon sticks, green cardamoms, cloves, black peppercorns, and red chilies and stir-fry for 5 minutes.

3 Place the yogurt in a bowl and whisk with a fork. Add the yogurt to the onions and stir well.

4 Add the meat and two-thirds of the chilies to the skillet and stir-fry the mixture for 5–7 minutes.

5 Gradually add the water to the skillet, stirring well. Cover and cook the beef and spice mixture for 1 hour, stirring and adding more water if necessary.

6 When thoroughly cooked through, remove the skillet from the heat and transfer the beef and spice mixture to a serving dish. Garnish with the remaining chopped chili.

65

classic vindaloo

serves six

⅔ cup malt vinegar

2 tbsp coriander seeds

1 tbsp cumin seeds

2 tsp chili powder

2 tsp ground turmeric

1 tsp cardamom seeds

2-inch/5-cm piece fresh gingerroot, coarsely chopped

4 garlic cloves, coarsely chopped

6 black peppercorns

6 whole cloves

1 cinnamon stick

salt

2 lb 4 oz/1 kg pork fillet, diced

6 curry leaves

3 tbsp ghee or vegetable oil

1 tsp black mustard seeds

⅔ cup water

freshly cooked rice, to serve

VARIATION

Serve with yellow rice: stir a pinch of ground turmeric with 1 tablespoon of boiling water until dissolved, then stir into the cooked rice until mixed.

---

1 Place the vinegar, coriander, cumin, chili powder, turmeric, cardamom, ginger, garlic, peppercorns, cloves, cinnamon, and a pinch of salt in a food processor or blender and process to make a paste, adding a little more vinegar if necessary. Place the pork in a large, shallow, nonmetallic dish and pour over the spice paste, turning meat to coat all over. Cover with plastic wrap and let marinate in the refrigerator for 1 hour. Arrange the curry leaves on top of the pork, then re-cover and let marinate for at least 8 hours or overnight.

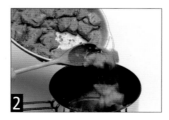

2 Heat the ghee in a large, heavy-bottom pan. Add the mustard seeds and cook over low heat, stirring frequently, until they begin to splutter and give off their aroma. Add the pork with the marinade, and the water. Bring to a boil, stirring constantly, then reduce the heat and simmer, covered, for 30 minutes.

3 Remove the lid from the pan and stir the curry. Simmer for an additional 30 minutes, or until the pork is tender. Transfer to a warmed serving dish and serve with rice.

COOK'S TIP

Remove the marinating meat from the refrigerator 30 minutes before you intend to begin cooking to bring it to room temperature.

chicken tikka

serves six

1 tsp finely chopped fresh
  gingerroot

1 garlic clove, crushed

½ tsp ground coriander

½ tsp ground cumin

1 tsp chili powder

3 tbsp plain yogurt

1 tsp salt

2 tbsp lemon juice

few drops of red food coloring
  (optional)

1 tbsp tomato paste

3 lb 5 oz/1.5 kg skinless, boneless
  chicken breasts

1 onion, sliced

3 tbsp vegetable oil

6 lettuce leaves

1 lemon, cut into wedges,
  to garnish

1 Blend the ginger, garlic, ground
  coriander, ground cumin, and chili
  powder together in a large bowl.

2 Add the yogurt, salt, lemon juice,
  red food coloring (if using), and
  the tomato paste to the spice mixture.

3 Using a sharp knife, cut the
  chicken into pieces. Add the
  chicken to the spice mixture and toss
  to coat well. Let marinate in the
  refrigerator for at least 3 hours,
  preferably overnight.

4 Preheat the broiler. Arrange the
  onion in the base of a flameproof
  dish. Carefully drizzle half of the oil
  over the onions.

5 Arrange the marinated chicken
  pieces on top of the onions and
  cook under the hot broiler, turning
  once and basting with the remaining
  oil, for 25–30 minutes.

6 Serve the chicken tikka on a be
  of lettuce and garnish with the
  lemon wedges.

COOK'S TIP
Chicken Tikka can be served
with Naan Bread (see page 181
Raita (see page 226), and
Mango Chutney (see page 230
or as an appetizer.

hicken with spinach

serves four

oz/225 g fresh spinach leaves,
  rinsed

fresh green chili, seeded
  and chopped

tbsp chopped fresh
  gingerroot

garlic cloves, chopped

tbsp water

tbsp ghee or vegetable oil

black peppercorns

bay leaf

onion, finely chopped

cup canned tomatoes,
  drained

tsp chili powder

tbsp Curry Paste (see page 11)

lt

cup chicken stock or water

tbsp plain yogurt, plus extra
  to garnish

skinless chicken thighs

1 Place the spinach in a large pan
with just the water clinging to the
leaves after rinsing, then cover and
cook for 4–5 minutes, or until wilted.
Transfer to a food processor or blender
and add the green chili, ginger, garlic,
and water. Process until smooth.

2 Heat the ghee in a karahi or pan.
Add the peppercorns and bay leaf
and cook over low heat, stirring
constantly, for 1–2 minutes, or until
they give off their aroma. Add the
onion and cook, stirring occasionally,
for 10 minutes, or until golden. Add
the tomatoes and cook for 2 minutes,
breaking them up with a wooden
spoon. Add the chili powder and Curry
Paste and season with salt to taste.
Cook, stirring constantly, for 2 minutes.

3 Stir in the spinach leaves and chili
purée with the stock and simmer
for 5 minutes. Add the yogurt,
1 tablespoon at a time, stirring well
after each addition, then simmer for an
additional 5 minutes. Finally, add the
chicken and stir well, then cover and
simmer for 30 minutes, or until tender
and cooked through. Serve immediately,
garnished with extra yogurt.

chicken masala

serves four

⅔ cup plain yogurt

4 tbsp lemon juice

2 tbsp corn oil

2 tsp Garam Masala (see page 11)

2 tsp ground cumin

1 tsp chopped fresh gingerroot

1 tsp chopped garlic

salt

8 skinless, boneless chicken thighs

1 tsp dried fenugreek

2 tsp amchoor (dried
 mango powder)

1 tsp dried mint

cilantro sprigs, to garnish

TO SERVE

tomato wedges

pappadams

1 Mix the yogurt, lemon juice, corn oil, Garam Masala, cumin, ginger, garlic, and a pinch of salt together in a bowl. Place the chicken thighs in a large, shallow, ovenproof dish. Pour over the yogurt mixture and turn the chicken to coat well. Cover with plastic wrap and let marinate in the refrigerator overnight.

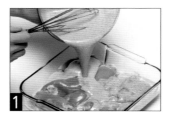

2 Preheat the oven to 375°F/190°C. Remove the plastic wrap from the chicken and cover the dish with foil. Bake the chicken in its marinade in the preheated oven for 45 minutes. Remove the chicken from the dish with a slotted spoon and cut into bite-size pieces, then spread out on a baking sheet.

3 Stir the fenugreek, amchoor, and mint into the remaining marinade, then pour over the chicken. Return to the oven and bake for an additional 10 minutes. Transfer to a warmed dish, then garnish with cilantro and serve with tomato wedges and pappadams.

COOK'S TIP

Fresh garlic adds a wonderfu flavor to many dishes, includi spicy curries. Store garlic bulbs a cool, dark place. They will l up to 6 months if kept correct

picy roast chicken

serves four

⅔ cup ground almonds

⅔ cup dry unsweetened coconut

⅔ cup vegetable oil

onion, finely chopped

tsp chopped fresh gingerroot

garlic clove, crushed

tsp chili powder

½ tsp Garam Masala (see page 11)

tsp salt

cup plain yogurt

chicken quarters, skinned

alad greens, to serve

) GARNISH

hopped cilantro

lemon, cut into wedges

1 Preheat the oven to 325°F/160°C. Dry-roast the almonds and coconut in a heavy-bottom pan, then reserve.

2 Heat the oil in a skillet. Add the onion and cook, stirring, until golden brown.

3 Place the ginger, garlic, chili powder, Garam Masala, and salt in a bowl and mix in the yogurt. Add the reserved almonds and coconut and mix well.

4 Add the onion to the spice mixture and blend, then reserve.

5 Arrange the chicken quarters in the base of a large, heatproof dish. Spoon the spice mixture over the chicken.

6 Cook in the preheated oven for 35–45 minutes. Check that the chicken is cooked thoroughly by piercing the thickest part of the meat with a sharp knife or a fine skewer—the juices will run clear when the chicken is cooked through. Garnish with the cilantro and lemon wedges and serve with a green salad.

COOK'S TIP

For an even spicier dish, add more chili powder and Garam Masala.

71

chicken dhansak

serves six

generous ½ cup chana dal

generous ½ cup moong dal

generous ½ cup toor dal

generous ½ cup masoor dal

scant ½ cup vegetable oil

2 tsp Garlic Paste (see page 11)

2 tsp Ginger Paste (see page 11)

6 chicken portions

2 cups canned tomatoes, drained

8 oz/225 g peeled pumpkin, diced

3 onions, chopped

4 oz/115 g fresh spinach, chopped

1 eggplant, diced

1 tbsp chopped fresh mint

salt

2 fresh green chilies, chopped

1½ tsp ground turmeric

1 tsp ground coriander

½ tsp ground cardamom

½ tsp ground cinnamon

½ tsp ground cloves

½ tsp chili powder

2 tbsp chopped cilantro,
   to garnish

1 Place the dals in a large pan and add enough water to cover. Bring to a boil, then reduce the heat and simmer, covered, for 40 minutes. Heat 3 tablespoons of the oil in a skillet. Add half the Garlic Paste and half the Ginger Paste and cook, stirring, for 1 minute. Add the chicken and cook until golden brown. Add to the dals.

2 Stir in the tomatoes, pumpkin, two-thirds of the onion, the spinach, eggplant, mint, and salt to taste. Bring to a boil, then cover and simmer for 45 minutes, or until the chicken is cooked. Transfer the chicken to a plate. Transfer the dal mixture to a food processor and process to a purée.

3 Heat the remaining oil in a cle pan. Add the remaining onion and cook over low heat for 10 min or until golden. Stir in the chilies a the remaining Garlic Paste and Gin Paste and cook, stirring, for 2 minu Add the remaining spices and cook 6 minutes, adding a little water if t mixture is very dry. Add to the dal mixture and stir, then cover and sim for 20 minutes. Add the chicken portions and simmer for an additio 20 minutes. Sprinkle with chopped cilantro and serve.

hicken drumsticks with herbs & spices

serves four

chicken drumsticks
½ tsp finely chopped fresh
   gingerroot
–2 garlic cloves, crushed
tsp salt
onions, chopped
large bunch of fresh
   cilantro, chopped
–6 fresh green chilies, chopped
½ cups vegetable oil
firm tomatoes, cut into wedges
large green bell peppers, seeded
   and coarsely chopped

Using a sharp knife, make
2–3 slashes in each chicken
mstick. Rub the ginger, garlic, and
over the drumsticks and reserve.

Place half of the chopped onion,
the cilantro, and chilies in a
rtar and grind to a paste using a
tle. Rub the paste over the chicken
msticks.

3 Heat the oil in a karahi or large,
heavy-bottom skillet. Add the
remaining chopped onion and cook
until golden brown. Remove the
onions from the skillet with a slotted
spoon and reserve.

4 Reduce the heat to medium–hot
and cook the drumsticks, in
batches if necessary, until cooked
through (10 minutes per batch).

5 When all of the chicken pieces are
cooked, remove them from the
skillet and keep warm.

6 Add the tomatoes and bell
peppers to the skillet and cook
them until they are tender but still firm.

7 Transfer the tomatoes and bell
peppers to a serving plate and
arrange the drumsticks on top. Garnish
with the reserved fried onions.

chicken tossed in black pepper

serves four–six

8 chicken thighs

1 tsp finely chopped fresh
 gingerroot

1 garlic clove, crushed

1 tsp salt

1½ tsp coarsely ground pepper

⅔ cup vegetable oil

1 green bell pepper, seeded and
 coarsely sliced

⅔ cup water

2 tbsp lemon juice

FRIED CORN & PEAS

¼ cup unsalted butter

2 cups frozen corn

2 cups frozen peas

½ tsp salt

½ tsp chili powder

1 tbsp lemon juice

chopped cilantro, to garnish

1 Using a sharp knife, bone the chicken thighs, if you prefer.

2 Mix the ginger, garlic, salt, and pepper together in a small bowl.

3 Add the chicken pieces to the pepper mixture and reserve.

4 Heat the oil in a large skillet. Add the chicken pieces and stir-fry for 10 minutes.

5 Reduce the heat and add the green bell pepper and the wat to the pan. Let the chicken mixture simmer for 10 minutes, then sprink over the lemon juice.

6 Meanwhile, make the fried co and peas. Melt the butter in a separate large skillet. Add the corn and peas and cook, stirring occasionally, for 10 minutes. Add th salt and chili powder and cook for a additional 5 minutes.

7 Sprinkle the lemon juice over the corn and peas and garnish with cilantro.

8 Transfer the chicken and peppe mixture to warmed serving pla and serve immediately with the frie corn and peas.

chicken jalfrezi

serves four

1 tsp mustard oil

3 tbsp vegetable oil

1 large onion, finely chopped

3 garlic cloves, crushed

1 tbsp tomato paste

2 tomatoes, peeled and chopped

1 tsp ground turmeric

½ tsp cumin seeds, ground

½ tsp coriander seeds, ground

½ tsp chili powder

½ tsp Garam Masala (see page 11)

1 tsp red wine vinegar

1 small red bell pepper, seeded
   and chopped

1 cup frozen fava beans

1 lb/450 g cooked chicken breasts,
   cut into bite-size pieces

salt

cilantro sprigs, to garnish

freshly cooked rice, to serve

1 Heat the mustard oil in a large skillet set over high heat for 1 minute, until it begins to smoke. Add the vegetable oil and reduce the heat, then add the onion and garlic and cook until they are golden.

2 Add the tomato paste, chopped tomatoes, ground turmeric, cumin, coriander, chili powder, Garam Masala, and red wine vinegar to the pan. Stir the mixture until fragrant.

3 Add the red bell pepper and fava beans and stir for 2 minutes, or until the pepper is softened. Stir in the chicken and salt to taste. Let simmer gently for 6–8 minutes, or until the chicken is heated through and the beans are tender.

4 Transfer to warmed serving plates, then garnish with cilantro sprigs and serve with rice.

COOK'S TIP

This dish is an ideal way of making use of leftover cooked poultry or game birds—turkey, duck, or quail. Any variety of bean works well, or substitute root vegetables, zucchini, potatoes, or broccoli. Leafy vegetables will not be so successful.

chicken & onions

serves four

1¼ cups vegetable oil

4 onions, finely chopped

1½ tsp finely chopped fresh
   gingerroot

1½ tsp Garam Masala (see page 11)

1 garlic clove, crushed

1 tsp chili powder

1 tsp ground coriander

3 green cardamoms

3 black peppercorns

3 tbsp tomato paste

8 chicken thighs, skinned

1¼ cups water

2 tbsp lemon juice

1 fresh green chili, finely chopped

¼ bunch of cilantro leaves,
   chopped

1 fresh green chili, cut into strips,
   to garnish

1 Heat the oil in a large skillet. Add the onions and cook, stirring occasionally, until golden brown.

2 Reduce the heat and add the ginger, Garam Masala, garlic, chili powder, ground coriander, cardamoms, and peppercorns. Stir well.

3 Add the tomato paste to the mixture in the skillet and stir-fry for 5–7 minutes.

4 Add the chicken thighs and to to coat with the spice mixture.

5 Pour the water into the pan, then cover and let simmer for 20–25 minutes.

6 Add the lemon juice, green ch and cilantro to the mixture and stir well until mixed.

7 Transfer the chicken and onior serving plates and garnish wit strips of green chili. Serve hot.

hicken korma

serves eight

/₂ tsp finely chopped fresh
 gingerroot

–2 garlic cloves, crushed

tsp Garam Masala (see page 11)

tsp chili powder

tsp salt

tsp black cumin seeds

green cardamoms, with husks
 removed and seeds crushed

tsp ground coriander

tsp ground almonds

cup plain yogurt

skinless, boneless chicken breasts

¼ cups vegetable oil

onions, sliced

cup water

bunch of cilantro, chopped

resh green chilies, chopped

shly cooked rice, to serve

1 Mix the ginger, garlic, Garam Masala, chili powder, salt, cumin seeds, cardamoms, ground coriander, almonds, and yogurt together in a small bowl.

2 Place the chicken breasts in a dish and spoon over the yogurt and spice mixture. Let chill.

3 Heat the oil in a large skillet. Add the onions and cook until golden brown.

4 Add the chicken breasts to the skillet and stir-fry for 5–7 minutes.

5 Add the water, then cover and let simmer for 20–25 minutes.

6 Add the cilantro and chilies and cook for an additional 10 minutes, gently stirring occasionally.

7 Transfer to a serving plate and serve with freshly cooked rice.

tandoori-style chicken

serves four

8 chicken drumsticks, skinned

⅔ cup plain yogurt

1½ tsp finely chopped fresh
   gingerroot

1–2 garlic cloves, crushed

1 tsp chili powder

2 tsp ground cumin

2 tsp ground coriander

1 tsp salt

½ tsp red food coloring (optional)

1 tbsp tamarind paste

⅔ cup water

⅔ cup vegetable oil, for basting

lettuce leaves

Naan Bread (see page 181),
   to serve

TO GARNISH

onion rings

1 lemon, cut into wedges

1 Using a sharp knife, make 2–3 slashes in each chicken drumstick. Place the yogurt in a large bowl. Add the ginger, garlic, chili powder, ground cumin, ground coriander, salt, and red food coloring (if using) and blend together.

2 Add the chicken to the yogurt and spice mixture and mix to coat well. Let the chicken marinate in the refrigerator for a minimum of 3 hours.

3 Mix the tamarind paste and water together in a separate bowl, then fold into the yogurt and spice mixture. Toss the drumsticks in this mixture and let marinate in the refrigerator for an additional 3 hours.

COOK'S TIP

Before serving the chicken drumsticks, make sure the chicken is tender and thoroughly cooked. A Raita, such as Mint Raita (see page 226), complements this dish perfectly.

4 Preheat the broiler to medium. Transfer the drumsticks to a heatproof dish and brush the drums with a little oil. Cook under the hot broiler for 30–35 minutes, turning t drumsticks occasionally and basting

5 Arrange the chicken on a bed lettuce and garnish with onio rings and lemon wedges. Serve wi Naan Bread.

chicken dopiaza

serves four

3 tbsp ghee or vegetable oil

8 baby onions or shallots, halved

3 dried red chilies

6 cardamoms

6 black peppercorns

2 whole cloves

2 bay leaves

2 onions, finely chopped

1 tsp Garlic Paste (see page 11)

1 tsp Ginger Paste (see page 11)

1 tsp ground cumin

1 tsp ground coriander

1 tsp chili powder

½ tsp ground turmeric

1 cup canned tomatoes

4 tbsp water

8 skinless chicken thighs

cilantro leaves, to garnish

freshly cooked rice, to serve

1 Heat 2 tablespoons of the ghee in a large, heavy-bottom pan or flameproof casserole. Add the baby onions and cook over low heat, stirring occasionally, for 10 minutes, or until golden. Remove with a slotted spoon and reserve until required.

2 Add the remaining ghee to the pan and cook the chilies, cardamoms, peppercorns, cloves, and bay leaves, stirring constantly, for 2 minutes, or until they give off their aroma. Add the chopped onions and cook, stirring frequently, for 5 minutes, or until softened.

3 Stir in the Garlic Paste, Ginger Paste, cumin, ground coriander, chili powder, and turmeric and cook, stirring constantly, for 2 minutes. Add the tomatoes and their can juices and the water. Stir well and simmer for 5 minutes, or until slightly thickened.

4 Add the chicken thighs and simmer for 20 minutes. Return the baby onions to the pan and cook for an additional 10 minutes, or until the chicken is tender and cooked through. Serve immediately with rice garnished with cilantro leaves.

VARIATION

You could use 8 skinless chicken drumsticks or 4 larger chicken portions. Increase the cooking time by 15 minutes for chicken portions.

COOK'S TIP

This dish can be prepared a day in advance and cooled, then covered and stored in the refrigerator. It is, however, not suitable for freezing.

chicken patties

serves six–eight

3 lb 5 oz/1.5 kg chicken, boned

½ tsp ground cumin

4 cardamom seeds, crushed

½ tsp ground cinnamon

1 tsp salt

1 tsp finely chopped fresh
   gingerroot

1 garlic clove, crushed

½ tsp ground allspice

½ tsp pepper

1¼ cups water

2 tbsp plain yogurt

2 fresh green chilies

1 small onion, chopped

½ bunch of cilantro, chopped

1 egg, beaten

1¼ cups vegetable oil

1 lemon, cut into wedges,
   to garnish

1 Place the chicken in a large pan. Add the ground cumin, cardamom seeds, ground cinnamon, salt, ginger, garlic, allspice, and pepper and pour in the water. Bring the mixture to a boil and boil until all of the water has been absorbed.

2 Place the mixture in a food processor and process to a smooth paste. Transfer the paste to a large bowl. Add the yogurt and blend together until well mixed.

3 Place the chilies, onion, and cilantro in the food processor and process until finely ground. Add to the chicken mixture and combine. Add the beaten egg and mix well.

4 With dampened hands, divide mixture into 12 portions and shape into small flat circles.

5 Heat the oil in a pan. Add the rounds in batches and cook gently, turning once. Drain thoroughly on paper towels and serve hot, garnished with lemon wedges.

COOK'S TIP

You can serve these patties with any dal, such as Onion Dal (see page 162), a green salad and Chapatis (see page 189).

uttered chicken

serves four–six

ant ⅔ cup unsalted butter

tbsp vegetable oil

onions, finely chopped

tsp finely chopped or crushed
fresh gingerroot

tsp Garam Masala (see page 11)

tsp ground coriander

tsp chili powder

tsp black cumin seeds

garlic clove, crushed

tsp salt

green cardamoms

black peppercorns

cup plain yogurt

tbsp tomato paste

chicken pieces, skinned

cup water

bay leaves

cup light cream

• GARNISH

opped cilantro

fresh green chilies, chopped

1 Heat the butter and oil in a large skillet. Add the onions and cook until golden brown, stirring. Reduce the heat.

2 Place the ginger in a bowl. Add the Garam Masala, ground coriander, chili powder, cumin seeds, garlic, salt, cardamoms, and peppercorns and blend. Add the yogurt and tomato paste and stir well.

3 Add the chicken pieces to the yogurt and spice mixture and mix to coat well.

4 Add the chicken to the onions in the skillet and stir-fry vigorously, making semicircular movements, for 5–7 minutes.

5 Add the water and bay leaves and let simmer for 30 minutes, stirring occasionally.

6 Add the cream and cook for an additional 10–15 minutes. Garnish with cilantro and chilies and serve.

duck curry

2-inch/5-cm piece fresh gingerroot

3 onions

2½ cups chicken stock

3 garlic cloves, finely chopped

4 whole cloves

salt

4 tbsp ghee or vegetable oil

1 tsp cayenne pepper

2 tsp coriander seeds,
   lightly crushed

6 lb/2.7 kg duck, cut into portions

large pinch of saffron threads

generous 1 cup ground almonds

1¼ cups single cream

1 tsp cardamom seeds,
   lightly crushed

1 Preheat the oven to 300°F/150°C. Finely chop the ginger and reserve. Cut 1 onion in half and finely chop the others. Place the stock in a large, heavy-bottom pan, then add the onion halves, ginger, garlic, cloves, and a pinch of salt and bring to a boil. Boil until reduced by half, then strain into a bowl and reserve until required. Discard the contents of the strainer.

2 Heat the ghee in a flameproof casserole. Add the chopped onions and cook over low heat for 10 minutes, or until golden. Stir in the cayenne and coriander seeds and cook for 1 minute, or until they give off their aroma. Add the duck portions and cook, turning frequently, until browned all over. Add the reserved stock, then season with salt to taste and bring to a boil. Reduce the heat, then cover and cook for 20 minutes.

3 Place the saffron in a bowl and add enough boiling water to cover. Let soak for 10 minutes. Mix almonds, cream, cardamom seeds, the saffron with its soaking liquid together. Pour the mixture into the casserole and stir well. Transfer to preheated oven and cook for an additional 20 minutes, or until the duck is tender. Serve immediately.

COOK'S TIP

It is best to use homemade stock for this dish, if possible. If you have to use a stock cube, don't add any salt in Step 1, because stock cubes tend to be very salty.

southern duck

serves four

2 tsp cumin seeds

2 tsp coriander seeds

1 tsp cardamom seeds

2 tsp Garam Masala (see page 11)

1 tsp chili powder

½ tsp ground turmeric

salt

6 boneless duck breasts

2 garlic cloves, finely chopped

2 onions, sliced

3¾ cups canned coconut milk

½ cup white wine vinegar

¾ cup water

2 tbsp chopped cilantro

COOK'S TIP

Using a sharp knife, trim off any excess fat from the duck breasts before cooking them, but do not remove the skin.

1 Place the cumin, coriander, and cardamom seeds, Garam Masala, chili powder, and turmeric into a mortar or spice grinder with a pinch of salt and grind finely. Reserve.

2 Place the duck breasts, skin-side down, in a large, heavy-bottom skillet and cook over medium heat for 10 minutes, or until the skin is golden brown. Turn over and cook for an additional 6–8 minutes, or until the second side is browned. Remove from the skillet with a slotted spoon and drain on paper towels.

3 Drain off all but about 1 tablespoon of the fat from skillet and return to the heat. Add garlic and onions and cook, stirring occasionally, for 8 minutes, or until golden brown. Stir in the ground mixture and cook, stirring constantly for 2 minutes, or until the spices give off their aroma.

4 Return the duck breasts to the skillet and stir in the coconut vinegar, and water. Bring to a boil then reduce the heat and simmer, covered, for 40–45 minutes, or until the duck is tender. Taste and add salt, if necessary. Stir in the chopped cilantro and serve immediately.

Fish Dishes

Fish is one of the most versatile ingredients and is equally delicious in spicy curries and creamy stews or when presented as fragrantly marinated kabobs. In this chapter, there are delicious recipes for both freshwater and sea fish, as well as many great ways of cooking shrimp.

Fish is eaten in the south and west of India, and traditional recipes are included, such as the delicious south Indian Fish in Coconut Sauce and Baked Fish with Coconut & Cilantro, a classic Parsee dish from the west coast. The fish is traditionally cooked in banana leaves, which are available from specialty Asian food stores, but waxed paper can be used instead.

fried fish in besan

serves four–six

²⁄₃ cup besan

1 tsp finely chopped fresh
   gingerroot

1 garlic clove, crushed

2 tsp chili powder

1 tsp salt

½ tsp ground turmeric

2 fresh green chilies, chopped

¼ bunch of cilantro, chopped

1¼ cups water

2 lb 4 oz/1 kg skinless cod fillet

1¼ cups oil

freshly cooked rice, to serve

TO GARNISH

2 lemons, cut into wedges

3 fresh green chilies, cut into strips

COOK'S TIP

Besan (gram flour) or chana dal
flour (lentil flour) is used to make
Pakoras (see page 194) and is
also used to bind kabobs. A
combination of besan and
ordinary whole-wheat flour
makes a delicious Gram Flour
Bread (see page 186).

1 Place the besan in a large bowl. Add the ginger, garlic, chili powder, salt, and turmeric and mix to blend well.

2 Add the chopped chilies and cilantro to the spiced mixture and stir to mix.

3 Pour in the water and stir to form a thick batter. Reserve.

4 Using a sharp knife, cut the cod into 10–12 pieces.

5 Carefully dip the pieces of cod into the batter, coating the cod all over. Shake off any excess batter.

6 Heat the oil in a heavy-bottom skillet. Add the battered cod and cook, in batches, over medium heat, turning once, until the fish is cooked through and golden.

7 Transfer the battered cod to a serving dish and garnish with lemon wedges and green chilies. S with freshly cooked rice.

fish in tomato sauce

serves four–six

1 lb 2 oz/500 g tomatoes

4 fresh green chilies

2 lb 4 oz/1 kg haddock fillets, skinned

salt

2 tsp ground turmeric

4 tbsp ghee or vegetable oil

2 onions, sliced

1 tbsp ground coriander

2 tsp Garam Masala (see page 11)

1 tsp chili powder

1 tsp sugar

2 tbsp plain yogurt

1 tbsp lemon juice

cilantro sprigs, to garnish

Pilaf Rice (see page 170), to serve

1 Peel, seed, and chop the tomatoes, then reserve. Using a sharp knife, slit the chilies lengthwise along 1 side, then seed and reserve. Remove any pin bones from the fish and cut into large chunks. Mix 1 teaspoon of salt and 1½ teaspoons of the turmeric together in a bowl, then rub the mixture all over the fish.

2 Heat the ghee in a large skillet. Add the fish, in batches if necessary, and cook over medium heat, stirring frequently, until golden brown all over. Remove with a slotted spoon and reserve. Add the onions, then reduce the heat and cook, stirring occasionally, for 10 minutes, or until golden brown.

3 Stir in the remaining turmeric, coriander, Garam Masala, chili powder, and sugar and cook, stirring for an additional 2 minutes. Increase the heat to medium and add the tomatoes, yogurt, lemon juice, and reserved chilies. Bring to a boil, then reduce the heat and simmer for 15 minutes.

4 Return the fish to the skillet. Stir gently to coat well in the sauce. Simmer for an additional 10 minutes, until the fish is cooked. Taste and add the seasoning, then garnish with cilantro and serve with Pilaf Rice.

unjabi-style fish

serves four

tbsp ghee or vegetable oil

onions, sliced

tsp Garlic Paste (see page 11)

tsp Ginger Paste (see page 11)

tbsp ground cumin

tsp ground coriander

tsp Garam Masala (see page 11)

tsp ground cinnamon

tsp cayenne pepper

cardamoms, lightly crushed

lt

cups canned tomatoes

cup light cream

tbsp lemon juice

lb 12 oz/800 g cod fillets,
  skinned and cut into 1½-inch/
  4-cm slices

opped cilantro, to garnish

shly cooked rice, to serve

Heat the ghee in a pan. Add the
  onions and cook over low heat,
ing occasionally, for 10 minutes, or
 golden. Add the Garlic Paste,
ger Paste, cumin, ground coriander,
am Masala, cinnamon, cayenne,
amoms, and a pinch of salt and
k, stirring, for 2 minutes, or until
spices give off their aroma.

2 Stir in the tomatoes and their can
  juices, cream, and lemon juice
and cook, stirring occasionally, for
5 minutes, or until slightly thickened.
Do not let the mixture boil.

3 Add the pieces of fish, then
  cover and simmer gently for
10 minutes, or until tender. Transfer to
warmed serving dishes and sprinkle
with chopped cilantro. Serve with rice.

fried trout with ginger

serves four

1 tsp Ginger Paste (see page 11)

1 tsp Garlic Paste (see page 11)

2 fresh green chilies, seeded and
finely chopped

1 tbsp chopped cilantro

¼ tsp ground turmeric

salt and pepper

4 trout, cleaned

vegetable oil, for brushing

TO GARNISH

cilantro sprigs

lime slices

1 Preheat the broiler to medium.
Mix the Ginger Paste, Garlic Paste, chilies, cilantro, turmeric, 1 teaspoon of pepper, and a pinch of salt together in a small bowl. Stir in enough water to make a smooth paste.

2 Using a sharp knife, slash the trout diagonally on both sides 2–3 times. Rub the spice paste into the fish, especially the slashes.

3 Brush with oil and cook under hot broiler for 15 minutes, turn once and brushing with more oil. Transfer to warmed serving plates a garnish with cilantro sprigs and lime slices. Serve immediately.

COOK'S TIP

Cilantro is used extensively in Indian cooking and imparts a distinctive flavor to dishes. Fine chop the stems as well as the leaves of the herb.

bengali-style fish

serves four–six

1 tsp ground turmeric

1 tsp salt

2 lb 4 oz/1 kg cod fillet, skinned and
    cut into pieces

6 tbsp corn oil

4 fresh green chilies

1 tsp finely chopped fresh
    gingerroot

1 garlic clove, crushed

2 onions, finely chopped

2 tomatoes, finely chopped

6 tbsp mustard oil

1¾ cups water

chopped cilantro, to garnish

Naan Bread (see page 181),
    to serve

COOK'S TIP

In the hot and humid eastern
plains that surround Bengal, the
mustard plant flourishes,
providing oil for cooking and
spicy seeds for flavoring. Fish
and seafood feature in many
meals, often flavored with
mustard oil.

1 Mix the turmeric and salt together in a small bowl.

2 Spoon the turmeric and salt mixture over the fish pieces.

3 Heat the corn oil in a skillet. Add the fish and cook until pale yellow. Remove the fish with a slotted spoon and reserve.

4 Place the chilies, ginger, garlic, onions, tomatoes, and mustard oil in a mortar and, using a pestle, grind to form a paste. Alternatively, process the ingredients in a food processor.

5 Transfer the spice paste to a skillet and dry-fry until golden brown.

6 Remove the skillet from the heat and gently place the fish pieces into the paste without breaking the fish up.

7 Return the skillet to the heat, then add the water and cook the fish, uncovered, over medium heat for 15–20 minutes.

8 Garnish with chopped cilantro and serve with Naan Bread.

eep-fried fish

serves six

red snapper fillets, halved

lt and pepper

cup lemon juice

egetable oil, for deep-frying

limes, cut into wedges, to garnish

ATTER

enerous ½ cup besan

tbsp rice flour

tsp chili powder

tsp ground turmeric

cup water

Season the fish to taste with salt
and pepper, then place in a large,
llow, nonmetallic dish and sprinkle
the lemon juice. Cover with plastic
p and let marinate in a cool place
30 minutes.

Meanwhile, make the batter. Sift
together the besan, rice flour, chili
der, and turmeric into a large
l. Gradually stir in the water to
e a smooth batter. Cover and let
for 30 minutes.

3 Heat the oil for deep-frying in
a deep-fat fryer or large,
heavy-bottom pan to 350–375°F/
180–190°C, or until a cube of bread
browns in 30 seconds. Dip the fish
pieces in the batter a few at a time, to
coat, and drain off the excess. Add to
the hot oil and deep-fry for 5 minutes,
or until golden brown and crisp.
Remove with a slotted spoon and drain
on paper towels. Keep warm while you
cook the remaining pieces of fish.
Serve, garnished with lime wedges.

COOK'S TIP

Make sure that the batter is
well blended before resting. If
you let the batter rest for more
than 30 minutes, stir it well
before using, because it may
have begun to separate.

angler fish kabobs

serves four

3 tbsp lime juice

1 tbsp finely chopped fresh mint

1 tbsp finely chopped
   cilantro

2 fresh green chilies, seeded and
   finely chopped

1 tsp Ginger Paste (see page 11)

½ tsp Garlic Paste (see page 11)

1 tsp ground coriander

salt

12 oz /350 g angler fish fillet, cubed

1 red bell pepper, seeded and cut
   into chunks

1 green bell pepper, seeded and cut
   into chunks

8 baby corn cobs, halved

8 white mushrooms

8 cherry tomatoes

½ small cauliflower, broken
   into florets

1 tbsp corn oil

Pilaf Rice (see page 170), to serve

TO GARNISH

1 lime, cut into wedges

cilantro sprigs

1 Mix the lime juice, mint, cilantro, chilies, Ginger Paste, Garlic Paste, ground coriander, and a pinch of salt together in a large, shallow, nonmetallic dish. Add the fish and stir to coat. Cover with plastic wrap and let marinate in a cool place for 30 minutes.

2 Preheat the broiler to medium. Drain the fish and reserve the marinade. Thread the angler fish, chunks of bell pepper, baby corn cobs, mushrooms, cherry tomatoes, and cauliflower florets onto 4 long or 8 short skewers.

3 Brush the kabobs with any remaining marinade and the and cook under the hot broiler, tur and basting frequently, for 10 min or until cooked. Serve immediately a bed of Pilaf Rice, garnished with wedges and cilantro sprigs.

COOK'S TIP

If using wooden or bamboo skewers, remember to soak them in a bowl of warm water while the fish is marinating to prevent them charring under the broiler.

VARIATION

Substitute large raw shrimp peeled but with their tails left intact, for the angler fish if you like.

fish in coconut sauce

serves six

1 tbsp ghee or vegetable oil

2 onions, sliced

2 tsp ground cumin

1 tsp Garlic Paste (see page 11)

1 tsp ground coriander

1 tsp ground turmeric

4 whole cloves

4 cardamoms, lightly crushed

6 curry leaves

3 cups canned coconut milk

2 lb 4 oz/1 kg angler fish tail

Chapatis (see page 189), to serve

COOK'S TIP

Try to make sure that all the pieces of fish are about the same size and thickness, so that they cook evenly. To test if the fish is cooked through, the flesh should be opaque and flake easily.

1 Heat the ghee in a large, heavy-bottom pan. Add the onions and cook over low heat, stirring occasionally, for 10 minutes, or until golden. Stir in the cumin, Garlic Paste, ground coriander, turmeric, cloves, and cardamoms and cook, stirring constantly, for 1–2 minutes, or until the spices give off their aroma. Add the curry leaves and coconut milk, then stir well and simmer for 20 minutes.

2 Meanwhile, remove and discard any gray membrane from the angler fish. Using a sharp knife, cut down either side of the central bone and remove and discard it. Cut each fillet in half across the center, then slice in half horizontally. Roll up each piece of fish as tightly as possible.

3 Gently add the fish rolls to the coconut sauce. Cover, then sim for an additional 10 minutes, or un the fish is tender and cooked throu Use the curry leaves as a garnish a serve immediately with Chapatis.

baked fish with coconut & cilantro

serves four

2 large lemon sole, cleaned
    and scaled

salt

5 tbsp lemon juice

scant 2 cups cilantro, chopped

½ cup dry unsweetened coconut

6 fresh green chilies, seeded
    and chopped

4 garlic cloves, chopped

1 tsp cumin seeds

1 tbsp sugar

vegetable oil, for brushing

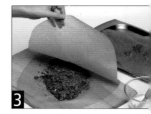

1 Using a sharp knife, slash the fish diagonally twice on both sides. Rub all over the inside and outside of the fish with salt and 4 tablespoons of the lemon juice. Place on a large plate, then cover and let marinate in a cool place for 30 minutes.

COOK'S TIP

Do not marinate the fish in the lemon juice for longer than an hour, otherwise the acid begins to denature the protein and "cook" the fish.

2 Preheat the oven to 400°F/200 Place the remaining lemon juic cilantro, coconut, chilies, garlic, cum seeds, and sugar in a food processo and process until smooth. Alternativ place the ingredients in a mortar an grind with a pestle.

3 Cut out 2 pieces of parchment paper or waxed paper large enough to enclose a fish completely and brush with a little oil. Rub the fi all over with the coconut and cilantr paste, then place each fish on a piec of parchment paper or waxed paper and fold in the sides to enclose. Place the packages on a large bakin sheet and bake in the preheated oven for 25–30 minutes, or until cooked through. Unwrap and serve immediately.

marinated fish

serves four

1 fresh green chili

4 red snapper, cleaned

½ cup lime juice

4 tbsp plain yogurt

1 tsp Garlic Paste (see page 11)

1 tsp Ginger Paste (see page 11)

1 tbsp coriander seeds

1 tsp Garam Masala (see page 11)

few drops red food coloring
   (optional)

¾ stick butter

2 tsp ground cumin

TO GARNISH

1 lime, cut into wedges

cilantro sprigs

1 Seed and chop the chili and reserve. Using a sharp knife, slash the fish diagonally several times on both sides and sprinkle with the lime juice. Place the yogurt, Garlic Paste, Ginger Paste, coriander seeds, chopped chili, and Garam Masala in a food processor and process to make a paste. Transfer to a large, shallow dish and stir in the red food coloring (if using). Add the fish, turning to coat. Cover with plastic wrap and let marinate in the refrigerator for 8 hours, turning occasionally.

COOK'S TIP

Do not let the butter turn brown when you are melting it over low heat, otherwise it will taste bitter and may spoil the finished dish.

2 Preheat the oven to 375°F/190°C. Remove the fish from the marinade and place o a wire rack in a large roasting pan. Cook in the preheated oven for 10 minutes.

3 Meanwhile, melt the butter in small pan over low heat. Rem the pan from the heat and stir in th cumin. Brush the butter all over the fish and return to the oven for an additional 6–7 minutes, or until cooked through. Transfer to warme plates and garnish with lime wedg and cilantro sprigs. Serve immediat

shrimp with tomatoes

serves four–six

3 onions

1 green bell pepper

1 tsp finely chopped fresh
gingerroot

1 garlic clove, crushed

1 tsp salt

1 tsp chili powder

2 tbsp lemon juice

12 oz /350 g frozen shrimp

3 tbsp vegetable oil

2 cups canned tomatoes

chopped cilantro, to garnish

freshly cooked rice, to serve

COOK'S TIP

Fresh gingerroot looks rather like
a knobbly potato. The skin
should be peeled, then the flesh
either grated, finely chopped, or
sliced. Ginger is also available
ground: this can be used as a
substitute for fresh gingerroot,
but the flavor of the fresh root is
far superior.

1 Using a sharp knife, slice the
onions and seed and slice the
green bell pepper.

2 Place the ginger, garlic, salt, and
chili powder in a small bowl and
mix well. Add the lemon juice and mix
to make a paste.

3 Place the shrimp in a bowl of cold
water and let thaw. Drain
thoroughly.

4 Heat the oil in a medium-size
skillet. Add the onions and cook
until golden brown.

5 Add the spice paste to the onions.
Reduce the heat to low and cook,
stirring and mixing well, for 3 minutes.

6 Add the canned tomatoes with
their juice and the sliced bell
pepper, and cook for 5–7 minutes,
stirring occasionally.

7 Add the thawed shrimp to the
pan and cook for 10 minutes,
stirring occasionally. Garnish with
cilantro and serve hot with freshly
cooked rice.

shrimp with bell peppers

serves four

1 lb/450 g frozen shrimp

½ bunch of cilantro

1 garlic clove, crushed

1 tsp salt

1 red bell pepper

1 green bell pepper

scant 5 tbsp unsalted butter

cilantro sprigs, to garnish

freshly cooked rice, to serve

1 Thaw the shrimp and rinse under cold running water twice. Drain the shrimp thoroughly and place in a large bowl.

2 Finely chop the cilantro and add to the shrimp with the garlic and salt. Reserve until required. Seed and slice the red and green bell peppers and reserve until required.

3 Melt the butter in a large skillet. Add the shrimp and stir-fry, stirring and tossing the shrimp gently, for 10–12 minutes.

4 Add the reserved bell peppers and cook for an additional 3–5 minutes, stirring occasionally.

5 Transfer the shrimp and bell peppers to a serving dish. Garnish with cilantro sprigs and serve with rice.

COOK'S TIP

When using frozen shrimp, mak sure that they are thoroughly thawed before using. Store the covered, in the refrigerator unt needed and always use the sar day as thawed.

andoori-style shrimp

serves four

)–12 raw jumbo shrimp

ant ½ cup unsalted butter

tsp finely chopped fresh
 gingerroot

garlic clove, crushed

tsp chili powder

tsp salt

tsp ground coriander

tsp ground cumin

bunch of cilantro, finely chopped

w drops of red food coloring
 (optional)

ettuce leaves

GARNISH

-2 fresh green chilies,
 finely chopped

emon, cut into wedges

COOK'S TIP

Though not essential, it is best
to shell the shrimp before
cooking them, because some
eople find it slightly awkward
to peel them at the table.

1 Preheat the broiler to high.
 Carefully shell the shrimp.

2 Transfer the shelled shrimp to a
 flameproof dish.

3 Melt the butter in a pan, then
 remove from the heat.

4 Add the ginger, garlic, chili
 powder, salt, ground coriander,
ground cumin, chopped cilantro,
and the red food coloring (if using)
to the butter and mix together well.

5 Brush the melted butter and spice
 mixture over the shrimp.

6 Cook the shrimp under the broiler,
 for 10 minutes, turning once.

7 Arrange the shrimp on a bed of
 lettuce and garnish with finely
chopped chilies and lemon wedges.
Serve immediately.

dried shrimp

serves four

7 oz/200 g dried shrimp

1¼ cups vegetable oil

2 onions, sliced

3 fresh green chilies, finely chopped

¼ bunch of cilantro,
    finely chopped

1½ tsp finely chopped fresh
    gingerroot

1–2 garlic cloves, crushed

pinch of ground turmeric

1 tsp salt

1 tsp chili powder, plus extra
    to garnish

2 tbsp lemon juice

Chapatis (see page 189), to serve

1 Soak the shrimp in a bowl of cold water for 2 hours. Drain the shrimp thoroughly and rinse under cold running water twice. Drain the shrimp again, thoroughly.

2 Heat ⅔ cup of the oil in a large skillet.

3 Add the onions, chilies, and the chopped cilantro to the skillet and stir-fry until the onions are golden brown.

VARIATION

You could use 1 lb/450 g fresh shrimp instead of the dried shrimp, if you prefer.

4 Add the ginger, garlic, turmer salt, and chili powder to the pan and stir-fry for an additional 2 minutes over low heat. Reserve required.

5 Heat the remaining oil in a pa Add the shrimp and cook, stir occasionally, until the shrimp are c

6 Add the shrimp to the onions blend together. Return the sh and onion mixture to the heat and fry for an additional 3–5 minutes. Sprinkle over the lemon juice.

7 Transfer the shrimp to a servi dish. Garnish with a pinch of powder and serve with Chapatis.

shrimp with spinach

serves four–six

8 oz/225 g frozen shrimp

12 oz /350 g canned spinach purée
   or frozen spinach, thawed
   and chopped

2 tomatoes

⅔ cup vegetable oil

½ tsp mustard seeds

½ tsp onion seeds

1 tsp finely chopped fresh
   gingerroot

1 garlic clove, crushed

1 tsp chili powder

1 tsp salt

1 Place the shrimp in a bowl of cold water and let stand until thawed thoroughly.

2 Drain the can of spinach purée (if using).

3 Using a sharp knife, cut the tomatoes into slices.

4 Heat the oil in a large skillet. Add the mustard and onion seeds to the skillet.

5 Reduce the heat and add the tomatoes, spinach, ginger, garlic, chili powder, and salt to the skillet and stir-fry for 5–7 minutes.

6 Drain the shrimp thoroughly and add to the spinach mixture in the skillet.

7 Gently stir the shrimp and spinach mixture until well blended, then cover and let simmer over low heat for 7–10 minutes.

8 Transfer the shrimp and spinach to a serving dish and serve hot.

ussels in coconut sauce

serves four

bsp ghee or vegetable oil

nion, finely chopped

sp Garlic Paste (see page 11)

sp Ginger Paste (see page 11)

sp ground cumin

sp ground coriander

sp ground turmeric

cups canned coconut milk

4 oz/1 kg live mussels, scrubbed and debearded

pped cilantro, to garnish

COOK'S TIP

prepare mussels, scrub them vell under cold running water nd pull off any beards that are still attached to them. Discard y with broken shells or that do ot shut when sharply tapped.

1 Heat the ghee in a large, heavy-bottom skillet. Add the onion and cook over low heat, stirring occasionally, for 10 minutes, or until golden brown.

2 Add the Garlic Paste and Ginger Paste and cook, stirring constantly, for 2 minutes. Add the cumin, ground coriander, turmeric, and a pinch of salt and cook, stirring constantly, for an additional 2 minutes. Stir in the coconut milk and bring the mixture to a boil.

3 Add the mussels, then cover and cook for 5 minutes, or until the mussels have opened. Discard any mussels that remain shut. Transfer the mussels, with the coconut sauce, to a large, warmed serving dish. Sprinkle with cilantro and serve immediately.

VARIATION

Substitute 2 cooked crabs for the mussels. Add the crab meat with the claws in Step 3 and cook until just heated through.

Vegetables

A great many people in India are vegetarians, and over the years Indians have used their imagination to create a vast number of different vegetarian dishes. Spinach, tomatoes, potatoes, green beans, and cauliflower are all commonly used in Indian cooking. Other popular ingredients, including eggplants, okra, and daikon, are less familiar in the Western culinary repertoire, despite the fact that they are now widely available. This chapter includes some simple but delicious vegetarian dishes. Serve them as an accompaniment to other curries, or as vegetarian dishes in their own right.

green bean & potato curry

serves four

1¼ cups vegetable oil

1 tsp white cumin seeds

1 tsp mixed mustard and
onion seeds

4 dried red chilies

3 tomatoes, sliced

1 tsp salt

1 tsp finely chopped fresh
gingerroot

1 garlic clove, crushed

1 tsp chili powder

1⅓ cups green beans, sliced

2 potatoes, peeled and diced

1¼ cups water

chopped cilantro

2 fresh green chilies, finely chopped

COOK'S TIP

Mustard seeds are often fried in oil or ghee (a cooking fat similar to clarified butter) to bring out their flavor before being combined with other ingredients.

1 Heat the oil in a large, heavy-bottom pan.

2 Add the white cumin seeds, mustard and onion seeds, and dried red chilies to the pan, stirring well.

3 Add the tomatoes to the pan and stir-fry the mixture for 3–5 minutes.

4 Mix the salt, ginger, garlic, an chili powder together in a bow Spoon the mixture into the pan an blend well.

5 Add the green beans and potatoes to the pan and stir-fr for 5 minutes.

6 Add the water, then reduce th heat and let simmer for 10–15 minutes, stirring occasional

7 Sprinkle over the chopped cila and chilies and serve.

potato curry

serves four

3 potatoes, peeled and rinsed

⅔ cup vegetable oil

1 tsp onion seeds

½ tsp fennel seeds

4 curry leaves

1 tsp ground cumin

1 tsp ground coriander

1 tsp chili powder

pinch of ground turmeric

1 tsp salt

1½ tsp amchoor (dried
mango powder)

COOK'S TIP

Traditionally, Semolina Dessert
(see page 252) is served to
follow potato curry.

1 Using a sharp knife, cut each potato into 6 slices.

2 Boil the potato slices in a pan of water until just cooked, but not mushy (test by piercing with a sharp knife or a skewer). Drain and reserve until required.

3 Heat the oil in a separate pan. Reduce the heat and add the onion seeds, fennel seeds, and curry leaves, stirring to mix.

4 Remove the pan from the heat and add the cumin, ground coriander, chili powder, turmeric, salt, and amchoor. Stir well until mixed.

5 Return the pan to the heat and stir-fry the mixture for 1 minute.

6 Pour this mixture over the cook potatoes and mix together, the stir-fry over low heat for 5 minutes.

7 Transfer the potato curry to warmed serving dishes and serve immediately.

pinach & cheese curry

serves four

/₄ cups vegetable oil

oz/200 g paneer cheese, cubed
(see Cook's Tip)

tomatoes, sliced

tsp ground cumin

/₂ tsp ground chili powder

tsp salt

4 oz/400 g fresh spinach leaves

fresh green chilies

COOK'S TIP

o make paneer, boil 4 cups milk
slowly over low heat, then add
2 tablespoons lemon juice,
stirring constantly until the milk
thickens and begins to curdle.
Strain the milk and let stand
under a heavy weight for
1½–2 hours to press to a flat
shape about ½ inch/1 cm thick.
Once set, the paneer can be cut
nto whatever shape is required.
It is also available from Asian
food stores.

1 Heat the oil in a large, heavy-bottom skillet. Add the cubed paneer and cook, stirring occasionally, until golden brown.

2 Add the tomatoes and stir-fry, breaking up the tomatoes, for 5 minutes.

3 Add the cumin, chili powder, and salt to the skillet and mix together well.

4 Add the spinach and stir-fry over low heat for 7–10 minutes.

5 Add the chilies and cook, stirring, for an additional 2 minutes.

6 Transfer to serving plates and serve hot.

vegetable patties

serves four

2 large potatoes, sliced

1 onion, sliced

½ cauliflower, cut into small florets

scant ½ cup peas

1 tbsp spinach purée

2–3 fresh green chilies

¼ bunch cilantro, chopped, plus
   extra to garnish

1 tsp finely chopped fresh
   gingerroot

1 garlic clove, crushed

1 tsp ground coriander

pinch of ground turmeric

1 tsp salt

scant 1 cup bread crumbs

1¼ cups vegetable oil

fresh chili strips, to garnish

1 Place the potatoes, onion, and cauliflower florets in a pan of water and bring to a boil. Reduce the heat and let simmer until the potatoes are cooked through. Remove the vegetables from the pan with a slotted spoon and drain thoroughly.

2 Add the peas and spinach purée to the vegetables and mix, mashing down with a fork.

3 Chop the chilies, then mix with the chopped cilantro, ginger, garlic, ground coriander, turmeric, and salt in a bowl.

4 Blend the spice mixture into the vegetables, mixing with a fork to make a paste. Spread the bread crumbs out on a large plate.

5 With dampened hands, divide the vegetable mixture into 10–12 small balls. Flatten them with the palm of your hands to make flat circles.

6 Dip each circle in the bread crumbs, coating well.

7 Heat the oil in a heavy-bottom skillet and shallow-fry the patties in batches, until golden brown, turning occasionally. Transfer to serving plate and garnish with chili strips and extra cilantro. Serve hot.

balti vegetables

serves four

3 tbsp ghee or vegetable oil

1 onion, chopped

1 tsp Garlic Paste (see page 11)

1 tsp Ginger Paste (see page 11)

2 tsp ground coriander

1 tsp chili powder

½ tsp ground turmeric

½ cauliflower, broken into florets

2 potatoes, diced

2 carrots, diced

1 cup frozen peas, thawed

1 small rutabaga, diced

¾ cup green beans, cut into
    2-inch/5-cm pieces

½ cup corn kernels, thawed if frozen

4 tomatoes, peeled and chopped

salt

4–8 tbsp vegetable stock
    or water

cilantro sprigs, to garnish

1 Heat the ghee in a large pan. Add the onion and cook over low heat, stirring occasionally, for 10 minutes, or until golden. Stir in the Garlic Paste and Ginger Paste and cook for 1 minute. Add the ground coriander, chili powder, and turmeric and cook, stirring, for 2 minutes, or until the spices give off their aroma.

2 Add the cauliflower, potatoes, carrots, peas, rutabaga, green beans, and corn and cook, stirring, for an additional 3 minutes. Add the tomatoes and salt to taste, then pour in 4 tablespoons of the stock.

3 Cover and simmer for 10 minu or until all the vegetables are tender. Check the mixture while it is cooking, and if the vegetables look if they might catch on the base of th pan, add more stock. Serve, garnish with cilantro sprigs.

kra curry

lb/450 g okra

cup vegetable oil

onions, sliced

fresh green chilies, finely chopped

curry leaves

tsp salt

tomato, sliced

tbsp lemon juice

opped cilantro

Rinse the okra and drain thoroughly. Using a sharp knife, p and discard the ends. Cut the a into 1-inch/2.5-cm long pieces.

COOK'S TIP

When you buy fresh okra, make sure they are not shriveled and at they do not have any brown spots. Fresh okra will keep, ghtly wrapped, for up to 3 days n the refrigerator. Okra have a remarkable glutinous quality which naturally thickens curries and casseroles.

2 Heat the oil in a large, heavy-bottom skillet. Add the onions, chilies, curry leaves, and salt and mix together. Stir-fry the vegetables for 5 minutes.

3 Add the tomato to the skillet and sprinkle over the lemon juice.

4 Gradually add the okra, mixing in gently with a slotted spoon. Stir-fry the vegetable mixture over medium heat for 12–15 minutes.

5 Add the cilantro, then cover and let simmer for 3–5 minutes.

6 Transfer to serving plates and serve hot.

vegetable curry

serves four

8 oz/225 g turnips or rutabaga,
    peeled

1 eggplant, trimmed

12 oz /350 g new potatoes, scrubbed

8 oz/225 g cauliflower

8 oz/225 g white mushrooms

1 large onion

8 oz/225 g carrots, peeled

6 tbsp vegetable ghee or oil

2 garlic cloves, crushed

2-inch/5-cm piece fresh gingerroot,
    finely chopped

1–2 fresh green chilies, seeded
    and chopped

1 tbsp paprika

2 tsp ground coriander

1 tbsp mild or medium curry
    powder or paste

1¾ cups vegetable stock

2 cups canned chopped tomatoes

salt

1 green bell pepper, seeded
    and sliced

1 tbsp cornstarch

⅔ cup coconut milk

2–3 tbsp ground almonds

cilantro sprigs, to garnish

1 Cut the turnips, eggplant, and
potatoes into ½-inch/1-cm cubes.
Divide the cauliflower into small florets.
Leave the mushrooms whole, or slice
thickly if preferred. Slice the onion and
carrots.

2 Heat the ghee in a large pan. Add
the onion, carrots, turnip, potato,
and cauliflower and cook gently for
3 minutes, stirring frequently. Add the
garlic, ginger, chilies, paprika, ground
coriander, and curry powder and cook
for 1 minute, stirring constantly.

3 Add the stock, canned tomato,
eggplant, and mushrooms and
season with salt to taste. Cover and
simmer gently for 30 minutes or until
tender, stirring occasionally. Add the
green bell pepper, then cover and
continue cooking for an additional
5 minutes.

4 Blend the cornstarch and coco
milk together until smooth. Stir
into the mixture, then add the groun
almonds and simmer for 2 minutes,
stirring. Taste and adjust the season
if necessary. Serve hot, garnished w
cilantro sprigs.

:uffed rice crêpes

serves six

up rice and scant ¼ cup urid dal,
or 1⅓ cups ground rice and
⅓ cup urid dal flour (ata)
2½ cups water
sp salt
bsp vegetable oil

LING

otatoes, diced
esh green chilies, chopped
sp ground turmeric
sp salt
up vegetable oil
sp mixed mustard and
onion seeds
ried red chilies
urry leaves
bsp lemon juice

To make the crêpes (dosas), soak
the rice and urid dal for 3 hours.
d the rice and urid dal to a smooth
istency, adding water if necessary.
and for an additional 3 hours to
ent. Alternatively, if you are using
nd rice and urid dal flour, mix
her in a bowl. Add the water and
nd stir until a batter is formed.

2 Heat 1 tablespoon of the oil in a
large, nonstick skillet. Using a
ladle, spoon the batter into the skillet.
Tilt the skillet to spread the mixture
over the base. Cover and cook over
medium heat for 2 minutes. Remove
the lid and turn the crêpes over very
carefully. Pour a little oil around the
edge, then cover and cook for an
additional 2 minutes. Repeat with the
remaining batter.

3 To make the filling, boil the
potatoes in a pan of water. Add
the chilies, turmeric, and salt and cook
until the potatoes are soft enough to
be lightly mashed.

4 Heat the oil in a pan. Add the
mustard and onion seeds, dried
red chilies, and curry leaves and cook
for 1 minute. Pour the spice mixture
over the mashed potatoes, then
sprinkle over the lemon juice and mix
well. Spoon the potato filling on one
half of each crêpe and fold the other
half over the filling. Serve hot.

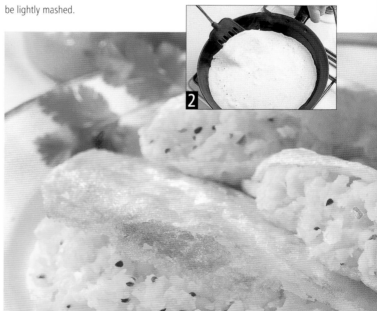

eggplant curry

serves four

1½ oz/40 g dried tamarind,
    coarsely chopped

½ cup boiling water

2 large eggplants, sliced

salt

2 tbsp ghee or vegetable oil

3 onions, sliced

1 tsp Garlic Paste (see page 11)

1 tsp Ginger Paste (see page 11)

4 curry leaves

1 fresh green chili, seeded and
    finely chopped

2 fresh red chilies, seeded and
    finely chopped

1 tbsp ground coriander

2 tsp cumin seeds

2 tsp yellow mustard seeds

2 tbsp tomato paste

generous 2 cups canned
    coconut milk

3 tbsp chopped cilantro, plus extra
    to garnish

1 Place the dried tamarind in a bowl, then add the boiling water and stir. Let soak for 30 minutes. Meanwhile, place the eggplant slices in a colander, sprinkling each layer with salt. Let drain for 30 minutes.

2 Strain the tamarind into a bowl, pressing down on the pulp with the back of a wooden spoon. Discard the contents of the strainer. Rinse the eggplant slices under cold running water and pat dry with paper towels.

3 Heat the ghee in a large pan. Add the onions and cook over low heat, stirring occasionally, for 10 minutes, or until golden. Stir in the Garlic Paste and Ginger Paste and cook, stirring constantly, for 2 minutes. Add the curry leaves, green and red chilies, ground coriander, cumin and mustard seeds, and tomato paste and cook, stirring constantly, for 2 minutes, or until the spices give off their aroma.

4 Add the tamarind liquid and coconut milk and bring to a boil. Add the eggplant slices, then cover and simmer for 12–15 minutes, or until the eggplant is tender. Uncover the pan and simmer for an additional 5 minutes, or until the sauce has thickened. Stir in the chopped cilantro and sprinkle the extra chopped herb on top, then serve immediately.

COOK'S TIP

Most contemporary varieties of eggplant no longer need salting to remove the bitter juices. However, doing so stops the vegetable from becoming too soggy.

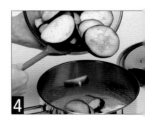

potatoes with spices & onions

serves four

6 tbsp vegetable oil

2 onions, finely chopped

1 tsp finely chopped fresh
gingerroot

1 garlic clove, crushed

1 tsp chili powder

1½ tsp ground cumin

1½ tsp ground coriander

1 tsp salt

14 oz/400 g canned new potatoes

1 tbsp lemon juice

BAGHAAR

3 tbsp vegetable oil

3 dried red chilies

½ tsp onion seeds

½ tsp mustard seeds

½ tsp fenugreek seeds

1 fresh green chili, finely chopped,
to garnish

1 Heat the oil in a large pan. Add the onions and cook, stirring, until golden brown. Reduce the heat, then add the ginger, garlic, chili powder, ground cumin, ground coriander, and salt and stir-fry for about 1 minute. Remove the pan from the heat and reserve until required.

2 Drain the water from the canned potatoes. Add the potatoes to the onion and spice mixture. Sprinkle over the lemon juice and mix well.

3 To make the baghaar, heat the oil in a separate pan. Add the red chilies, onion seeds, mustard seeds, and fenugreek seeds and cook until the seeds turn a shade darker. Remove the pan from the heat and pour over the potatoes.

4 Garnish with the chopped chili and serve immediately.

COOK'S TIP

You could also serve these as unusual accompaniment to pl. roast lamb or lamb chops.

potatoes & peas

serves two–four

⅔ cup vegetable oil

3 onions, sliced

1 garlic clove, crushed

1 tsp finely chopped fresh
gingerroot

1 tsp chili powder

½ tsp ground turmeric

1 tsp salt

2 fresh green chilies, finely chopped

1⅓ cups water

3 potatoes

1 cup peas

chopped cilantro, to garnish

1 Heat the oil in a large skillet. Add the onions and cook, stirring occasionally, until golden brown.

2 Mix the garlic, ginger, chili powder, turmeric, salt, and chilies together in a bowl. Add the spice mixture to the onions in the skillet.

3 Stir in ⅔ cup of the water, then cover and cook until the onions are cooked through.

4 Meanwhile, using a sharp kn cut each potato into 6 slices.

5 Add the potato slices to the mixture in the skillet and stir-f for 5 minutes.

6 Add the peas and the remain ⅔ cup of the water to the pa then cover and cook for 7–10 min Transfer the potatoes and peas to serving plates and serve garnished with chopped cilantro.

COOK'S TIP

Turmeric is an aromatic root
which is dried and ground to
produce the distinctive bright
yellow-orange powder used in
many Indian dishes. It has a
warm, aromatic smell and a full,
somewhat musty taste.

·ied cauliflower

serves four

tbsp vegetable oil

tsp onion seeds

tsp mustard seeds

tsp fenugreek seeds

dried red chilies

small cauliflower, cut into small

florets

tsp salt

green bell pepper, seeded

and diced

VARIATION

For a weekend feast or a special
occasion, this dish looks great
made with baby cauliflowers
nstead of florets. Peel off most of
the outer leaves, leaving a few
mall leaves for decoration. Blanch
he baby cauliflowers whole for 4
minutes, then cook as above.

COOK'S TIP

nion seeds are small and black.
hey may be labeled as kalonji in
Asian food stores. Onion seeds
can be used instead of pepper,
but have a spicier taste.

1 Heat the oil in a large, heavy-
bottom pan.

2 Add the onion seeds, mustard
seeds, fenugreek seeds, and the
dried red chilies to the pan, stirring
to mix.

3 Reduce the heat and gradually
add the cauliflower and salt
to the pan. Stir-fry for 7–10 minutes,
coating the cauliflower in the spice
mixture.

4 Add the bell pepper and stir-fry
the mixture for 3–5 minutes.

5 Transfer the spicy fried cauliflower
to a serving dish and serve hot.

daikon curry

serves four

1 lb/450 g daikon, preferably
  with leaves

1 tbsp moong dal

1¼ cups water

⅔ cup vegetable oil

1 onion, thinly sliced

1 garlic clove, crushed

1 tsp dried chili flakes

1 tsp salt

Chapatis (see page 189), to serve

1 Rinse, then peel and slice the daikon, together with its leaves if wished.

2 Place the daikon, the leaves (if using), and the moong dal in a pan and pour over the water. Bring to a boil and cook until the daikon is soft.

3 Drain the daikon thoroughly, and use your hands to squeeze out any excess water.

4 Heat the oil in a pan. Add the onion, garlic, dried chili flakes, and salt and cook, stirring occasionally, until the onions have softened and turned a light golden brown color.

5 Stir the daikon mixture into the spiced onion mixture and mix well. Reduce the heat and continue cooking, stirring frequently, for 3–5 minutes.

6 Transfer the daikon curry to individual serving plates and serve hot with Chapatis.

COOK'S TIP

Daikon looks a bit like a parsnip without the tapering end and is now sold in many supermarkets as well as in Asian grocery stores.

ggplants & yogurt

serves four

eggplants

tbsp vegetable oil

onion, sliced

tsp white cumin seeds

tsp chili powder

tsp salt

tbsp plain yogurt

tsp mint sauce

esh mint leaves, shredded,

to garnish

Preheat the oven to 325°F/160°C. Rinse the eggplants and pat dry h paper towels.

Place the eggplants in an ovenproof dish. Bake in the heated oven for 45 minutes. nove the baked eggplants from oven and let cool.

Slice the eggplants in half, then, using a spoon, scoop out the plant flesh and reserve. Heat the oil heavy-bottom pan. Add the onion cumin seeds and cook, stirring, for 2 minutes.

4 Add the chili powder, salt, yogurt, and mint sauce to the pan and stir well to mix.

5 Add the eggplants to the onion and yogurt mixture and stir-fry for 5–7 minutes, or until all of the liquid has been absorbed and the mixture is quite dry.

6 Transfer the eggplant and yogurt mixture to a serving dish and garnish with mint leaves.

tomato curry

serves four

2 cups canned tomatoes

1 tsp finely chopped fresh
   gingerroot

1 garlic clove, crushed

1 tsp chili powder

1 tsp salt

½ tsp ground coriander

½ tsp ground cumin

4 tbsp vegetable oil

½ tsp onion seeds

½ tsp mustard seeds

½ tsp fenugreek seeds

pinch of white cumin seeds

3 dried red chilies

2 tbsp lemon juice

3 hard-cooked eggs

¼ bunch of cilantro, chopped

1 Place the tomatoes in a large bowl. Add the ginger, garlic, chili powder, salt, ground coriander, and cumin to the tomatoes and blend well. Heat the oil in a pan. Add the onion, mustard, fenugreek and white cumin seeds, and the dried red chilies, and stir-fry for 1 minute. Remove the pan from the heat.

2 Add the tomato mixture to the spicy oil mixture and return to heat. Stir-fry the mixture for 3 minut then reduce the heat and cook with the lid ajar for 7–10 minutes, stirrin occasionally.

3 Sprinkle over the lemon juice. Transfer the tomato curry to a serving dish and keep warm until required.

4 Shell and quarter the hard-coo eggs, then gently add them, y end down, to the tomato curry.

5 Garnish with chopped cilantro and serve hot.

COOK'S TIP

This tomato curry can be made in advance and frozen, because it freezes particularly well.

kashmiri vegetables

serves four

3 tbsp ghee or vegetable oil

2 tbsp slivered almonds

8 cardamom seeds

8 black peppercorns

2 tsp cumin seeds

1 cinnamon stick

2 fresh green chilies, seeded
  and chopped

1 tsp Ginger Paste (see page 11)

1 tsp chili powder

3 potatoes, cut into chunks

salt

8 oz/225 g okra cut into 1-inch/
  2.5-cm pieces

½ cauliflower, broken into florets

⅔ cup plain yogurt

⅔ cup vegetable stock or water

freshly cooked rice, to serve

1 Heat 1 tablespoon of the ghee in a heavy-bottom pan. Add the almonds and cook over low heat, stirring constantly, for 2 minutes, or until golden.

2 Remove the almonds from the pan with a slotted spoon and drain on paper towels, then reserve. Place the cardamom seeds, peppercorns, cumin seeds, and cinnamon stick in a spice grinder or mortar and grind finely.

3 Add the remaining ghee to the pan and heat. Add the chilies and cook, stirring frequently, for 2 minutes. Stir in the Ginger Paste, chili powder, and ground spices and cook, stirring constantly, for 2 minutes, or until they give off their aroma.

4 Add the potatoes and season salt to taste, then cover and co stirring occasionally, for 8 minutes. A the okra and cauliflower and cook an additional 5 minutes.

5 Gradually stir in the yogurt and stock and bring to a boil. Cover and simmer for an additiona 10 minutes, or until all the vegetab are tender. Garnish with the almon and serve with freshly cooked rice.

VARIATION

Use sweet potatoes instead o
ordinary potatoes to give the
dish a delicately sweet flavor.

eggplants in pickling spices

2 tsp ground coriander

2 tsp ground cumin

2 tsp dry unsweetened coconut

2 tsp sesame seeds

1 tsp mixed mustard and
    onion seeds

1¼ cups vegetable oil

3 onions, sliced

1 tsp chopped fresh gingerroot

1 garlic clove, crushed

½ tsp ground turmeric

1½ tsp chili powder

1½ tsp salt

3 eggplants, halved lengthwise

1 tbsp tamarind paste

1¼ cups water

BAGHAAR

⅔ cup vegetable oil

1 tsp mixed onion and
    mustard seeds

1 tsp cumin seeds

4 dried red chilies

3 tbsp finely chopped
    cilantro

1 fresh green chili, finely chopped

TO GARNISH

3 hard-cooked eggs, cut into fourths

cilantro sprigs

1 Dry-roast the ground coriander, cumin, coconut, sesame seeds, and mustard and onion seeds in a pan. Using a pestle and mortar, grind briefly. Alternatively, use a food processor. Heat the oil in a skillet. Add the onions and cook until golden. Reduce the heat and add the ginger, garlic, turmeric, chili powder, and salt, stirring. Let cool, then grind this mixture to form a paste.

2 Make 4 cuts across each eggp half. Blend the spices with the onion paste. Spoon this mixture int the slits in the eggplants.

3 Mix the tamarind paste and 3 tablespoons of the water together to make a paste. Reserve.

4 For the baghaar, heat the oil i large skillet. Add the onion ar mustard seeds, cumin seeds, and chilies and cook briefly. Reduce the heat, then gently place the stuffed eggplants into the baghaar and sti gently. Stir in the tamarind paste ar the remaining water and cook for 15–20 minutes. Add the cilantro a chili. When cool, transfer to a servi dish and serve garnished with the hard-cooked eggs and cilantro spri

umplings in yogurt sauce

serves four

cup besan

tsp chili powder

tsp salt

tsp baking soda

onion, finely chopped

fresh green chilies, chopped

bunch of cilantro, chopped

cup water

¼ cups vegetable oil

)GURT SAUCE

¼ cups plain yogurt

tbsp besan

cup water

tsp chopped fresh gingerroot

garlic clove, crushed

½ tsp chili powder

½ tsp salt

tsp ground turmeric

tsp ground coriander

tsp ground cumin

GHAAR

cup vegetable oil

tsp white cumin seeds

dried red chilies

1 To make the dumplings, sift the besan into a large bowl. Add the chili powder, salt, baking soda, onion, chopped chilies, and cilantro and mix. Add the water and mix to make a thick paste. Heat the oil in a skillet. Place teaspoonfuls of the paste in the oil and cook, turning once, over medium heat until a crisp golden brown. Reserve.

2 To make the sauce, place the yogurt in a bowl and whisk in the besan and water. Add all of the spices and mix well.

3 Push this mixture through a large strainer into a pan. Bring to a boil over low heat, stirring constantly. If the yogurt sauce becomes too thick, add a little extra water.

4 Pour the sauce into a deep serving dish and arrange all of the dumplings on top. Keep warm.

5 To make the baghaar, heat the oil in a skillet. Add the cumin seeds and the dried red chilies and cook until darker in color. Pour the dressing over the dumplings and serve hot.

141

stuffed bell peppers

serves four

scant ½ cup vegetable oil

1 onion, finely chopped

1 potato, diced

½ cup peas, thawed if frozen

½ cup fava beans

2 oz/55 g small cauliflower florets

scant ½ cup carrot, diced

½ cup corn kernels

2 tsp amchoor (dried
    mango powder)

1 tsp Garam Masala (see page 11)

½ tsp chili powder

salt

4 large or 8 small green bell peppers

VARIATION

Substitute other vegetables in
the filling, such as broccoli,
chopped mushrooms, diced
zucchini, and eggplant.

1 Preheat the oven to 325°F/160°C. Heat 4 tablespoons of the vegetable oil in a heavy-bottom pan. Add the onion and cook over low heat, stirring occasionally, for 5 minutes, or until softened. Add the potato and cook, stirring occasionally, for an additional 5 minutes.

2 Add the peas, fava beans, cauliflower, carrot, corn, amchoor, Garam Masala, and chili powder and season with salt to taste. Stir well, then cover and cook for 15 minutes, or until all the vegetables are tender. Remove the pan from the heat and let cool.

3 Cut the tops off the bell peppers to make "lids," then seed. Heat the remaining vegetable oil in a skillet and cook the bell peppers, turning frequently, for 3 minutes. Remove with a slotted spoon and drain on paper towels. Spoon the vegetable mixture into the bell peppers and arrange them in a single layer in an ovenproof dish. Bake in the preheated oven for 20 minutes, then serve immediately.

COOK'S TIP

Chili powder is made from drie
red chilies and is usually very
hot, so use with caution. It is
available from most large
supermarkets.

chickpea curry

serves four

6 tbsp vegetable oil

2 onions, sliced

1 tsp finely chopped fresh
gingerroot

1 tsp ground cumin

1 tsp ground coriander

1 garlic clove, crushed

1 tsp chili powder

2 fresh green chilies

½ bunch of cilantro, chopped

⅔ cup water

1 large potato

1½ cups canned chickpeas, drained

1 tbsp lemon juice

COOK'S TIP

Using canned chickpeas saves
time, but you can use dried
chickpeas if you prefer. Soak
them overnight, then boil them
for 15–20 minutes, or until soft.

---

1 Heat the oil in a large pan. Add the onions and cook, stirring occasionally, until golden brown.

2 Reduce the heat, then add the ginger, ground cumin, ground coriander, garlic, chili powder, green chilies, and chopped cilantro to the pan and stir-fry for 2 minutes.

3 Add the water to the mixture the pan and stir to mix. Peel a dice the potato.

4 Add the diced potato and the drained chickpeas to the mixt in the pan, then cover and let simm stirring occasionally, for 5–7 minute

5 Sprinkle the lemon juice over the curry.

6 Transfer the chickpea curry to serving dishes and serve hot.

otato & cauliflower curry

serves four

cup vegetable oil

tsp white cumin seeds

dried red chilies

nions, sliced

sp finely chopped fresh
gingerroot

arlic clove, crushed

sp chili powder

sp salt

ch of ground turmeric

otatoes

cauliflower, cut into small florets

resh green chilies (optional)

unch of cilantro, chopped

up water

COOK'S TIP

Always handle chilies with
caution, preferably wearing
ober gloves, because the juices
are extremely pungent. Wash
your hands thoroughly after
reparing and handling chilies
d do not put your fingers near
your eyes, as this can be
very painful.

---

1 Heat the oil in a large pan. Add
the white cumin seeds and dried
red chilies, stirring to mix.

2 Add the onions to the pan and
cook, stirring occasionally, until
golden brown.

3 Mix the ginger, garlic, chili
powder, salt, and turmeric
together in a bowl. Add the spice
mixture to the onions and stir-fry for
2 minutes.

4 Add the potatoes and cauliflower
to the onion and spice mixture,
stirring to coat the vegetables in the
spice mixture.

5 Reduce the heat and add the
green chilies (if using), cilantro,
and water to the pan. Cover and let
simmer for 10–15 minutes.

6 Transfer the potato and
cauliflower curry to warmed
serving plates and serve immediately.

green pumpkin curry

⅔ cup vegetable oil

2 onions, sliced

½ tsp white cumin seeds

1 lb/450 g green pumpkin, cubed

1 tsp amchoor (dried
   mango powder)

1 tsp finely chopped fresh
   gingerroot

1 garlic clove, crushed

1 tsp dried chili flakes

½ tsp salt

1¼ cups water

1 Heat the oil in a large skillet. Add the onions and cumin seeds and cook, stirring occasionally, until a light golden brown color.

2 Add the cubed pumpkin to the skillet and stir-fry for 3–5 minutes over low heat.

3 Mix the amchoor, ginger, garlic, dried chili flakes, and salt together in a bowl.

4 Add the spice mixture to the pumpkin mixture, stirring well to mix.

5 Add the water, then cover and cook over low heat for 10–15 minutes, stirring occasiona

6 Transfer to warmed serving p and serve hot.

COOK'S TIP

Cumin seeds are popular in Indian cooking because of their warm, pungent flavor and aroma. The seeds are sold whole or ground, and are included as one of the flavorings in Garam Masala (see page 11).

VARIATION

You can use ordinary pumpkin for this recipe, if you prefer.

stuffed eggplants

serves four

2 large eggplants

2 carrots, diced

2 potatoes, diced

2 zucchini, diced

⅔ cup vegetable stock

or ½ vegetable stock cube
dissolved in ⅔ cup hot water

½ tsp ground coriander

½ tsp ground cumin, plus extra
for sprinkling

½ tsp ground cardamom

½ tsp ground turmeric

¼ tsp ground cinnamon

¼ tsp cayenne pepper

¼ tsp ground cloves

¼ tsp ground mace

1 onion, thinly sliced

salt

1 tbsp chopped fresh mint

fresh mint sprigs, to garnish

COOK'S TIP

This is a terrific recipe for anyone
following a lowfat eating plan,
because steaming and simmering
the vegetables is a healthy way
of cooking.

1 Preheat the oven to 375°F/190°C. Halve the eggplants lengthwise and, using a sharp knife, cut all around the edges without piercing the skins. Cut a crisscross pattern in the flesh and carefully scoop out with a spoon, leaving the shells intact. Steam the shells over a pan of boiling water for 5 minutes, or until tender, but not disintegrating. Remove and let cool. Place the carrots and potatoes in the steamer and cook for 3 minutes, then add the zucchini and cook for an additional 3 minutes. Transfer the vegetables to a bowl.

2 Chop the eggplant flesh. Bring the stock to a boil in a pan. Stir in the coriander, cumin, cardamom, turmeric, cinnamon, cayenne, cloves, and mace and add the onion. Simmer, stirring occasionally, for 5 minutes. Add the eggplant flesh and simmer for an additional 5 minutes. Stir in the carrots, potatoes, and zucchini, then add salt to taste and remove the pan from the heat. Add the mint.

3 Arrange the eggplant shells in single layer in an ovenproof d Divide the vegetable mixture betwe them and sprinkle very lightly with little extra ground cumin. Cover wit foil and bake in the preheated over 30 minutes, or until tender. Serve garnished with mint sprigs.

egg curry

serves four

4 tbsp vegetable oil

1 onion, sliced

1 red chili, finely chopped

½ tsp chili powder

½ tsp finely chopped fresh
    gingerroot

1–2 garlic cloves, crushed

4 eggs

1 firm tomato, sliced

¼ bunch of cilantro, chopped,
    to garnish

COOK'S TIP

Eggs contain high quality
protein, fat, iron, and vitamins A,
B, and D, although they are also
high in cholesterol. Both the
leaves and finely chopped stems
of cilantro are used in Indian
cooking, to flavor dishes and as
edible garnishes. Cilantro has
a very distinctive and
pronounced taste.

1 Heat the oil in a large pan. Ad
   the onion and cook until just
softened and a light golden color.

2 Add the chili, chili powder, gin
   and garlic and stir-fry over low
heat for 1 minute.

3 Add the eggs and tomato slice
   the mixture in the pan and
continue cooking, stirring to break
the eggs when they begin to cook,
3–5 minutes.

4 Sprinkle over the chopped
   cilantro. Transfer the egg curry
serving plates and serve hot.

nixed vegetables

serves four

/₄ cups vegetable oil

tsp mustard seeds

tsp onion seeds

tsp white cumin seeds

-4 curry leaves, chopped

lb/450 g onions, finely chopped

tomatoes, chopped

red and ½ green bell pepper,
seeded and sliced

tsp finely chopped fresh
gingerroot

garlic clove, crushed

tsp chili powder

tsp ground turmeric

tsp salt

/₄ cups water

potatoes, peeled and cut
into pieces

cauliflower, cut into small florets

carrots, peeled and sliced

fresh green chilies, finely chopped

bunch of cilantro, finely chopped

tbsp lemon juice

shly cooked rice, to serve

1 Heat the oil in a large pan. Add the mustard, onion, and cumin seeds along with the curry leaves and cook until they turn a shade darker.

2 Add the onions to the pan and cook over medium heat until golden brown.

3 Add the tomatoes and bell peppers and stir-fry for 5 minutes.

4 Add the ginger, garlic, chili powder, turmeric, and salt and mix well.

5 Add 1¼ cups of the water, then cover and let simmer for 10–12 minutes, stirring occasionally. Add the potatoes, cauliflower, carrots, green chilies, and cilantro and stir-fry for 5 minutes.

6 Add the remaining water and the lemon juice, stirring well. Cover and let simmer for 15 minutes, stirring occasionally.

7 Transfer the mixed vegetables to warmed serving plates and serve immediately with rice.

zucchini & fenugreek seeds

serves four

6 tbsp vegetable oil

1 onion, finely chopped

3 fresh green chilies, finely chopped

1 tsp finely chopped fresh
  gingerroot

1 garlic clove, crushed

1 tsp chili powder

1 lb/450 g zucchini, sliced

2 tomatoes, sliced

2 tsp fenugreek seeds

chopped cilantro, to garnish

Chapatis (see page 189), to serve

1 Heat the oil in a large, heavy-bottom skillet. Add the onion, green chilies, ginger, garlic, and chili powder, stirring well until mixed.

2 Add the sliced zucchini and tomatoes to the skillet and stir-fry for 5–7 minutes.

3 Add the fenugreek seeds to the zucchini mixture in the skillet and stir-fry for an additional 5 minutes.

4 Remove the skillet from the heat and transfer the zucchini and fenugreek seed mixture to serving dishes. Garnish with cilantro and serve hot with Chapatis.

COOK'S TIP

Fresh fenugreek is sold in bunches. Both the leaves and the flat, yellowish-brown seeds are used, but the stems and root should be discarded, because they have a bitter taste.

ry split okra

serves four

lb/450 g okra

cup vegetable oil

/₂ oz/100 g dried onions

tsp amchoor (dried
    mango powder)

tsp ground cumin

tsp chili powder

tsp salt

Trim the ends off the okra, then
carefully split down the center
hout cutting through completely.

Heat the oil in a large pan. Add
the dried onions and cook
l crisp.

Remove the onions from the pan
with a slotted spoon and let drain
oughly on paper towels.

When cool enough to handle,
coarsely tear the dried onions and
e in a large bowl.

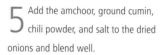

COOK'S TIP

Amchoor is made from
dried ground mangoes. It has a
slightly sour taste. Amchoor is
sold in jars from specialty Asian
food stores.

5 Add the amchoor, ground cumin,
chili powder, and salt to the dried
onions and blend well.

6 Spoon the onion and spice
mixture into the split okra.

7 Reheat the oil in the pan. Gently
add the okra to the hot oil and
cook over low heat for 10–12 minutes.

8 Transfer the cooked okra to a
warmed serving dish and
serve immediately.

3read, Beans & Grains

The most common Indian breads are chapatis, parathas, and pooris and are cooked almost every day in most Indian households. They are made as individual portions, and you should allow for 2 per person.

Rice is served with almost every meal in India, so the Indians have created a variety of ways of cooking it. Whatever the dish, the aim is to produce dry, separate grains of rice that are cooked yet still have some "bite" to them. Basmati rice is the best choice, because it cooks very well and gives an excellent result.

There are at least 30 different types of lentil to be found in India, but the most commonly used ones are moong, masoor, chana, and urid. Rich in protein, lentils make ideal accompaniments to vegetable curries. Lentils are also delicious cooked with a variety of meats.

lemon dal

serves four

scant ½ cup masoor dal

1 tsp finely chopped fresh
   gingerroot

1 garlic clove, crushed

1 tsp chili powder

½ tsp ground turmeric

1¾ cups water

1 tsp salt

3 tbsp lemon juice

2 fresh green chilies

¼ bunch of cilantro, chopped

BAGHAAR

⅔ cup vegetable oil

4 whole garlic cloves

6 dried red chilies

1 tsp white cumin seeds

1 lemon, cut into slices, to garnish

1 Rinse the dal twice under cold running water, removing any stones. Place in a large pan.

2 Add the ginger, garlic, chili powder, and turmeric to the dal. Stir in 1¼ cups of the water and bring to a boil over a medium heat with the lid left slightly ajar. Cook for 30 minutes, or until the dal is soft enough to be mashed.

3 Remove the pan from the heat and mash the dal with a potato masher. Add the salt, lemon juice, and remaining water, then stir and mix well. It should be a fairly smooth consistency.

4 Seed and finely chop the green chilies, then add to the pan with the cilantro and keep warm.

5 To make the baghaar, heat the oil in a pan. Add the garlic, red chilies, and cumin seeds and cook for 1 minute. Turn off the heat, and when the heat has been reduced pour the baghaar over the dal. If the dal is too runny, cook, uncovered, over medium heat for 3–5 minutes.

6 Transfer the dal to a serving d and garnish with lemon slices Serve hot.

COOK'S TIP

This dish is a good accompaniment to Beef Korma with Almonds (see page 60).

rained dal with meatballs

1 Rinse the dal twice under cold running water, removing any stones. Place the dal in a pan and cover with 2½ cups of the water. Add the ginger, garlic, turmeric, and chili powder and boil for 20 minutes, or until the dal is soft and mushy. Add the salt, stirring.

2 Remove the pan from the heat and mash the dal with a potato masher, then push it through a strainer. Add the lemon juice and stir in the remaining water. Transfer to a clean pan and bring to a boil over low heat. Reserve.

3 To make the meatballs, follow the recipe for Beef Patties on page 55, but shape into small balls rather than flat circles. Drop the meatballs gently into the dal mixture and keep warm.

4 Prepare the baghaar. Heat the oil in a pan. Add the garlic, dried red chilies, and cumin seeds and cook for 2 minutes. Pour the baghaar over the dal mixture, stirring to mix.

5 For the potato wafers, rub the salt over the potato shavings. Heat the oil in a skillet. Add the potatoes and cook, turning occasionally, until crisp. Garnish the meatballs with the potato wafers, chilies, and chopped cilantro.

black-eye peas

serves four

scant 1 cup dried black-eye peas

1¼ cups vegetable oil

2 onions, sliced

1 tsp finely chopped fresh
gingerroot

1 garlic clove, crushed

1 tsp chili powder

1½ tsp salt

1½ tsp ground coriander

1½ tsp ground cumin

⅔ cup water

2 fresh red chilies, cut into strips

½ bunch of cilantro, chopped

1 tbsp lemon juice

1 Rinse the black-eye peas under cold running water, then soak in a bowl of water overnight.

2 Place the black-eye peas in a pan of water and bring to a boil, then cook over low heat for 30 minutes. Drain the beans thoroughly and reserve.

3 Heat the oil in a separate pan. Add the onions and cook until golden brown. Add the ginger, garlic, chili powder, salt, ground coriander, and ground cumin and stir-fry the mixture for 3–5 minutes.

4 Add the water to the pan, then cover and cook until all of the water has completely evaporated.

5 Add the boiled black-eye peas, red chilies and cilantro to the beans and stir to blend together. Stir-fry the bean mixture for 3–5 minutes.

6 Transfer the black-eye peas to a serving dish and sprinkle over the lemon juice. Serve hot or cold.

COOK'S TIP

Black-eye peas are oval-shaped gray or beige beans with a dark dot in the center. They have a slightly smoky flavor and are so canned as well as dried.

hite lentils

serves two–four

ant ½ cup urid dal

tsp finely chopped fresh
  gingerroot

½ cups water

:sp salt

:sp coarsely ground pepper

:bsp ghee

garlic cloves, peeled but
  kept whole

resh red chilies, finely chopped

sh mint leaves, to garnish

Rinse the dal twice under cold
water, removing any stones.

Place the dal and ginger in a
large pan.

Add the water, then cover and
bring to a boil. Cook over
ium heat for 30 minutes. Check to
whether the dal is cooked by
ing it between your forefinger and
nb. If the dal is a little hard in
center, cook for an additional
minutes. If necessary, remove the
nd cook until any remaining water
evaporated.

4 Add the salt and pepper to the
dal and mix well, then reserve.

5 Heat the ghee in a separate pan.
Add the garlic cloves and red
chilies, and stir well to mix.

6 Pour the garlic and chili mixture
over the dal and garnish with the
mint leaves.

7 Transfer the white lentils to
serving dishes and serve hot.

dry moong dal

serves four

scant ¾ cup moong dal

1 tsp finely chopped fresh
    gingerroot

½ tsp ground cumin

½ tsp ground coriander

1 garlic clove, crushed

½ tsp chili powder

2½ cups water

1 tsp salt

BAGHAAR

scant ½ cup unsalted butter

5 dried red chilies

1 tsp white cumin seeds

1 Rinse the dal twice under cold running water, removing any stones.

2 Place the dal in a pan. Add the ginger, ground cumin, ground coriander, garlic, and chili powder and stir to mix.

3 Pour in the water to cover the dal mixture. Cook over medium heat, stirring, for 20 minutes, or until the dal is soft but not mushy.

4 Add the salt and stir to mix. Transfer to a serving dish and keep warm.

5 Meanwhile, make the baghaar. Melt the butter in a pan. Add the dried red chilies and cumin seeds and cook until they begin to pop.

6 Pour the baghaar over the dal and serve hot.

COOK'S TIP

Dried red chilies are the quicke
way to add heat to a dish.

hana dal cooked with rice

serves six

ant ½ cup chana dal

¼ cups basmati rice

bsp ghee

onions, sliced

sp finely chopped fresh
gingerroot

garlic clove, crushed

tsp ground turmeric

sp salt

tsp chili powder

sp Garam Masala (see page 11)

bsp plain yogurt

ups water

cup milk

sp saffron threads

black cardamoms

black cumin seeds

bsp lemon juice

esh green chilies

bunch of cilantro, chopped

1 Rinse the dal twice under cold running water, removing any stones, then soak in a bowl of water for 3 hours. Rinse the rice and reserve.

2 Heat the ghee in a skillet. Add the onions and cook until golden brown. Using a slotted spoon, remove half of the onion with a little of the ghee and place in a bowl.

3 Add the ginger, garlic, turmeric, 1 teaspoon of the salt, the chili powder, and Garam Masala to the mixture remaining in the skillet and stir-fry for 5 minutes. Stir in the yogurt and add the dal and ⅔ cup of the water. Cook, covered, for 15 minutes. Reserve.

4 Meanwhile, boil the milk with the saffron and reserve.

5 Boil the remaining water and add the remaining salt, cardamoms, cumin seeds, and the rice, and cook, stirring, until the rice is half cooked. Drain, and place half of the following ingredients—fried onion, saffron milk, lemon juice, green chilies, and cilantro—on top of the dal mixture. Place the remaining rice on top of this and the rest of the fried onion, saffron milk, lemon juice, chilies, and cilantro on top of the rice. Cover tightly with a lid and cook for 20 minutes over very low heat. Mix with a slotted spoon before serving.

161

onion dal

serves four

scant ½ cup masoor dal

6 tbsp vegetable oil

1 small bunch of scallions, trimmed
   and chopped, including the
   green part

1 tsp finely chopped fresh
   gingerroot

1 garlic clove, crushed

½ tsp chili powder

½ tsp ground turmeric

1¼ cups water

1 tsp salt

TO GARNISH

1 fresh green chili, finely chopped

¼ bunch of cilantro, chopped

1 Rinse the dal twice, removing any
stones and reserve.

2 Heat the oil in a pan. Add the
scallions and cook until lightly
browned.

3 Reduce the heat and add the
ginger, garlic, chili powder, and
turmeric to the pan. Stir-fry the
scallions with the spices.

4 Add the dal and mix to
blend together.

5 Add the water to the dal mixtu
in the pan, then reduce the he
further and cook for 20–25 minutes

6 When the dal is cooked
thoroughly, add the salt and s
gently with a wooden spoon to mix

7 Transfer the onion dal to a ser
dish and garnish with the
chopped green chili and cilantro.
Serve immediately.

fried spicy rice

serves four–six

2½ cups basmati rice

1 onion

2 tbsp ghee

1 tsp finely chopped fresh
    gingerroot

1 garlic clove, crushed

1 tsp salt

1 tsp black cumin seeds

3 cloves

3 green cardamoms

2 cinnamon sticks

4 peppercorns

3 cups water

1 Rinse the rice thoroughly under cold running water.

2 Slice the onion. Melt the ghee in a large skillet. Add the onion and cook until a crisp golden brown color.

3 Add the ginger, garlic, and salt to the skillet, stirring to mix.

4 Add the rice, cumin seeds, cloves, cardamoms, cinnamon sticks, and peppercorns to the mixture in the skillet and stir-fry for 3–5 minutes.

5 Add the water and bring to a Reduce the heat, then cover a cook until the rice is tender.

6 Drain the fried spicy rice and transfer to a serving dish. Serve immediately.

COOK'S TIP

Cardamom pods contain numerous tiny black seeds which have a warm flavor and are highly aromatic—green cardamoms are considered the best because of their fine delicate flavor. Green cardamoms are also prized for their digestive properties, and some Indians chew them raw after they have eaten extra-spicy curries, to aid digestion and sweeten the breath.

pinach & chana dal

serves four–six

bsp chana dal

bsp vegetable oil

sp mixed onion and
mustard seeds

dried red chilies

–16 oz/400–450 g canned
spinach, drained

sp finely chopped fresh
gingerroot

sp ground coriander

sp ground cumin

sp salt

sp chili powder

bsp lemon juice

resh green chili, to garnish

Rinse the lentils twice under cold
running water, then soak in a
l of warm water for at least
urs, preferably overnight.

COOK'S TIP

Very similar in appearance to
moong dal—the yellow split
eas—chana dal has slightly less
shiny grains. It is used as a
binding agent and can be
ought from Asian food stores.

2 Place the lentils in a pan, then
cover with water and boil for
30 minutes.

3 Heat the oil in a pan. Add the
onion and mustard seeds and
dried red chilies and cook, stirring, until
they turn a shade darker.

4 Add the drained spinach to the
pan, mixing gently.

5 Add the root ginger, ground
coriander, cumin, salt, and chili
powder to the pan. Reduce the heat
and gently stir-fry the mixture for
7–10 minutes.

6 Add the dal to the pan and
blend into the spinach mixture
well, stirring gently so that it does not
break up.

7 Transfer the mixture to a serving
dish. Sprinkle over the lemon
juice and garnish with the green chili.
Serve immediately.

oil-dressed dal

serves four

generous ¼ cup masoor dal

scant ¼ cup moong dal

1¾ cups water

1 tsp finely chopped fresh
   gingerroot

1 garlic clove, crushed

2 fresh red chilies, chopped

1 tsp salt

BAGHAAR

2 tbsp ghee

1 onion, sliced

1 tsp mixed mustard and
   onion seeds

1 Rinse the dals twice under cold running water, removing any stones.

2 Place the dals in a large pan and pour over the water, stirring. Add the ginger, garlic, and red chilies and bring to a boil for 15–20 minutes, over medium heat, half covered with a lid, until soft.

3 Remove the pan from the heat and mash the dals with a potato masher. Add more water if necessary to form a thick sauce.

4 Add the salt to the dal mixture and stir well. Transfer the dal to a heatproof serving dish and keep warm.

> ### COOK'S TIP
> This dish makes a very good accompaniment, especially for a dry vegetarian or meat curry. It also freezes well—simply reheat it in a pan or covered in the oven.

5 Just before serving, melt the ghee in a small pan. Add the onion and cook until golden brown. Add the mustard and onion seeds stir to mix.

6 Pour the onion mixture over the dal while still hot and serve immediately.

spiced rice & lentils

serves four

1 cup basmati rice

¾ cup masoor dal

2 tbsp ghee

1 small onion, sliced

1 tsp chopped fresh gingerroot

1 garlic clove, crushed

½ tsp ground turmeric

2½ cups water

1 tsp salt

Chutney (see pages 227–231),
   to serve

COOK'S TIP

Many Indian recipes specify
ghee as the cooking fat.
This is because it is similar to
clarified butter in that it can be
heated to a very high
temperature without burning.
Ghee adds a nutty flavor to
dishes and a glossy shine to
sauces. You can buy ghee in
cans, and a vegetarian version is
also available. Store at room
temperature or keep in
the refrigerator.

---

1 Mix the rice and dal and rinse
twice under cold running water,
rubbing with your fingers and
removing any stones. Reserve.

2 Heat the ghee in a large pan. Add
the onion and cook, stirring
occasionally, for 2 minutes.

3 Reduce the heat, then add the
ginger, garlic, and turmeric and
stir-fry for 1 minute.

VARIATION

Moong dal may be substituted
for masoor dal in this recipe.

4 Add the rice and dal to the
mixture in the pan and blend
together, mixing gently.

5 Add the water and bring to a b
Reduce the heat and cook,
covered, for 20–25 minutes.

6 Just before serving, add the sa
and mix well.

7 Transfer to a serving dish and
serve immediately with a Chut
of your choice.

pilaf rice

serves two–four

1 cup basmati rice

2 tbsp ghee

3 green cardamoms

2 cloves

3 peppercorns

½ tsp salt

½ tsp saffron threads

1¾ cups water

1 Rinse the rice twice under cold running water and reserve.

2 Heat the ghee in a pan. Add the cardamoms, cloves, and peppercorns to the pan and cook, stirring, for 1 minute.

3 Add the rice and stir-fry for an additional 2 minutes.

4 Add the salt, saffron, and water to the rice mixture and reduce the heat. Cover the pan and let simmer over low heat until the water has evaporated.

5 Transfer to a serving dish and serve hot.

COOK'S TIP

The most expensive of all spice saffron threads are the stamen of a type of crocus. They give dishes a rich, golden color, as well as adding a distinctive, slightly bitter taste. Saffron is sold as a powder or in thread. Saffron threads are more expensive, but do have a superior flavor. Some books recommend substituting grour turmeric—but though the colo are similar, the tastes are not

omato rice with bell pepper

serves four

cups basmati rice

tbsp ghee or vegetable oil

tsp onion seeds

tsp black onion seeds

onion, thinly sliced

yellow bell pepper, seeded
and sliced

tomatoes, sliced

potato, diced

tsp Garlic Paste (see page 11)

tsp Ginger Paste (see page 11)

tsp chili powder

cup frozen fava beans or peas

tbsp chopped cilantro

lt

cups water

antro sprigs, to garnish

Rinse the rice in several changes
of water and let soak for
minutes.

2 Meanwhile, heat the ghee in a
large, heavy-bottom pan. Add
the onion and black onion seeds and
cook over low heat, stirring, for
1–2 minutes, or until they give off their
aroma. Add the onion and cook,
stirring occasionally, for 5 minutes, or
until softened. Drain the rice.

3 Add the yellow bell pepper,
tomatoes, potato, Garlic Paste,
Ginger Paste, and chili powder and
cook, stirring constantly, for 3 minutes.
Add the fava beans and cilantro and
add salt to taste, then cook, stirring, for
2 minutes.

4 Add the rice and stir until the
grains glisten and the ingredients
are thoroughly blended. Pour in the
water and bring to a boil over high
heat. Cover tightly, then reduce the
heat and let simmer for 15 minutes.

5 Remove the pan from the heat
and let stand, still covered, for
5 minutes. Serve garnished with
cilantro sprigs.

COOK'S TIP

The word "basmati" means
fragrant in Hindi, and this type of
rice is very aromatic. However,
you can use other varieties
of long-grain rice for this dish,
if you prefer.

brown rice with fruit & nuts

serves four–six

4 tbsp ghee or vegetable oil

1 large onion, chopped

2 garlic cloves, crushed

1-inch/2.5-cm piece fresh
   gingerroot, finely chopped

1 tsp chili powder

1 tsp cumin seeds

1 tbsp mild or medium curry
   powder or paste

scant 1½ cups brown rice

3¾ cups boiling vegetable stock

2 cups canned chopped tomatoes

salt and pepper

1 cup no-soak dried apricots or
   peaches, cut into slivers

1 red bell pepper, seeded and diced

¾ cup frozen peas

1–2 small, slightly green bananas

⅓–½ cup toasted mixed nuts

1 Heat the ghee in a large skillet.
Add the onion and cook gently
for 3 minutes.

2 Stir in the garlic, ginger, chili
powder, cumin seeds, curry
powder, and rice. Cook gently for
2 minutes, stirring constantly, until the
rice is coated in the spiced oil.

3 Pour in the boiling stock, stirring
to mix. Add the tomatoes and
season to taste with salt and pepper.
Bring the mixture to a boil, then reduce
the heat and let simmer gently,
covered, for 40 minutes, or until the
rice is almost cooked and most of the
liquid is absorbed.

4 Add the apricots, red bell pepp
and peas to the rice mixture in
skillet. Cover and continue cooking
10 minutes.

5 Remove the skillet from the he
and let stand for 5 minutes
without uncovering.

6 Peel and slice the bananas.
Uncover the rice mixture and t
with a fork to mix. Add the toasted
nuts and sliced banana and toss lig

7 Transfer the brown rice, fruit, a
nuts to a serving dish and ser

lamb biryani

serves six

⅔ cup milk

1 tsp saffron threads

5 tbsp ghee

3 onions, sliced

2 lb 4 oz/1 kg lean cubed lamb

7 tbsp plain yogurt

1½ tsp finely chopped fresh
   gingerroot

1–2 garlic cloves, crushed

2 tsp Garam Masala (see page 11)

2 tsp salt

¼ tsp ground turmeric

2½ cups water

2¼ cups basmati rice

2 tsp black cumin seeds

3 cardamoms

4 tbsp lemon juice

2 fresh green chilies

¼ bunch of cilantro, chopped

1 Boil the milk in a pan with the saffron and reserve. Heat the ghee in a pan. Add the onions and cook until golden. Remove half of the onions and ghee from the pan and place in a bowl.

2 Mix the meat, yogurt, ginger, garlic, Garam Masala, 1 teaspoon of the salt, and turmeric together in a large bowl.

3 Return the pan with the ghee and onions to the heat. Add the meat mixture and stir for 3 minutes, then add the water. Cook over low heat for 45 minutes, stirring occasionally. Check to see whether the meat is tender: if not, add ⅔ cup water and cook for an additional 15 minutes. Once all the water has evaporated, stir-fry for 2 minutes, then reserve.

4 Meanwhile, place the rice in a pan. Add the cumin seeds, cardamoms, remaining salt, and enough water for cooking, and coo[k] over medium heat until the rice is h[alf] cooked. Drain. Remove half of the [rice] and place in a bowl.

5 Spoon the meat mixture on to[p of] the rice in the pan. Add half e[ach] of the saffron milk, lemon juice, chi[li] and cilantro. Add the reserved onio[n] and ghee, and the other half of the [] rice, saffron milk, lemon juice, chilie[s] and cilantro. Cover and cook over l[ow] heat for 15–20 minutes, or until the rice is cooked. Stir well and serve h[ot].

VARIATION
Substitute the lamb with chicke[n] if you prefer.

shrimp pilaf

serves four

- 1 lb/450 g frozen shrimp
- ⅔ cup milk
- ½ tsp saffron threads
- 1 tsp chili powder
- 1 tsp caraway seeds
- 2 cinnamon sticks
- 2 green cardamoms
- 2 onions, sliced
- 2 bay leaves
- 1 tsp finely chopped fresh gingerroot
- 1 tsp salt
- 2¼ cups basmati rice
- 5 tbsp ghee
- 4 tbsp lemon juice
- ½ bunch of fresh mint leaves

1 Thaw the frozen shrimp by placing them in a bowl of cold water for 2 hours.

2 Boil the milk in a pan and add the saffron. Reserve until required.

3 Place the chili powder, caraway seeds, cinnamon sticks, green cardamoms, half the onion, the bay leaves, ginger, and salt in a mortar and, using a pestle, grind to a fine paste. Reserve.

4 Place the rice in a pan of boiling water and when the rice is half cooked, remove the pan from the heat, drain, and reserve.

5 Heat the ghee in a pan. Add the remaining onion and cook until golden brown. Transfer to a bowl and mix with the lemon juice and mint.

6 Add the spice paste and shrimp to the pan and stir-fry for 5 minutes. Remove the shrimp and spices with a slotted spoon and place in a bowl.

7 Place the half-cooked rice in the pan and pour the shrimp mixture over the top. Pour half of the lemon juice, onion and mint mixture, and of the saffron milk over the shrimp. Arrange the other half of the rice on top and pour over the remaining ingredients.

8 Cover and cook over low heat 15–20 minutes. Mix well before transferring to a serving dish.

~hicken biryani

serves six

~ tsp finely chopped fresh
 gingerroot

~2 garlic cloves, crushed

~bsp Garam Masala (see page 11)

~sp chili powder

~tsp ground turmeric

~ cardamom seeds, crushed

~ cups plain yogurt

~sp salt

~b 5 oz/1.5 kg chicken, skinned
 and cut into 8 pieces

~cup milk

~nch of saffron threads

~bsp ghee

~nions, sliced

~ cups basmati rice

~innamon sticks

~lack peppercorns

~sp black cumin seeds

~resh green chilies

~bunch of cilantro,
 finely chopped

~bsp lemon juice

1 Mix the ginger, garlic, Garam
Masala, chili powder, turmeric,
cardamom seeds, the yogurt, and
1 teaspoon of the salt together in a
bowl. Add the chicken pieces and mix
well. Let chill for 3 hours.

2 Boil the milk in a pan. Place the
saffron in a bowl, then pour over
the boiling milk. Reserve.

3 Heat the ghee in a large, heavy-
bottom pan and cook the onions
until golden brown. Remove half of
the onions and ghee from the pan
and reserve.

4 Place the rice, cinnamon sticks,
peppercorns, and cumin seeds
in a pan of water. Bring the rice to a
boil, then remove the pan from the
heat when half cooked. Drain and
place in a bowl. Stir in the remaining
teaspoon of salt.

5 Chop the chilies. Add the chicken
to the pan containing the onions.
Add half each of the chilies, cilantro,
lemon juice, and saffron milk. Add the
rice, then the remaining ingredients,
including the fried onions. Cover
and cook over low heat for 1 hour.
Check that the chicken is well cooked
before serving.

vegetable pilaf

serves four–six

2 potatoes

1 eggplant

7 oz/200 g carrots

⅓ cup green beans

4 tbsp ghee

2 onions, sliced

¾ cup plain yogurt

2 tsp finely chopped fresh
gingerroot

2 garlic cloves, crushed

2 tsp Garam Masala (see page 11)

2 tsp black cumin seeds

½ tsp ground turmeric

3 black cardamoms

2 cinnamon sticks

2 tsp salt

1 tsp chili powder

1¼ cups milk

½ tsp saffron threads

3 cups basmati rice

5 tbsp lemon juice

1 Peel and cut the potatoes into 6 pieces. Cut the eggplant into 6 pieces, then peel and slice the carrots and cut the green beans into pieces. Heat the ghee in a skillet. Add the potatoes, eggplant, carrots, and beans, turning with a spatula. Remove from the skillet and reserve.

2 Add the onions to the skillet and cook until soft. Add the yogurt, ginger, garlic, Garam Masala, 1 teaspoon of the cumin seeds, turmeric, 1 cardamom, 1 cinnamon stick, 1 teaspoon of the salt, and the chili powder and stir-fry for 3–5 minutes. Return the vegetables to the skillet and cook for 4–5 minutes.

3 Boil the milk in a pan and add the saffron. Half cook the rice with the remaining salt, cinnamon stick, cardamoms, and cumin seeds in a separate pan of boiling water. Drain the rice, leaving half in the pan while transferring the other half to a bowl.

4 Pour the vegetable mixture on of the rice in the pan. Pour hal of the lemon juice and half of the saffron milk over the vegetables an rice, then cover with the remaining and pour the remaining lemon juice and saffron milk over the top. Cove and return to the heat. Cook over l heat for 20 minutes. Serve hot.

tomato rice

serves four

⅔ cup vegetable oil

2 onions, sliced

1 tsp onion seeds

1 tsp finely chopped fresh
   gingerroot

1 garlic clove, crushed

½ tsp ground turmeric

1 tsp chili powder

1½ tsp salt

2 cups canned tomatoes

2¼ cups basmati rice

2½ cups water

1 Heat the oil in a large pan.
Add the onions and cook until
golden brown.

2 Add the onion seeds, ginger,
garlic, turmeric, chili powder, and
salt, stirring well.

3 Reduce the heat, then add the
tomatoes and stir-fry for
10 minutes, breaking up the tomatoes.

4 Add the rice to the tomato
mixture, stirring gently to coat
the rice in the mixture.

5 Pour in the water, stirring to
incorporate. Cover the pan and
cook over low heat until the water has
been absorbed and the rice is cooked.

6 Transfer the tomato rice to a
warmed serving dish and
serve immediately.

COOK'S TIP

Onion seeds are always used
whole in Indian cooking. The
are often used in pickles
sprinkled over the top of Naa
Bread (see page 181). Ironicall
onion seeds don't have anythi
to do with the vegetable, bu
they look similar to the plant
seed, hence the name.

aan bread

sp sugar

sp fresh yeast

warm water

cups all-purpose flour, plus extra
for dusting

bsp ghee

sp salt

ant ¼ cup unsalted butter, melted

sp poppy seeds

Place the sugar and yeast in a
small bowl or pitcher with the
m water and mix well until the
st has dissolved. Let stand for
minutes, until the mixture is frothy.

Place the flour in a large bowl.
Make a well in the center and
the ghee and salt. Pour in the
st mixture and, using your hands,
well to form a dough. Add more
er if required.

Turn the dough out onto a floured
counter and knead for 5 minutes,
ntil smooth.

4 Return the dough to the bowl,
then cover and let rise in a warm
place for 1½ hours, or until it has
doubled in size.

5 Preheat the broiler to very hot.
Turn the dough out onto a floured
counter and knead for an additional
2 minutes. Break off small balls with
your hands and pat them into circles
about 5 inches/13 cm in diameter and
½ inch/1 cm thick.

6 Place the dough circles onto a
greased sheet of foil and cook
under the hot broiler for 7–10 minutes,
turning twice and brushing with the
butter and sprinkling with the
poppy seeds.

7 Serve warm immediately, or keep
wrapped in foil until required.

COOK'S TIP

A tandoor oven throws out a
ferocious heat; this bread is
traditionally cooked on the side
wall of the oven where the heat
is only slightly less than in the
center. For an authentic effect,
leave your broiler on for a long
time to heat up before the first
dough round goes under.

parathas

makes twelve

generous 2 cups whole-wheat flour
(urid dal flour [ata] or chapati
flour), plus extra for dusting

⅓ cup all-purpose flour

salt

2 tbsp ghee, melted

COOK'S TIP

Press each paratha down gently
with a spatula or flat spoon
while you are cooking it to make
sure that it cooks evenly on
both sides.

1 Sift the whole-wheat flour, all-
purpose flour, and a pinch of
salt into a large bowl. Make a well in
the center of the flours and add
2 teaspoons of the ghee. Rub it into
the flour with your fingertips, then
gradually knead in enough cold water
to make a soft dough. Cover with
plastic wrap and let rest for at least
30 minutes.

2 Divide the dough into 12 equal-
size pieces and roll into balls. Keep
covered the balls that you are not
working on, to prevent them drying out.
Roll out a ball of dough on a lightly
floured counter to a 4-inch/10-cm circle
and brush with ghee. Fold in half, then
brush with ghee again and fold in half
once more. Either shape into a ball and
roll out to a 7-inch/18-cm round or roll
into a 6-inch/15-cm triangle. Repeat
with the remaining balls, stacking the
parathas interleaved with plastic wrap.

3 Heat a heavy-bottom skillet or
griddle pan. Add 1–2 paratha
a time and cook for 1 minute, then
over with a spatula and cook for an
additional 2 minutes. Brush with gh
and flip back to the first side and co
until golden. Brush with ghee, then
over again and cook until golden. K
warm while you cook the remaining
parathas in the same way.

arathas stuffed with vegetables

serves four–six

DUGH

enerous 1⅓ cups whole-wheat
  flour (urid dal flour [ata] or
  chapati flour)

tsp salt

enerous ¾ cup water

ant ½ cup ghee, plus extra for
  rolling out and frying

LLING

potatoes, peeled and cut
  into pieces

tsp ground turmeric

tsp Garam Masala (see page 11)

tsp finely chopped fresh gingerroot

bunch of cilantro, chopped

fresh green chilies, finely chopped

tsp salt

To make the parathas, mix the
  flour, salt, water, and ghee
ether in a bowl to form a dough.

2 Divide the dough into 8–12 equal
  portions. Roll each portion out
onto a floured counter. Brush the
center of the dough portions with
½ teaspoon of ghee. Fold the dough
portions in half, then roll into a pipelike
shape and flatten with the palms of
your hand, then roll around your finger
to form a coil. Roll out again, using
flour to dust as and when necessary, to
form a circle 7 inches/18 cm in
diameter.

3 To make the filling, place the
  potatoes in a pan of water and
cook until soft enough to be mashed.
Remove the pan from the heat and
mash the potatoes with a potato
masher.

4 Blend the turmeric, Garam
  Masala, ginger, cilantro, chilies,
and salt together in a bowl.

5 Add the spice mixture to the
  mashed potato and mix well.
Spread 1 tablespoon of the spicy
potato mixture on half the dough
round and cover with another dough
round. Seal the edges well.

6 Heat 2 teaspoons of the ghee in a
  heavy-bottom skillet. Place the
parathas gently in the skillet in batches
and cook, turning and moving them
about gently with a flat spoon, until
golden.

7 Remove the parathas from the
  skillet and serve immediately.

lightly fried bread

serves five

generous 1⅓ cups whole-wheat flour
  (urid dal flour (ata) or chapati
  flour), plus extra for dusting
½ tsp salt
1 tbsp ghee, plus extra for frying
1¼ cups water

COOK'S TIP

In India, breads are cooked on
a tava, a traditional flat griddle.
A large skillet makes an
adequate substitute.

1 Place the whole-wheat flour
and the salt in a large bowl
and mix well.

2 Make a well in the center of the
flour. Add the ghee and rub it in
well. Gradually pour in the water and
work to form a soft dough. Let the
dough rest for 10–15 minutes.

3 Carefully knead the dough for
5–7 minutes. Divide the dough
into about 10 equal-size portions.

4 Roll out each dough portion on a
lightly floured counter to form a
flat crêpe shape.

5 Using a sharp knife, lightly dra
lines in a criss cross pattern or
each dough portion.

6 Heat a heavy-bottom skillet.
Gently place the dough portion
one by one, into the skillet.

7 Cook the bread for 1 minute,
then turn over and spread wit
1 teaspoon of ghee. Turn the bread
over again and cook gently, moving
around the skillet with a spatula, ur
golden. Turn the bread over once
again, then remove from the skillet
keep warm while you cook the
remaining batches.

gram flour bread

scant ⅔ cup whole-wheat flour (urid
   dal flour [ata] or chapati flour),
   plus extra for dusting

½ cup besan (gram flour)

½ tsp salt

1 small onion

¼ bunch of cilantro, very finely
   chopped

2 fresh green chilies, finely chopped

⅔ cup water

2 tsp ghee

1 Sift the whole-wheat and gram
   flours together in a large bowl.
Add the salt to the flour and mix well.

2 Finely chop the onion and add to
   the flour mixture with the cilantro
and chilies. Mix well.

3 Add the water and mix to form a
   soft dough. Cover the dough and
let stand for 15 minutes.

4 Knead the dough for
   5–7 minutes.

5 Divide the dough into 8 equal-
   size portions.

6 Roll out the dough portions on a
   lightly floured counter to circles
about 7 inches/18 cm in diameter.

7 Place the dough portions
   individually in a skillet and cook
over medium heat, turning 3 times and
lightly greasing each side with the
ghee each time. Transfer the bread to
serving plates and serve hot.

COOK'S TIP

Also called gram flour, besan is
   pale yellow flour made from
   ground chickpeas. In Indian
   kitchens it is used to make
breads, bhajias, and batters and
to thicken sauces and stabilize
yogurt when it is added to hot
   dishes. Buy it from Indian
   groceries or large health food
stores and store in a cool, dark
place in an airtight container.

pooris

serves ten

generous 1⅓ cups whole-wheat flour
   (urid dal flour (ata) or chapati flour)
½ tsp salt
⅔ cup water
2½ cups vegetable oil, plus extra
   for oiling

1 Place the flour and salt in a large
  bowl and stir well.

2 Make a well in the center of the
  flour. Gradually pour in the water
and mix together to form a dough,
adding more water if necessary.

3 Knead the dough until it is
  smooth and elastic and let rest
in a warm place for 15 minutes.

COOK'S TIP

You can make pooris in advance,
if you prefer. Wrap in foil and
reheat in a hot oven for
10 minutes when required.

4 Divide the dough into 10 equal
  portions and with lightly oiled
hands, pat each into a smooth ball.

5 Roll out each ball on a lightly
  oiled counter to form a thin circle.

6 Heat the oil in a deep skillet.
  Deep-fry the circles in batches
a few seconds, turning once, until
golden in color.

7 Remove the pooris and drain on
  paper towels. Serve hot.

hapatis

serves five–six

nerous 1⅓ cups whole-wheat flour
(urid dal flour [ata] or chapati
flour), plus extra for dusting

tsp salt

nerous ¾ cup water

Place the flour in a large bowl.
Add the salt and mix well.

Make a well in the center of the
flour and gradually pour in the
er, mixing well with your fingers to
a supple dough.

3 Knead the dough for
7–10 minutes. Ideally, let the
dough rest for 15–20 minutes, but
if time is short roll out the dough
straightaway. Divide the dough into
10–12 equal-size portions. Roll
out each piece of dough on a
well floured counter.

3

COOK'S TIP

Ideally, chapatis should be eaten
as they come out of the skillet,
but if that is not practical keep
them warm after cooking by
wrapping them up in foil. In
India, chapatis are sometimes
cooked on a naked flame, which
makes them puff up. Allow about
2 per person.

---

4 Place a heavy-bottom skillet on a
high heat. When steam begins to
rise from the skillet, reduce the heat
to medium.

5 Place a chapati in the skillet and
when the chapati begins to
bubble turn it over. Carefully press
down on the chapati with a clean dish
towel or a wooden spatula and turn
the chapati over once again. Remove
the chapati from the skillet and keep
warm while you make the others.

6 Repeat the process until all of the
chapatis are cooked.

Snacks & Side Dishes

In India, people enjoy holding tea parties at about 5 or 6 o'clock in the afternoon, and little snacks such as the ones in this chapter are served. They are ideal for cocktail or other drinks parties, when you would like to offer something more interesting than the usual peanuts and chips. The basic quantities are for 4 people, but you can multiply according to the number on your guest list. Accompaniments—a simple Cucumber Salad or a Mint Raita, for example—always add color and variety to a meal. Most take very little time to prepare, but taste delicious. None of these accompaniments has to be made in large quantities, because they are taken in only small amounts: variety is better than quantity!

onion bhajias

makes about twenty-four

½ tsp onion seeds

½ tsp cumin seeds

½ tsp fennel seeds

½ tsp black onion seeds

generous 1½ cups besan

1 tsp baking powder

1 tsp ground turmeric

½ tsp chili powder

pinch of asafetida

salt

3 onions, thinly sliced

2 fresh green chilies, seeded and
    finely chopped

3 tbsp chopped cilantro

vegetable oil, for deep-frying

COOK'S TIP

Do not overcrowd the fryer or
pan when deep-frying, because
you need room to turn the
bhajias over. Lower the bhajias
slowly into the hot oil to
prevent any splashes.

1 Heat a large, heavy-bottom skillet
and dry-fry the onion, cumin,
fennel, and black onion seeds for a few
seconds, stirring constantly, until they
give off their aroma. Remove from the
heat and tip into a mortar. Crush lightly
with a pestle and tip into a large bowl.

2 Sift the besan, baking powder,
turmeric, chili powder, asafetida,
and a pinch of salt into the bowl and
add the onions, chilies, and chopped
cilantro. Mix thoroughly, then gradually
stir in enough cold water to make a
thick batter.

3 Heat the oil in a deep-fat fry
large, heavy-bottom pan to
350–375°F/180–190°C, or until a
cube of bread browns in 30 secon
Drop spoonfuls of the mixture into
hot oil and cook until golden brow
turning once. Remove with a slot
spoon and drain on paper towels
Serve hot.

VARIATION

You can use this batter to m
bhajias with a variety of oth
vegetables, such as cauliflow
florets or sliced mushroom

pakoras

serves four

6 tbsp besan

½ tsp salt

1 tsp chili powder

1 tsp baking powder

1½ tsp white cumin seeds

1 tsp pomegranate seeds

1¼ cups water

¼ bunch of cilantro,
    finely chopped

vegetables of your choice:
    cauliflower, cut into small florets;
    onions, cut into rings; potatoes,
    sliced; eggplants, sliced; or fresh
    spinach leaves

vegetable oil, for deep-frying

1 Sift the besan into a large bowl.

2 Add the salt, chili powder, baking powder, cumin, and pomegranate seeds and blend together well.

3 Pour in the water and beat well to form a smooth batter.

4 Add the chopped cilantro and mix. Reserve.

5 Dip the prepared vegetables of your choice into the batter, carefully shaking off any excess.

6 Heat the oil in a large heavy-bottom skillet. Place the batte vegetables in the oil and deep-fry, batches, turning once.

7 Repeat this process until all o batter has been used up.

8 Transfer the battered vegetab to paper towels and drain thoroughly. Serve immediately.

COOK'S TIP

When deep-frying, it is important to use oil at the correct temperature. If the oil is too hot, the outside of the food will burn, as will the spices, before the inside is cooked. If the oil is too cool, the food will be sodden with oil before a crisp batter forms. Draining on paper towels is essential, because it absorbs excess oil and moisture.

al fritters

serves four

cup moong dal, soaked for
2–3 hours, then drained

cup urid dal, soaked for
2–3 hours, then drained

2 tbsp water

nion, finely chopped

resh green chili, chopped

nch/2.5-cm piece fresh
gingerroot, finely chopped

osp chopped cilantro

sp baking soda

etable oil, for deep-frying

utney (see pages 227–231),
o serve

1 Place the dals in a food processor with the water and process to make a thick paste. Transfer to a large bowl and stir in the onion, chili, ginger, cilantro, and baking soda. Season with salt to taste, then mix thoroughly and let stand for 5 minutes.

VARIATION

Substitute ½–1 teaspoon of chili powder for the fresh chili, if you like. Serve with either Mango or Tamarind Chutney (see pages 230–231).

2 Heat the oil in a deep-fat fryer or large, heavy-bottom pan to 350–375°F/180–190°C, or until a cube of bread browns in 30 seconds. Drop small spoonfuls of the mixture into the hot oil and deep-fry for 3–4 minutes, or until golden.

3 Remove the fritters with a slotted spoon and drain on paper towels. Keep warm while you cook the remaining fritters. Serve immediately with the Chutney of your choice.

fried eggplants in yogurt

serves four

generous ¾ cup plain yogurt

generous ¼ cup water

1 tsp salt

1 eggplant

⅔ cup vegetable oil

1 tsp white cumin seeds

6 dried red chilies

COOK'S TIP

Rich in protein and calcium, yogurt plays an important part in Indian cooking. It is used as a marinade, as a creamy flavoring in curries and sauces, and as a cooling accompaniment to hot dishes.

VARIATION

Finely chop and seed the dried red chilies, if you prefer.

1 Place the yogurt in a bowl and whisk with a fork. Add the water and salt to the yogurt and mix well.

2 Transfer the yogurt mixture to a serving bowl and reserve.

3 Using a sharp knife, slice the eggplant thinly.

4 Heat the oil in a large skillet. the eggplant slices and cook, batches, over medium heat, turning occasionally, for 5 minutes, until th begin to turn crisp. Remove from th skillet, then transfer to a serving pl and keep warm.

5 When all of the eggplant slice have been cooked, reduce the heat and add the cumin seeds and dried red chilies to the skillet. Cook 1 minute, stirring.

6 Spoon the yogurt on top of th eggplants, then pour over the cumin and chilli mixture. Serve immediately.

spicy corn

serves four

1¾ cups frozen or canned corn

1 tsp ground cumin

1 garlic clove, crushed

1 tsp ground coriander

1 tsp salt

2 fresh green chilies, chopped

1 onion, finely chopped

3 tbsp unsalted butter

4 dried red chilies, crushed

½ tsp lemon juice

¼ bunch of cilantro, shredded, plus
   extra to garnish

1 Thaw the corn (or drain if using canned corn) and reserve.

2 Place the ground cumin, garlic, ground coriander, salt, half of the green chili, and the onion in a mortar or a food processor and grind to form a smooth paste.

3 Heat the butter in a large skillet. Add the onion and spice mixture and cook over medium heat, stirring occasionally, for 5–7 minutes.

4 Add the crushed red chilies to the skillet and stir to mix.

5 Add the corn and stir-fry for an additional 2 minutes.

COOK'S TIP

Cilantro is an essential ingredient in Indian cooking, along with coriander seeds from the same plant. Coriander seeds are often dry-roasted before use to develop their flavor.

6 Add the remaining green chili, lemon juice, and the shredded cilantro to the skillet, stirring occasionally to mix.

7 Transfer the spicy corn mixture a warmed serving dish. Garni with cilantro and serve hot.

dian-style omelet

serves two–four

small onion, very finely chopped
fresh green chilies, finely chopped
bunch of cilantro, finely chopped
eggs
sp salt
bsp vegetable oil
antro sprigs, to garnish
sp green salad, to serve

1 Mix the onion, chilies, and cilantro together in a large bowl.

2 Place the eggs in a separate bowl and whisk together. Add the onion mixture and mix together. Add the salt and whisk together well.

3 Heat 1 tablespoon of the oil in a skillet. Place a ladleful of the omelet mixture into the skillet.

4 Cook the omelet, turning once and pressing down with a wooden spatula to make sure that the egg is cooked right through, until the omelet is golden brown.

5 Repeat the same process with the remaining omelet mixture. Keep the cooked omelets warm in the meantime.

6 Garnish with cilantro sprigs and serve the omelets immediately with a crisp green salad.

COOK'S TIP

Indian cooks use a variety of vegetable oils, and peanut or corn oils make good alternatives for most dishes, although sometimes more specialty ones, such as coconut oil, mustard oil, and sesame oil, are called for.

shrimp patties

makes eight

10 oz/280 g cooked shrimp, peeled, deveined, and chopped

1 onion, finely chopped

1 fresh green chili, seeded and finely chopped

½-inch/1-cm piece fresh gingerroot, finely chopped

1 tbsp chopped cilantro

2 tbsp fresh white bread crumbs

¼ tsp ground turmeric

1 tbsp lime juice

1 egg, lightly beaten

⅔ cup dried bread crumbs

3 tbsp ghee or vegetable oil

cilantro sprigs, to garnish

VARIATION

To make chicken patties, substitute the same quantity of ground cooked chicken for the shrimp.

1 Mix the shrimp, onion, chili, ginger, cilantro, fresh bread crumbs, turmeric, lime juice, and beaten egg in a large bowl, kneading well with your hands until the mixture is thoroughly blended.

2 Divide the mixture into 8 equal-size portions, then form each portion into a ball between the palms of your hands and flatten into patties. Spread the dried bread crumbs out on a large plate and dip each patty in turn into the bread crumbs to coat evenly.

3 Heat the ghee in a large, hea᠎ bottom skillet. Add the patties 2 batches if necessary, and cook fo 5–6 minutes on each side, until go brown. Remove with a spatula and drain on paper towels. Keep each batch warm while you cook the remainder. Garnish with cilantro sp and serve immediately.

COOK'S TIP

If possible, use natural dried bread crumbs for coating the patties rather than colored brea᠎ crumbs. You may need to pres᠎ the bread crumbs onto the patties to coat.

vegetable sambar

serves six

4 cups canned tomatoes

2 tbsp dry unsweetened coconut

2 tbsp lemon juice

1 tbsp yellow mustard seeds

scant ¼ cup raw or muscovado
   sugar

2 tbsp ghee or vegetable oil

2 onions, sliced

4 cardamom pods, lightly crushed

6 curry leaves, plus extra to garnish

2 tsp ground coriander

2 tsp ground cumin

1 tsp ground turmeric

1 tsp Ginger Paste (see page 11)

scant 1 cup toor dal

1 lb/450 g sweet potatoes,
   cut into chunks

2 lb/900 g potatoes, cut into chunks

2 carrots, sliced

2 zucchini, cut into chunks

1 eggplant, cut into chunks

salt

1 Place the tomatoes and their can juices, coconut, 1 tablespoon of the lemon juice, the mustard seeds, and sugar in a food processor or blender and process until smooth.

2 Heat the ghee in a large, heavy-bottom pan. Add the onion and cook over low heat, stirring occasionally, for 10 minutes, or until golden. Add the cardamoms, curry leaves, coriander, cumin, turmeric, and Ginger Paste and cook, stirring constantly, for 1–2 minutes, or until the spices give off their aroma. Stir in the tomato mixture and dal and bring to a boil. Reduce the heat, then cover and simmer for 10 minutes.

3 Add the sweet potatoes, potatoes, and carrots. Re-cover the pan and simmer for an additional 15 minutes. Add the zucchini, eggplant, and remaining lemon juice and salt to taste, then re-cover and simmer for an additional 10–15 minutes, or until the vegetables are tender. Serve garnished with curry leaves.

VARIATION

You can use any vegetables that you have to hand to make this dish. Add fibrous ones with the sweet potatoes and softer ones with the zucchini.

soft dumplings in yogurt with masala

serves four

1⅓ cups urid dal flour (ata)

1 tsp baking powder

½ tsp ground ginger

1¼ cups water

vegetable oil, for deep-frying

YOGURT SAUCE

1¾ cups plain yogurt

⅔ cup water

generous ⅓ cup sugar

MASALA

⅓ cup ground coriander

⅓ cup ground white cumin

1–2 tsp dried chili flakes

3½ oz/100 g citric acid

chopped fresh red chilies,
   to garnish

1 Place the urid dal flour in a large bowl. Add the baking powder and ground ginger and stir well. Add the water and mix to form a batter.

2 Heat the oil in a deep pan or skillet. Pour in the batter, 1 teaspoon at a time, and deep-fry the dumplings until golden brown, reducing the heat when the oil gets too hot. Set the dumplings aside.

3 To make the yogurt sauce, place the yogurt in a separate bowl. Add the water and sugar and mix together with a whisk or fork. Reserve until required.

4 To make the masala, dry-roast ground coriander and the cumin in a pan until a little darker in color. Add the dried chili flakes and citric and blend well together.

5 Sprinkle 1 tablespoon of the masala over the dumplings and garnish with chopped red chilies. S with the reserved yogurt mixture.

amosas

serves ten–twelve

STRY

up self-rising flour

sp salt

bsp butter, cut into small pieces

bsp water

LING

otatoes, boiled

sp finely chopped fresh
gingerroot

arlic clove, crushed

sp white cumin seeds

sp mixed onion and
mustard seeds

sp salt

sp dried red chili flakes

bsp lemon juice

mall fresh green chilies,
finely chopped

etable oil, for deep-frying

1 Sift the flour and salt into a large bowl. Add the butter and rub it into the flour until the mixture resembles fine bread crumbs.

2 Pour in the water and mix with a fork to form a dough. Pat the dough into a ball and knead for 5 minutes, or until the dough is smooth. Add a little flour if the dough is sticky. Cover and reserve.

3 To make the filling, mash the boiled potatoes gently and mix with the ginger, garlic, cumin seeds, onion and mustard seeds, salt, dried red chili flakes, lemon juice, and green chili.

4 Break small balls off the dough and roll each one out very thinly to form a round. Cut in half, then dampen the edges and shape into cones. Fill the cones with a little of the filling, then dampen the top and bottom edges of the cones and pinch together to seal. Reserve.

5 Fill a deep pan one-third full with oil and heat to 350°–375°F/ 180°–190°C, or until a small cube of bread browns in 30 seconds. Lower the samosas into the oil, a few at a time, and deep-fry for 2–3 minutes or until golden brown. Remove from the oil and drain thoroughly on paper towels. Serve hot or cold.

205

samosas with meat filling

1 quantity Samosa Pastry
(see page 205)
vegetable oil, for deep-frying
cilantro sprigs, to garnish
FILLING
2 tbsp ghee or vegetable oil
1 onion, chopped
1 lb/450 g fresh ground lamb
1 tsp Garlic Paste (see page 11)
1 tsp Ginger Paste (see page 11)
salt and pepper

COOK'S TIP

Frozen samosas do not need to be thawed before deep-frying. However, if you prefer to thaw them, this will not adversely affect them.

1 To make the filling, heat the ghee in a karahi or large, heavy-bottom skillet. Add the onion and cook over low heat, stirring frequently, for 10 minutes, or until golden. Add the lamb, Garlic Paste, and Ginger Paste and season to taste with salt and pepper. Cook, breaking up the meat with a wooden spoon, for 10 minutes, or until the mixture is fairly dry. Transfer to a bowl with a slotted spoon and let cool.

2 Break small balls off the dough and roll each one out very thinly to form a circle. Cut in half, then dampen the edges and form into cones. Fill the cones with some of the filling, then dampen the top and bottom edges and pinch together to seal. Reserve.

3 Fill a deep-fat fryer or large, heavy-bottom pan one-third with vegetable oil and heat to 350–375°F/180–190°C, or until a cube of bread browns in 30 secon Carefully lower the samosas into th hot oil, in batches, and deep-fry fo 2–3 minutes, or until golden brow Remove with a slotted spoon and on paper towels. Keep warm while cook the remaining samosas. Serv or cold, garnished with cilantro sp

VARIATION

If you don't want to go to th bother of making the samos pastry yourself, you can use spring roll wrappers instead

bombay potatoes

serves six

1 lb 2 oz/500 g new potatoes, diced

1 tsp ground turmeric

salt

4 tbsp ghee or vegetable oil

6 curry leaves

1 dried red chili

2 fresh green chilies, chopped

½ tsp black onion seeds

1 tsp mixed mustard and
   onion seeds

½ tsp cumin seeds

½ tsp fennel seeds

¼ tsp asafetida

2 onions, chopped

5 tbsp chopped cilantro

juice of ½ lime

1 Place the potatoes in a large, heavy-bottom pan and pour in just enough cold water to cover. Add ½ teaspoon of the turmeric and a pinch of salt and bring to a boil. Simmer for 10 minutes, or until tender, then drain and reserve until required.

2 Heat the ghee in a large, heavy-bottom skillet. Add the curry leaves and dried red chili and cook, stirring frequently, for a few minutes, or until the chili is blackened. Add the remaining turmeric, the fresh chilies, the black onion, mustard, onion, cumin, and fennel seeds and the asafetida, onions, and chopped cilantro and cook, stirring constantly, for 5 minutes, or until the onions have softened.

3 Stir in the potatoes and cook over low heat, stirring frequently, for 10 minutes, or until heated through. Squeeze over the lime juice and serve.

COOK'S TIP

Asafetida is thought to aid digestion and combat flatulenc It is best bought as a powder rather than as a resin, althoug the powder quickly loses its flavor and must be stored in a sealed jar.

picy potato cakes

makes eight

/450 g potatoes, diced

nion, grated

sp Garam Masala (see page 11)

sp chili powder (optional)

osp lemon juice

osp chopped cilantro

:

osp ghee or butter

ntro sprigs, to garnish

Cook the potatoes in a pan of
lightly salted boiling water for
5 minutes, or until tender, but still
Meanwhile, place the grated
n in a clean dish towel and wring
to squeeze out the excess
ture. Transfer the onion to a large
l and stir in the Garam Masala,
powder (if using), lemon juice, and
ped cilantro. Season with salt
ste.

2 Drain the potatoes and add to the
bowl. Mash coarsely with a fork or
potato masher. Divide the mixture into
8 equal-size portions, then form each
portion into a ball between the palms
of your hands and flatten into a cake.

3 Heat the ghee in a large, heavy-
bottom skillet. Add the potato
cakes, in batches, if necessary, and
cook for 2 minutes on each side, until
golden brown and crisp. Remove from
the skillet with a spatula and drain on
paper towels. Serve warm or cold
garnished with cilantro sprigs.

chickpea snack

serves 2–4

1½ cups canned chickpeas,
   drained

1 onion

2 potatoes

2 tbsp tamarind paste

6 tbsp water

1 tsp chili powder

2 tsp sugar

1 tsp salt

TO GARNISH

1 tomato, cut into fourths

2 fresh green chilies, chopped

2–3 tbsp chopped cilantro

1 Place the drained chickpeas in a large bowl.

2 Chop the onion and reserve. Peel and dice the potatoes. Place the potatoes in a pan of water and boil until cooked through. Drain and reserve until required.

3 Mix the tamarind paste and water together in a small bowl.

4 Add the chili powder, sugar, and 1 teaspoon of salt to the tamarind paste mixture and mix together. Pour the mixture over the chickpeas.

COOK'S TIP

Cream-colored and resembling hazelnuts in appearance, chickpeas have a nutty flavor and slightly crunchy texture. Indian cooks also grind chickpeas to make a flour called besan or gram flour, which is used to make breads, thicken sauces, and to make batters for deep-fried dishes.

5 Add the onion and the diced potatoes, and stir to mix. Sea with a little salt to taste.

6 Transfer to a serving bowl an garnish with tomato, chilies, chopped cilantro.

deep-fried diamond pastries

serves four

1 cup all-purpose flour
1 tsp baking powder
½ tsp salt
1 tbsp black cumin seeds
scant ½ cup water
1¼ cups vegetable oil

1 Place the all-purpose flour in a large bowl.

2 Add the baking powder, salt, and the cumin seeds and stir to mix.

3 Add the water to the dry ingredients and mix to form a soft, elastic dough.

COOK'S TIP

Black cumin seeds are used here for their strong aromatic flavor. White cumin seeds cannot be used as a substitute.

4 Roll out the dough on a clean counter until ¼ inch/5 mm thi

5 Using a sharp knife, score the dough to form diamond shape Re-roll the dough trimmings and cu out more diamond shapes until all the dough has been used up.

6 Heat the oil in a large pan to 350°–375°F/180°–190°C, or until a cube of bread browns in 30 seconds.

7 Carefully place the pastry diamonds in the hot oil, in batches if necessary, and deep-fry u golden brown.

8 Remove the diamond pastries with a slotted spoon and let d on paper towels. Serve with a dal f dipping or store in an airtight conta and serve when required.

›iced semolina

serves four

:up vegetable oil

sp mixed onion and
 mustard seeds

Iried red chilies

:urry leaves (fresh or dried)

bsp coarse semolina

:up cashew nuts

sp salt

:up water

COOK'S TIP

:urry leaves are very similar in
ppearance to bay leaves but are
ery different in flavor. They can
e bought both fresh and dried.
They are used to flavor lentil
dishes and vegetable curries.

1 Heat the oil in a large, heavy-
 bottom pan.

2 Add the mixed onion and
 mustard seeds, dried red chilies,
and curry leaves and stir-fry for
1 minute, stirring constantly.

3 Reduce the heat and add the
 coarse semolina and the cashew
nuts to the mixture in the pan. Quickly
stir-fry for 5 minutes, moving the
mixture around all the time so that it
does not catch and burn.

4 Add the salt to the mixture
 and continue to stir-fry,
stirring constantly.

5 Add the water and cook, stirring
 constantly, until the mixture
begins to thicken.

6 Serve the spiced semolina warm
 as a teatime snack.

cool cucumber salad

serves four

8 oz/225 g cucumber

1 fresh green chili (optional)

2 tbsp finely chopped
    cilantro

2 tbsp lemon juice

½ tsp salt

1 tsp sugar

fresh mint leaves, to garnish

1 Using a sharp knife, slice the cucumber thinly and cut the slices in half. Arrange the cucumber slices on a round serving plate. Using a sharp knife, chop the green chili (if using). Sprinkle the chopped chili over the cucumber.

2 To make the dressing, place the cilantro, lemon juice, salt, and sugar in a bowl and mix together, then reserve.

3 Place the cucumber in the refrigerator and let chill for at least 1 hour, or until required. Transfer the cucumber to a serving dish. Pour the dressing over the cucumber just before serving and garnish with a few mint leaves.

COOK'S TIP

Much of the heat in Indian dish
comes from the use of fresh
green chilies, although dried a
ground red chilies are also
commonplace in Indian kitchen
In southern India, with its
searingly hot temperatures,
chilies are used in copious
amounts because they cause t
body to perspire, which has a
cooling effect. Numerous
varieties of fresh chili grow in
India, from fairly mild to hot. A
a general rule, the smaller the
chili, the hotter it will be. Fres
chilies will keep for about 5 da
in the refrigerator. To store
cilantro, put the roots in a glas
of water and keep in a cool pla
for up to 4 days.

omato kachumbar

serves six

cup lime juice

sp sugar

t

omatoes, chopped

cucumber, chopped

callions, chopped

esh green chili, seeded
and chopped

osp chopped cilantro

bsp chopped fresh mint

1 Mix the lime juice, sugar, and a pinch of salt together in a large bowl and stir until the sugar has completely dissolved.

2 Add the tomatoes, cucumber, scallions, chili, cilantro, and mint and toss well to mix.

3 Cover with plastic wrap and let chill in the refrigerator for at least 30 minutes. Toss the vegetables before serving.

COOK'S TIP

Chop all the vegetables into fairly small, even-size pieces for the best texture and presentation. You can use whatever vegetables you have in the refrigerator, as long as they can be eaten raw.

hot salad

serves four

½ cauliflower

1 green bell pepper

1 red bell pepper

½ cucumber

4 carrots

2 tbsp butter

salt and pepper

COOK'S TIP

In India, you can buy snacks and accompaniments along the roadside. While you can buy many of them from Asian stores, they are fresher and more satisfying made at home.

1 Rinse the cauliflower and cut into small florets, using a sharp knife. Seed and cut the bell peppers into thin strips. Cut the cucumber into thick slices, then into fourths. Peel the carrots and cut them into thin slices.

2 Melt the butter in a large pan, stirring constantly.

3 Add the cauliflower, bell peppers, cucumber, and carrots and stir-fry for 5–7 minutes. Season to taste with salt and pepper. Cover with a lid, then reduce the heat and let simmer for 3 minutes.

4 Transfer the vegetables to a serving dish, toss to mix and serve immediately.

VARIATION

You can replace the vegetables this recipe with those of your choice, if you prefer.

weet & sour fruit

serves four

oz/400 g canned mixed

fruit cocktail

oz/400 g canned guavas

arge bananas

apples

sp coarsely ground pepper

sp salt

bsp lemon juice

tsp ground ginger

sh mint leaves, to garnish

COOK'S TIP

Ginger is one of the most popular spices in India and also one of the oldest. It can be bought as fresh gingerroot in most large supermarkets. It should always be peeled before use and can be finely chopped or grated. Ground ginger is also useful to have in your pantry. The lemon juice in this recipe adds a sharp flavor to the dish and also prevents the bananas and apples discoloring when the flesh is exposed to the air.

1 Drain the fruit cocktail and place the fruit in a deep mixing bowl.

2 Mix the guavas and their syrup with the drained fruit cocktail.

3 Peel the bananas and cut into slices. Core and dice the apples.

4 Add the fresh fruit to the bowl containing the canned fruit and mix together.

5 Add the pepper, salt, lemon juice, and ginger and stir to mix.

6 Serve as a snack, garnished with a few mint leaves.

onion kachumbar

serves four

2 red onions or 1 Spanish onion,
    thinly sliced

1 fresh green chili, seeded
    and chopped

1 tbsp lime juice

¼ tsp chili powder

1 tbsp chopped cilantro

salt

1 Place the onion slices in a large serving bowl. Sprinkle with the chopped chili, lime juice, chili powder, cilantro, and salt to taste.

2 Toss well to coat the onion slices in the flavorings. Cover the bowl with plastic wrap.

3 Let stand in a cool place, but not the refrigerator, for 30 minutes, to enable the onion to release its juices. Toss the mixture again and taste and adjust the seasoning, if necessary, before serving.

COOK'S TIP

Red and Spanish onions are much sweeter than brown onions and are, therefore, a better choice for serving raw in this salad. No Indian meal is complete without an appetizing collection of small side dishes, which invariably include a simple salad. This one is the perfect foil for tandoori dishes and kabobs.

mixed rice, nuts & raisins

serves four

scant ¼ cup chana dal

1¼ cups vegetable oil

2 tsp onion seeds

6 curry leaves

7 oz/200 g parva (flaked rice)

2 tbsp peanuts

scant ¼ cup raisins

generous ⅓ cup sugar

2 tsp salt

2 tsp chili powder

2 oz/55 g sev (optional)

1 Rinse the dal under cold running water, removing any stones. Soak in a bowl of water for at least 3 hours.

2 Heat the oil in a pan. Add the onion seeds and curry leaves and cook, stirring constantly, until the onion seeds are crisp and golden.

3 Add the parva (flaked rice) to the mixture in the pan and cook until crisp and golden (do not let it burn).

4 Remove the mixture from the pan and let drain on paper towels so that any excess oil is soaked up. Transfer to a bowl.

5 Cook the peanuts in the remaining oil, stirring constan[t]. Add the peanuts to the flaked rice mixture, stirring to mix well. Add th[e] raisins, sugar, salt, and chili powde[r] and mix together. Mix in the sev (if using). Transfer to a serving dish

6 Reheat the oil remaining in th[e] pan and cook the drained dal until golden. Add to the other ingredients in the serving dish and mix together.

7 This dish can be eaten straightaway or stored in an airtight container until you need it.

COOK'S TIP
Sev are very thin sticks made o[f] besan and can be bought in Asian food stores.

hrimp sambal

serves four

z/250 g cooked peeled
shrimp, chopped

ard-cooked eggs, shelled
and sliced

arge onion, finely chopped

-inch/3-cm piece fresh
gingerroot, finely chopped

sp chili powder

bsp canned coconut milk

sp cumin seeds

GARNISH

me, cut into wedges

ntro sprigs

COOK'S TIP

you shell the eggs immediately
ter hard-cooking them, you can
void any discoloration around
e yolk. To cool the cooked eggs
quickly, rinse them under cold
running water.

1 Place the shrimp, hard-cooked eggs, onion, ginger, chili powder, and coconut milk in a serving bowl and mix well. Season with salt to taste.

2 Place the cumin seeds in a mortar and lightly crush with a pestle.

3 Sprinkle the crushed cumin seeds over the sambal, then cover with plastic wrap and let chill in the refrigerator for at least 30 minutes. Serve garnished with lime wedges and cilantro sprigs.

chickpea salad

serves four

1½ cups canned chickpeas

4 carrots

1 bunch of scallions

1 cucumber

½ tsp salt

½ tsp pepper

3 tbsp lemon juice

1 red bell pepper, seeded and
   thinly sliced

1 Drain the chickpeas and place them in a large salad bowl.

2 Using a sharp knife, peel and slice the carrots. Cut the scallions into thin strips. Slice the cucumber, then cut into thick fourths. Add the carrots, scallions, and cucumber to the chickpeas and mix.

3 Stir in the salt and pepper and sprinkle with the lemon juice.

4 Gently toss the salad ingredie together using 2 serving spoo

5 Using a sharp knife, slice the bell pepper thinly.

6 Arrange the slices of red bell pepper on top of the chickpe salad. Serve the salad immediately let chill in the refrigerator and serv when required.

COOK'S TIP
Using canned chickpeas rather than the dried ones speeds up the cooking time.

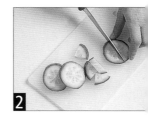

ggplant purée

serves six

arge eggplants, halved
lengthwise

bsp chopped cilantro

sp ground coriander

sp ground cumin

sp ground turmeric

omatoes, finely chopped

bsp ghee or vegetable oil

nion, finely chopped

sp Ginger Paste (see page 11)

sp Garlic Paste (see page 11)

esh green chili, finely chopped

bsp lemon juice

esh mint sprig, to garnish

apatis (see page 189), to serve

3 Heat the ghee in a heavy-bottom skillet. Add the onion and cook over low heat, stirring occasionally, for 5 minutes, or until softened. Stir in the Ginger Paste, Garlic Paste, and chili and cook, stirring constantly, for 2 minutes. Add the eggplant mixture, then season with salt to taste and cook, stirring frequently, until the liquid has evaporated and the purée is thickened and fairly smooth. Sprinkle with the lemon juice, then spoon into a warmed serving bowl and garnish with a mint sprig. Serve immediately with Chapatis.

Preheat the oven to 350°F/180°C. Place the eggplants, cut-sides up, shallow, ovenproof dish, then with foil and bake for 1 hour, or the flesh is very soft. Let cool.

Scoop the eggplant flesh into a bowl and mash well. Beat in the tro, ground coriander, cumin, eric, and tomatoes with a den spoon.

COOK'S TIP

Before baking the eggplants in the oven, use a sharp knife to slash the flesh of each half 2 or 3 times.

223

lime pickle

serves four

12 limes, halved and seeded

4 oz/115 g salt

scant ½ cup chili powder

2 tbsp mustard powder

2 tbsp ground fenugreek

1 tbsp ground turmeric

1¼ cups mustard oil

½ oz/15 g yellow mustard
    seeds, crushed

½ tsp asafetida

COOK'S TIP

If you are absolutely certain that the jar won't crack when you add the hot oil in Step 3, then there is no need to transfer the lime mixture to a bowl to cool.

1 Cut each lime half into 4 pieces and pack them into a large, sterilized jar (see Cook's Tip, page 223), sprinkling over the salt at the same time. Cover and let stand in a warm place for 10–14 days, or until the limes have turned brown and softened.

2 Mix the chili powder, mustard powder, fenugreek, and turmeric together in a small bowl and add to the jar of limes. Stir to mix, then re-cover and let stand for 2 days.

3 Transfer the lime mixture to a heatproof bowl. Heat the oil in a heavy-bottom skillet. Add the mustard seeds and asafetida and cook, stirring constantly, until the oil is very hot and just beginning to smoke. Pour the oil and spices over the limes and mix well. Cover and let cool. When cool, pack into a sterilized jar and seal, then store in a sunny place for 1 week before serving.

raitas

serves four

MINT RAITA

generous ¾ cup plain yogurt

4 tbsp water

1 small onion, finely chopped

½ tsp mint sauce

½ tsp salt

3 fresh mint leaves, to garnish

CUCUMBER RAITA

8 oz/225 g cucumber

1 onion

½ tsp salt

½ tsp mint sauce

1¼ cup plain yogurt

⅔ cup water

fresh mint leaves, to garnish

EGGPLANT RAITA

1 eggplant

1 tsp salt

1 small onion, finely chopped

2 fresh green chilies, finely chopped

generous ¾ cup plain yogurt

3 tbsp water

1 To make the mint raita, place the yogurt in a bowl and whisk with a fork. Gradually add the water, whisking well. Add the onion, mint sauce, and salt and blend together. Garnish with the fresh mint leaves.

2 To make the cucumber raita, peel and slice the cucumber. Using a sharp knife, chop the onion finely. Place the cucumber and onion in a large bowl, then add the salt and the mint sauce. Add the yogurt and the water, place the mixture in a blender and blend well. Transfer to a serving bowl and serve garnished with a few fresh mint leaves.

3 To make the eggplant raita, rinse the eggplant and remove the top end. Discard the top and chop the rest into small pieces. Boil the eggplant in a pan of water until soft and mushy. Drain the eggplant and mash. Transfer to a serving bowl and add the salt, the onion, and chilies, mixing well. Whisk the yogurt with the water in a separate bowl and pour over the eggplant mixture. Mix well and serve.

ne jewels chutney

serves four

sp coriander seeds

sp cumin seeds

sp onion seeds

sp aniseed

cup almonds, chopped

pe mango, peeled, pitted,
and sliced

ating apple, cored and chopped

anana, peeled and sliced

resh pineapple slices, chopped

or 4 canned pineapple slices in
juice, drained, and chopped

z/225 g canned peaches in fruit
juice, drained and chopped

cup dried dates, pitted
and sliced

erous ⅓ cup raisins

ried red chilies

oz/40 g piece fresh gingerroot,
chopped

up raw or muscovado sugar

cup white wine or
malt vinegar

1 Heat a heavy-bottom skillet. Add the coriander seeds, cumin seeds, onion seeds, aniseed, and almonds and cook over low heat, stirring constantly, for 1–2 minutes, or until the spices give off their aroma. Remove the skillet from the heat and reserve.

2 Place the mango, apple, banana, pineapple, peaches, dates, raisins, chilies, ginger, and sugar in a heavy-bottom pan. Pour in the vinegar, then add a pinch of salt and bring to a boil, stirring constantly. Reduce the heat and simmer gently, stirring frequently, for 15 minutes, or until thickened.

3 Stir in the spice mixture and cook, stirring frequently, for an additional 5 minutes. Remove from the heat and let cool. Either serve immediately or ladle into a sterilized jar (see Cook's Tip) and seal.

COOK'S TIP

To sterilize jars, boil clean jars in a pan of water for 10 minutes. Transfer to a preheated oven, 275°F/140°C, place upside down and dry for 15 minutes.

sesame seed chutney

serves four

8 tbsp sesame seeds

2 tbsp water

½ bunch of cilantro,
   finely chopped

3 fresh green chilies, chopped

1 tsp salt

2 tsp lemon juice

1 fresh red chili, chopped,
   to garnish

COOK'S TIP

Dry-roasting coaxes all of the flavor out of dried spices and gives dishes well-harmonized flavors that do not taste raw. Dry-roasting only takes a few minutes and you will be able to tell when the spices are ready because of the wonderful aroma they release. Be sure to stir the spices constantly and never take your eyes off the pan, because the spices can burn very quickly.

1 Place the sesame seeds in a large, heavy-bottom pan and dry-roast them. Remove the pan from the heat and let cool.

2 Once cooled, place the sesame seeds in a mortar or food processor and grind to form a fine powder. Add the water to the sesame seeds and mix to form a smooth paste.

3 Finely chop the cilantro and add to the sesame seeds with the chilies. Grind once again.

4 Add the salt and lemon juice to the mixture and grind again.

5 Remove the mixture from the food processor or mortar. Transfer to a serving dish and garnish with chopped chili. Serve.

mango chutney

serves four

2 lb 4 oz/1 kg fresh mangoes

4 tbsp salt

2½ cups water

2½ cups sugar

1¾ cups vinegar

2 tsp finely chopped fresh
gingerroot

2 garlic cloves, crushed

2 tsp chili powder

2 cinnamon sticks

scant ½ cup raisins

generous ½ cup dates, pitted

1 Using a sharp knife, halve and pit the mangoes—cut down on either side of the large pit and score the flesh, then turn inside out and cut off the mango cubes. Place the mango in a large bowl. Add the salt and water and let stand overnight. Drain the liquid from the mangoes and reserve.

2 Bring the sugar and vinegar to a boil in a large pan over low heat, stirring. Gradually add the mango cubes to the sugar and vinegar mixture, stirring to coat the mango in the mixture.

3 Add the ginger, garlic, chili powder, cinnamon sticks, rais and dates, and bring to a boil aga stirring occasionally. Reduce the he and cook for 1 hour, or until the mi thickens. Remove from the heat an cool. Remove the cinnamon sticks discard. Spoon the chutney into cle dry jars and cover tightly with lids. stand in a cool place so the flavors fully develop.

COOK'S TIP

When choosing mangoes, sele ones that are shiny with unblemished skins. To test if th are ripe, gently cup the mango your hand and squeeze it gently—it should give slightly the touch if ready for eating.

amarind chutney

serves four–six

bsp tamarind paste

bsp water

sp chili powder

tsp ground ginger

tsp salt

sp sugar

2 tbsp finely chopped cilantro,

to garnish

COOK'S TIP

egetable dishes are often given a sharp, sour flavor with the addition of tamarind. This is made from the semidried, mpressed pulp of the tamarind tree. You can buy bars of the ungent-smelling pulp in Asian ood stores. Store it in a tightly sealed plastic bag or airtight container. Alternatively, for reater convenience, keep a jar f tamarind paste in your pantry and use as required. Although marind is much more sour than mon, lemon is often used as a substitute.

1 Place the tamarind paste in a small bowl.

2 Gradually add the water to the tamarind paste, gently whisking with a fork to form a smooth, runny consistency.

3 Add the chili powder and the ginger to the mixture and blend well.

4 Add the salt and the sugar and mix well.

5 Transfer the chutney to a serving dish and garnish with chopped cilantro. Serve.

Desserts

Indian desserts are quite rich and very sweet, so it is an excellent idea to offer a wide variety of fresh fruit—mangoes, guavas, or melon, for example—as well. These are best served chilled, especially in the summer months.

This chapter offers simple, everyday desserts, such as Indian Rice Pudding, as well as more exotic creations. Among Indian people, some desserts such as Indian Bread Pudding, Carrot Dessert, and Indian Vermicelli Pudding are served only on special occasions, such as religious festivals. Few Indian restaurants in the West offer much in the way of special Indian desserts, so these recipes will come as a pleasant—and mouthwatering—surprise.

indian bread pudding

COOK'S TIP

To make khoya, first bring
3¾ cups milk to a boil in a large,
heavy-bottom pan, watching the
milk carefully so that it doesn't
burn. Reduce the heat and boil
for 35 minutes, stirring
occasionally.

1 Cut the slices of bread
into fourths.

2 Heat the ghee in a skillet. Add the
bread slices and cook, turning
once, until a crisp golden brown color.

3 Place the fried bread in the
bottom of a heatproof dish and
reserve.

4 To make a syrup, place the sugar,
water, and cardamom seeds in a
pan and bring to a boil until the syrup
thickens.

5 Pour the syrup over the fried
bread in the dish.

6 Place the milk, evaporated milk
and saffron in a separate pan
bring to a boil over low heat until the
milk has halved in volume.

7 Pour the milk over the syrup-
coated bread.

8 Decorate with the pistachios,
chopped almonds, and varak
(if using). Serve the bread pudding
with or without cream.

coconut sweet

1 Place the butter in a heavy-bottom pan and melt over low heat, stirring constantly.

2 Add the dry unsweetened coconut to the melted butter, stirring to mix.

3 Stir in the condensed milk and the pink food coloring (if using) and mix constantly for 7–10 minutes.

4 Remove the pan from the heat and let the coconut mixture cool slightly.

5 Once cool enough to handle, shape the coconut mixture into long blocks and cut into equal-size rectangles. Let set for 1 hour, then serve.

VARIATION

If you prefer, you could divide the coconut mixture in two, and add the pink food coloring to only one half of the mixture. This way, you will have an attractive combination of pink and white coconut sweets.

COOK'S TIP

Coconut is used extensively in Indian cooking to add flavor and creaminess to various dishes. The best flavor comes from freshly grated coconut, although ready-prepared dry unsweetened coconut, as used here, makes an excellent standby. Freshly grated coconut freezes successfully, so is well worth preparing when you have the time.

mond slices

serves six–eight

ggs

cup ground almonds

cups milk powder

up sugar

sp saffron threads

nt 1 stick unsalted butter

cup slivered almonds

Preheat the oven to 325°F/160°C. Beat the eggs together in a bowl reserve until required.

Place the ground almonds, milk powder, sugar, and saffron in a bowl and stir to mix well.

2

4

5

3 Melt the butter in a small pan.

COOK'S TIP

These almond slices are best eaten hot, but they may also be served cold. They can be made a day or even a week in advance and reheated. They also freeze beautifully.

4 Pour the melted butter over the dry ingredients and mix well with a wooden spoon.

5 Add the reserved beaten eggs to the mixture and stir to blend well.

6 Spread the mixture in a shallow 6–8-inch/15–20-cm square ovenproof dish and bake in the preheated oven for 45 minutes. Test whether the cake is cooked through by piercing with the tip of a knife or a skewer—it will come out clean if it is cooked thoroughly.

7 Using a sharp knife, cut the almond cake into slices.

8 Decorate the almond slices with slivered almonds and transfer to a serving dish. Serve hot or cold.

almond & pistachio dessert

serves four–six

scant ¾ stick unsalted butter

2 cups ground almonds

1 cup sugar

⅔ cup light cream

8 almonds, chopped

10 pistachio nuts, chopped

1 Melt the butter in a medium-size, preferably nonstick pan, stirring well.

2 Add the ground almonds, sugar, and cream to the melted butter in the pan, stirring well. Reduce the heat and stir constantly for 10–12 minutes, scraping the base of the pan.

3 Increase the heat until the mixture turns a little darker in color.

4 Transfer the almond mixture to a shallow serving dish and smooth the top with the back of a spoon.

5 Decorate the dessert with the chopped almonds and pistachios.

6 Leave the dessert to set for 1 hour, then cut into diamond shapes and serve cold.

COOK'S TIP

You could use a variety of shape cookie cutters to cut the desse into different shapes, rather tha diamonds, if you prefer. This almond dessert can be ma in advance and stored in an airtight container in the refrigerator for several days.

arrot dessert

COOK'S TIP

his dessert tastes better made
ith pure ghee. However, if you
e trying to limit your fat intake,
se vegetable ghee instead. A
uicker way to grate the carrots
is to use a food processor.

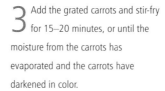

1 Peel and grate the carrots,
then reserve.

2 Heat the ghee in a large, heavy-
bottom skillet.

3 Add the grated carrots and stir-fry
for 15–20 minutes, or until the
moisture from the carrots has
evaporated and the carrots have
darkened in color.

4 Add the milk, evaporated milk,
cardamoms, and sugar to the
carrot mixture and continue to stir
for an additional 30–35 minutes,
or until the mixture is a rich brownish-
red color.

5 Transfer the carrot mixture to
individual serving dishes.

6 Decorate with the pistachio nuts
and varak (if using) and serve.

239

sweet potato dessert

2 lb 4 oz/1 kg sweet potatoes

3¾ cups milk

generous ¾ cup sugar

few chopped almonds, to decorate

COOK'S TIP

Sweet potatoes are longer than ordinary potatoes and have a pinkish or yellowish skin with yellow or white flesh. As their name suggests, they taste slightly sweet.

1 Using a sharp knife, peel the sweet potatoes, then rinse under cold water and cut them into slices.

2 Place the sweet potato slices in a large pan. Cover with 2½ cups of the milk and cook slowly until the sweet potato is soft enough to be mashed.

3 Remove the pan from the heat and mash the sweet potatoes with a potato masher to remove all the lumps.

4 Add the sugar and remaining milk to the mashed sweet potatoes, and carefully stir to blend together.

5 Return the pan to the heat and let the mixture simmer until it begins to thicken (it should reach the consistency of a cream of chicken soup).

6 Transfer the sweet potato dessert to a serving dish.

7 Decorate with the chopped almonds and serve.

sweet saffron rice

serves four

1 cup basmati rice

1 cup sugar

pinch of saffron threads

1¼ cups water

2 tbsp ghee

3 cloves

3 cardamoms

scant ¼ cup golden raisins

TO DECORATE

few pistachio nuts (optional)

varak (silver leaf) (optional)

1 Rinse the rice twice under cold running water, then bring to a boil in a pan of water, stirring. Remove the pan from the heat when the rice is half cooked, then drain thoroughly and reserve.

2 Boil the sugar, saffron, and water together in a separate pan, stirring, until the syrup thickens. Reserve until required.

3 Heat the ghee, cloves, and cardamoms in a separate pan, stirring occasionally. Remove the pan from the heat.

4 Return the rice to low heat and add the golden raisins, stirring. Pour the syrup over the rice mixture and stir.

5 Pour the ghee mixture over the rice and let simmer over low for 10–15 minutes. Check to see whether the rice is cooked; if not, a little water, then cover and let simm Serve warm, decorated with pistach nuts and varak (silver leaf, if using)

VARIATION

For a stronger saffron flavor, pla the saffron threads on a piece foil and toast them lightly unde hot broiler for a few moments (take care not to burn them). Crush finely before adding to th sugar to make the syrup.

ooris stuffed with chana dal halva

serves four–six

nerous 1 cup coarse semolina

cup all-purpose flour, plus extra
for dusting

tsp salt

tsp ghee

cup milk

LING

bsp chana dal

cups water

bsp ghee, plus extra for frying

green cardamoms, husks removed
and seeds crushed

loves

bsp sugar

bsp ground almonds

sp saffron threads

nt ⅓ cup golden raisins

Place the semolina, flour, and salt
in a bowl and mix. Add the ghee
rub it in with your fingers. Add the
and mix to form a dough. Knead
dough for 5 minutes, then cover
let rise for about 3 hours. Knead
dough on a floured counter for
ninutes.

2 Roll out the dough until it
measures 10 inches/25 cm square
and divide into 10 portions. Roll out
each of these into 5-inch/13-cm circles
and set aside. To make the filling, soak
the dal for at least 3 hours, if time
allows. Place the dal in a pan and add
the water. Bring to a boil over medium
heat until all of the water has
evaporated and the dal is soft enough
to be mashed into a paste.

3 Heat the ghee in a separate pan.
Add the cardamom seeds and
cloves and reduce the heat, then add
the dal paste and stir for 5–7 minutes.

4 Fold in the sugar and almonds
and cook, stirring, for 10 minutes.
Add the saffron and golden raisins and
blend until thickened, stirring, for
5 minutes. Spoon the filling onto one
half of each pastry round. Dampen the
edges with water and fold the other
half over to seal.

5 Heat the ghee in a skillet. Add the
pooris and cook over low heat
until golden. Transfer the pooris to
paper towels, then drain and serve.

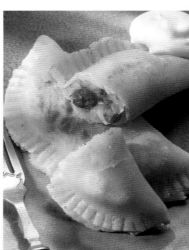

almond sherbet

COOK'S TIP

An electric coffee grinder or spice mill will greatly cut down the time taken to grind the almonds. If using a coffee grinder that is also used for coffee, always remember to clean the grinder thoroughly afterward, otherwise you will end up with strange-tasting coffee! A pestle and mortar will take longer and is also not as good for large quantities.

In India, ice-cool sherbets such as this one are served on special occasions, such as religious festivals. They would be served on the very finest tableware and decorated with varak (edible silver leaf).

1 Soak the almonds in a bowl of water for at least 3 hours or preferably overnight.

2 Using a sharp knife, chop the almonds into small pieces. Grind to a fine paste in a food processor or using a pestle and mortar.

3 Add the sugar to the almond paste and grind once again to form a fine paste.

4 Add the milk and water and m well (in a blender if you have c

5 Transfer the almond sherbet to large serving dish.

6 Let the almond sherbet chill ir refrigerator for 30 minutes. St just before serving.

istachio dessert

serves four–six

a cups water

a cups pistachio nuts

cups whole milk powder

a cups sugar

ardamoms, husks removed and
seeds crushed

bsp rose water

v saffron threads

DECORATE

cup slivered almonds

sh mint leaves

1 Boil 2½ cups of the water in a
pan. Remove the pan from the
heat and soak the pistachio nuts in
this water for 5 minutes. Drain the
pistachio nuts thoroughly and remove
the skins.

2 Grind the pistachio nuts in a food
processor or use a pestle
and mortar.

3 Add the dried milk powder to the
ground pistachio nuts and
mix well.

COOK'S TIP

It is best to buy whole pistachio
nuts and grind them yourself,
rather than using packets
of ready-ground nuts. Freshly
ground nuts have the best flavor,
as grinding releases their
natural oils.

4 To make the syrup, place the
remaining water and the sugar in
a pan and heat gently. When
the liquid begins to thicken, add
the cardamom seeds, rose water,
and saffron.

5 Add the syrup to the pistachio
mixture and cook for 5 minutes,
stirring, until the mixture thickens. Let
the mixture cool slightly.

6 Once cooled enough to handle,
roll the pistachio mixture into
balls. Decorate with the slivered
almonds and mint leaves and let set
before serving.

245

deep-fried sweetmeats in syrup

serves six–eight

5 tbsp whole milk powder

1½ tbsp all-purpose flour

1 tsp baking powder

1½ tbsp unsalted butter

1 egg

1 tsp milk to mix (if required)

10 tbsp ghee

SYRUP

3 cups water

8 tbsp sugar

2 green cardamoms, with husks removed and seeds crushed

large pinch of saffron threads

2 tbsp rose water

1 Place the milk powder, flour, and baking powder in a bowl.

2 Place the butter in a pan and heat until melted, stirring.

3 Whisk the egg in a bowl. Add the melted butter and whisked egg to the dry ingredients and blend together (add the teaspoon of milk at this stage, if necessary) to form a soft dough.

4 Break the dough into 12 small pieces and shape, in the palms of your hands, into small, smooth balls.

5 Heat the ghee in a deep skillet. Reduce the heat and then start cooking the dough balls, 3–4 at a time, tossing and turning gently with slotted spoon until a dark golden brown color. Remove the sweetmeats from the pan and let stand in a deep serving bowl.

6 To make the syrup, boil the water and sugar in a pan for 7–10 minutes. Add the crushed cardamom seeds and saffron, and pour over the sweetmeats.

7 Pour the rose water sparingly over the top. Let soak for 10 minutes for the sweetmeats to absorb plenty of the syrup. Serve the sweetmeats hot or cold.

ground almonds cooked in ghee & milk

serves two–four

2 tbsp ghee

2 tbsp all-purpose flour

generous 1 cup ground almonds

1¼ cups milk

scant ¼ cup sugar

fresh mint leaves, to decorate

COOK'S TIP

Ghee comes in two forms and can be bought from Asian food stores. It is worth noting that pure ghee, made from melted butter, is not suitable for vegans, although there is a vegetable ghee available from specialty Asian food stores and some healthfood stores.

1 Place the ghee in a small, heavy-bottom pan. Melt the ghee over low heat, stirring so that it does not burn.

2 Reduce the heat and add the flour, stirring vigorously to remove any lumps.

3 Add the almonds to the ghee flour mixture, stirring constant

4 Gradually add the milk and su to the mixture in the pan and bring to a boil. Continue cooking fo 3–5 minutes, or until the liquid is smooth and reaches the consistenc cream of chicken soup.

5 Transfer to a serving dish, decorate with mint leaves and serve hot.

VARIATION

You could use coconut milk in this recipe, for a delicious alternative.

fruit & nut ice cream

serves six

5 cups canned evaporated milk,
  unopened
3 egg whites
3 cups confectioners' sugar
generous 1¼ cups chopped pistachio
  nuts, plus extra to decorate
¾ cup slivered almonds
scant ¼ cup candied cherries,
  coarsely chopped, plus extra to
  decorate
½ cup golden raisins
1 tsp ground cardamom

1 Begin preparing the day before you want to serve the ice cream. Place the cans of evaporated milk on their sides in a large, heavy-bottom pan. Pour in enough water to come about three-quarters of the way up their sides and bring to a boil. Reduce the heat, then cover tightly and simmer for 20 minutes. Remove from the heat and let cool, then chill for 24 hours. Place a large bowl in the refrigerator to chill.

2 The next day, whisk the egg whites in a spotlessly clean, greasefree bowl until soft peaks form. Pour the evaporated milk into the chilled bowl and whisk until doubled in size. Fold in the egg whites, then the sugar. Gently fold in the pistachio nuts, almonds, cherries, golden raisins, and ground cardamom.

COOK'S TIP

Don't forget to remove the labels from the cans before boiling the evaporated milk.

3 Cover the bowl with plastic w and freeze for 1 hour. Remove bowl from the freezer and beat the mixture. Spoon into a freezerproof container and freeze for 3 hours or preferably overnight, until set.

4 Scoop the ice cream into dishe Decorate with chopped pistac nuts and candied cherries and serve

ce pudding

serves eight–ten

nerous ⅓ cup basmati rice

ups milk

bsp sugar

rak (silver leaf) or chopped
pistachio nuts, to decorate

oris (see page 188), to serve

COOK'S TIP

Varak (varaq, vark) is edible
silver leaf that is used in India
to decorate elaborate dishes
prepared for the most special
ccasions and celebrations, such
as weddings. It is pure silver
hat has been beaten until it is
wafer-thin. It comes with a
iece of backing paper which is
eeled off as the varak is laid on
he cooked food. It is extremely
elicate and so must be handled
with care. You can buy varak
from Asian food stores.
Remember that because it is
pure silver it should be stored
in an airtight bag or box to
avoid tarnishing.

1 Rinse the rice and place in a large
pan. Add 2½ cups of the milk
and bring to a boil over very low
heat. Cook until the milk has been
completely absorbed by the rice,
stirring occasionally.

2 Remove the pan from the heat.
Mash the rice, making swift,
round movements in the pan, for at
least 5 minutes, until all of the lumps
have been removed.

VARIATION

If you prefer, you can substitute
American or Patna long-grain rice
for the basmati rice.

3 Return the pan to the heat and
gradually add the remaining milk.
Bring to a boil over low heat, stirring
occasionally.

4 Add the sugar and continue to
cook, stirring constantly, for
7–10 minutes or until the mixture is
quite thick in consistency.

5 Transfer the rice pudding to a
heatproof serving bowl. Decorate
with varak (silver leaf) or chopped
pistachio nuts and serve on its own or
with Pooris.

semolina dessert

serves four

6 tbsp ghee

3 cloves

3 cardamoms

8 tbsp coarse semolina

½ tsp saffron threads

scant ⅓ cup golden raisins

10 tbsp sugar

1¼ cups water

1¼ cups milk

cream, to serve

TO DECORATE

scant ⅓ cup dry unsweetened
    coconut, toasted

scant ¼ cup chopped almonds

scant ¼ cup pistachio nuts, soaked
    and chopped (optional)

1 Place the ghee in a pan and melt over medium heat.

2 Add the cloves and cardamoms to the melted butter and reduce the heat, stirring to mix. Add the semolina and stir until it turns a shade darker.

3 Add the saffron, golden raisins, and sugar to the mixture, stirring to mix well.

4 Pour in the water and milk an stir the mixture constantly unt the semolina has softened. Add m water if it becomes too solid.

5 Remove the pan from the hea and transfer the semolina to a serving dish.

6 Decorate the semolina dessert with the toasted dry unsweete coconut, chopped almonds, and pistachio nuts (if using). Serve with little cream drizzled over the top.

COOK'S TIP

Cloves are used to give flavo
and aroma to both sweet and
savory dishes. They should be
used with caution because the
flavor can be overwhelming
if too many are used, and
should be removed before the
dish is served.

mango ice cream

serves six

⅔ cup heavy cream

2 tbsp superfine sugar

generous 1¾ cups mango juice

½ tsp ground cinnamon

slivered almonds, to decorate

COOK'S TIP

Don't beat the cream too vigorously—only whisk it enough to make a smooth mixture and to dissolve the sugar.

1 Pour the cream into a large bowl, then add the sugar and whisk lightly until dissolved. Stir in the mango juice and cinnamon.

2 Pour the mixture into 6 freezerproof molds and cover with foil, then place in the freezer for 3 hours or preferably overnight, until set. During the first hour of freezing, gently shake the molds 3 times.

3 To serve, dip the bases of the molds in hot water, then invert onto individual serving plates. Decorate with slivered almonds and serve immediately.

dian vermicelli pudding

Soak the pistachio nuts (if using)
in a bowl of water for at least
urs. Peel the pistachios and mix
with the slivered almonds. Chop
nuts finely and reserve

COOK'S TIP

You can find seviyan (Indian
ermicelli) in Asian food stores.
is dessert can be served warm
or cold.

2 Melt the ghee in a large pan and
lightly fry the seviyan. Reduce the
heat immediately (the seviyan will turn
golden brown very quickly, so be
careful not to burn it), and if necessary
remove the pan from the heat. Do not
worry if some bits are a little darker
than others.

3 Add the milk to the seviyan and
bring to a boil slowly, taking care
that it does not boil over.

4 Add the evaporated milk, sugar,
and the pitted dates to the
mixture in the pan. Let simmer for
10 minutes, uncovered, stirring
occasionally. When the consistency
begins to thicken, pour the pudding
into a serving bowl.

5 Decorate the pudding with the
prepared pistachio nuts and
almonds and serve.

indian fruit & custard

1 tbsp blanched almonds

4 cups milk

1¾ cups evaporated milk

1 tbsp rose water

1 tsp ground cardamom

a few drops of yellow food
    coloring (optional)

fresh fruit, such as mango and
    papaya slices and mixed berries

1 tbsp pistachio nuts, chopped,
    to decorate (optional)

1 Dry-fry the almonds in a heavy-bottom pan over low heat, stirring constantly, for 1–2 minutes, or until golden. Remove the pan from the heat and reserve.

2 Bring the milk to a boil in a separate pan, then reduce the heat and simmer for 30 minutes, or until reduced by about half. Strain into a clean pan, then place over very low heat and stir in the evaporated milk, rose water, and cardamom. Add a few drops of food coloring to tint the custard an attractive golden yellow, if you like. Simmer gently, stirring frequently to prevent the custard catching on the base of the pan, for 15 minutes, or until thickened and smooth.

3 Pour the custard into a bowl and stir in the reserved almonds. Cover with plastic wrap and let cool, then chill in the refrigerator for at least 1 hour and up to 8 hours. Slice the fruit just before serving. Divide the custard between individual serving plates, arrange the fruit beside it and sprinkle with the pistachios (if using).

COOK'S TIP

Reducing milk as a basis for desserts is a popular technique India. Evaporated milk also features in a number of favorite desserts.

Thai

Introduction

Anyone who loves Thai food will appreciate that it is a unique cuisine, distinctly different from the cooking of the countries which border it, but with many culinary influences from far beyond its geographical frontiers. Thai cooking owes many of its characteristics to climate and culture, but a

history of many centuries of invasions and emigration has played a large part in shaping its cuisine. The roots of the Thai nation can be traced back to the first century A.D., the time of the Chinese Han Dynasty, when the T'ai tribes occupied parts of South China along valuable trade routes between the East and West. Over the years, the T'ai had a close but often stormy relationship with the Chinese, and eventually began to emigrate south to the lands of what is now northern Thailand, bordering Burma and Cambodia, then sparsely occupied by Buddhist and Hindu communities.

ime, the T'ai established
independent Kingdom
ukhothai (translated as
wn of happiness"), which
ntually became Siam.

ports of Siam were the
rance to an important trade
te, and ships from all over
ope and Japan docked
re, or sailed inland along
rivers, bringing foreign
ds, teas, spices, silks,
per, and ceramics. In the
h century, the Portuguese
oduced the chili to
theast Asia. The plant
rished immediately in the
on's soils and climates,
continues to thrive.
le with Arab and Indian
rchants was important, and
hy Muslims settled in Siam.
Siam became the Kingdom
hailand in 1939 after a
od of political upheaval,
twenty-first century
iland still reflects much of
past centuries of mixed
ures, witnessed by the
ependence, pride, creativity,
passion of the nation.
love of life is apparent in
way they take pleasure

in entertaining and eating.
To a visitor, they seem to eat
all day long. The streets and
waterways are lined with food
vendors selling a huge variety
of tasty snacks from their stalls,
carts, bicycles, and boats.

Parties and celebrations are
extremely popular, and during
the many festivals, the colorful,
often elaborate, and carefully
prepared festive foods
show a respect for custom
and tradition. Visitors are
entertained with an unending
succession of trays of tasty
snacks, platters of exotic fruits,
and Thai beer, or local whiskey.
When a meal is served, all the
dishes are served together, so
the cook can enjoy the food
along with the guests.

Presenting food beautifully
is a source of great pride in
Thailand. Vegetables and fruits
are sometimes carved into
elaborate shapes for use as
garnishes—intricate patterns
and skilled artistry are an
integral part of Thai culture,
which exhibits a deep
appreciation of all things
beautiful.

Everyday life in Thailand
is closely tied to the seasons,
marked by the harvesting of
crops and the vagaries of the
monsoon climate. Food is
taken seriously, with great care
taken in choosing the freshest
of ingredients, and thoughtfully
balancing delicate flavors and
textures. Throughout Thailand,
rice is the most important
staple food, the center of every
meal. And coconut, in its
various forms, has an almost
equal place. Cooks in every
region are expert at making
the most of any ingredient
available locally, so the
character of many classic
Thai dishes will vary according
to the region in which they
are cooked.

Fundamentals of Thai Cooking

The essential ingredients you need in order to cook Thai food are listed here. Of these, the most important are coconut, lime, chili, rice, garlic, lemongrass, gingerroot, and cilantro. With these you can create many traditional Thai dishes. Although many recipes have long lists of ingredients, the cooking methods involved in making them are simple enough even for inexperienced cooks to follow.

Balance is the guiding principle of Thai cooking, the five extremes of flavor—bitter, sour, hot, salty, and sweet— being carefully and skillfully balanced in each dish and over several courses. Every dish therefore contributes to the balance of the entire meal.

Basil

Three varieties of sweet basil are used in Thai cooking, but the variety commonly sold in the West also works well. Asian food stores often sell the seeds for Thai basil, so you can grow your own.

Chilies

The many varieties of chili v in heat from very mild to fi hot, so choose carefully. Th small red or green Thai chil are often used—they are v hot, and if you prefer a mil heat, you should remove th seeds. Red chilies are gene slightly sweeter and milder than green chilies. Larger chilies tend to be milder. Dried crushed chilies are us for seasoning.

Cilantro

This is a herb with a punge citrus-like flavor, widely use savory dishes. It wilts quite quickly, so retains its freshn best if bought with a root attached. Alternatively, you grow your own. It will mak your cooking taste even be

Coconut Milk

This is made from grated, pressed fresh coconut. It is very widely in cans and lon packages, in powdered for and in blocks as creamed

...onut. Coconut cream is
...mmed from the top, and is
...htly thicker and richer.

...langal
...elative of ginger, with a
...der, aromatic flavor. It is
...ailable fresh or dried.

...rlic
...e pungent cloves of this
...b are used abundantly in
...ai cooking. Fresh garlic is
...ed whole, crushed, sliced,
...chopped in savory dishes
...d curry pastes. Pickled garlic
...n be useful to have in the
...recupboard because it
...akes an attractive garnish.

...nger
...sh gingerroot is peeled and
...ated, chopped, or sliced for a
...rm, spicy flavor.

...ffir Lime Leaves
...ese leaves have a distinctive
...ne scent, and can be bought
...sh, dried, or frozen.

...mongrass
...aromatic tropical grass with
...emon scent similar to lemon

balm. Strip off the fibrous outer
leaves and slice or chop the
insides finely, or bruise and use
whole. It can also be bought in
dried, powdered form.

Palm Sugar
This is a rich, brown, unrefined
sugar made from the coconut
palm and sold in blocks. The
best way to use it is to crush it
with a mallet. Turbinado sugar
is a good substitute.

Rice Vinegar
Mirin, or sweet rice vinegar,
is a savory flavoring. Sherry
or white wine vinegar can be
substituted.

Soy Sauce
Dark and light soy sauce are
used for seasoning. The light
sauce is saltier than the dark
and is used in stir-fries and
with light meats. Dark soy
adds a rich flavor and color to
braised and red meat dishes.

Tamarind Paste
The pulp of the tamarind fruit is
usually sold in blocks. It gives a
sour/sweet flavor. Soak the

pulp in a bowl of hot water
for 30 minutes, then press out
the juice and discard the pulp
and seeds.

Thai Curry Paste
This flavoring varies in heat,
with yellow the mildest, red
variable, and green the hottest.

Thai Fish Sauce
Called nam pla, this is used
like salt for seasoning savory
dishes, and has a distinctive,
intense aroma.

Soups

Soups are part of almost every Thai meal, including breakfast. Lunch is often a large bowl of soup—a thin stock-based broth, usually  spiked with fresh red or green chilies, and with the addition of fine noodles, rice, egg strips or tiny fish balls, and meat balls or cubes of tofu. In restaurants, soups are often served in a large "firepot" with a central funnel of burning coals to keep the contents hot.

The soups featured in this section are perfect for any time of the day and whatever the occasion, whether it is a formal dinner party or a summer barbecue lunch. They all use traditional Thai ingredients, and the most typical ones can be easily found in Asian food stores and supermarkets.

chili-spiced shrimp won ton soup

serves four

WON TONS

6 oz/175 g cooked, shelled shrimp

1 garlic clove, crushed

1 scallion, finely chopped

1 tbsp dark soy sauce

1 tbsp Thai fish sauce

1 tbsp chopped cilantro

1 small egg, separated

12 won ton skins

SOUP

2 small fresh red Thai chilies

2 scallions

4 cups clear beef stock

1 tbsp Thai fish sauce

1 tbsp dark soy sauce

1 tbsp rice wine or dry sherry

handful of cilantro leaves,
    to garnish

1 Finely chop the shrimp. Place them in a bowl and stir in the garlic, scallion, soy sauce, fish sauce, cilantro, and egg yolk.

2 Lay the won ton skins on a counter in a single layer and place about 1 tablespoon of the filling mixture in the center of each. Brush the edges with egg white and fold each one into a triangle, pressing lightly to seal. Bring the 2 bottom corners of the triangle around to meet in the center, securing with a little egg white to hold in place.

3 To make the soup, slice the chilies at a steep diagonal angle to make long thin slices. Slice the scallions on the same angle.

4 Place the stock, fish sauce, so sauce, and rice wine in a larg pan and bring to a boil. Add the c and scallions. Drop the won tons i the pan and simmer for 4–5 minu or until thoroughly heated.

5 Serve the soup and won tons small bowls and garnish with cilantro at the last moment.

ce soup with eggs

Heat the oil in a large pan or
preheated wok.

Add the garlic and pork and
stir-fry gently for 1 minute, or
l the meat is broken up but
browned.

Add the scallions, ginger, chili,
and stock, stirring until boiling.
l the rice, then reduce the heat and
mer for 2 minutes.

4 Add the fish sauce and season
to taste with salt and pepper.
Carefully break the eggs into the soup
and simmer over very low heat for
3–4 minutes, or until set.

5 Ladle the soup into large bowls,
allowing 1 egg per portion.
Garnish with shredded cilantro and
serve immediately.

COOK'S TIP

If you prefer, beat the eggs
together and cook like an omelet
until set, then cut into ribbon-like
strips and add to the soup just
before serving.

tom yam gung

serves four

1¾ cups light chicken stock

2 fresh kaffir lime leaves,
    chopped

2-inch/5-cm piece lemongrass,
    chopped

3 tbsp lemon juice

3 tbsp Thai fish sauce

2 small hot fresh green chilies,
    seeded and finely chopped

1 tsp sugar

8 small shiitake mushrooms or
    8 Chinese straw mushrooms,
    halved

1 lb/450 g raw shrimp, shelled if
    necessary and deveined

scallion strips, to garnish

TOM YAM SAUCE

4 tbsp vegetable oil

5 garlic cloves, finely chopped

1 large shallot, finely chopped

2 large hot dried red chilies,
    roughly chopped

1 tbsp dried shrimp (optional)

1 tbsp Thai fish sauce

2 tsp sugar

1 First make the tom yam sauce. Heat the oil in a pan. Add the garlic and cook for a few seconds until the garlic just browns. Remove with a slotted spoon and reserve. Add the shallot to the same oil and cook until browned and crisp. Remove with a slotted spoon and reserve. Add the chilies and cook until they darken. Remove from the oil and drain on paper towels. Remove the pan from the heat and reserve the oil.

2 Grind the dried shrimp, if using, in a food processor or spice grinder, then add the reserved chilies, garlic, and shallots. Grind to a smooth paste. Return the pan with the original oil to low heat, then add the paste and warm through. Add the fish sauce and sugar and mix. Remove the pan from the heat.

3 Heat the stock and 2 tablespo of the tom yam sauce togethe in a separate pan. Add the lime lea lemongrass, lemon juice, fish sauce chilies, and sugar and simmer for 2 minutes.

4 Add the mushrooms and shrimp and cook for an additi 2–3 minutes, or until the shrimp ar cooked. Ladle into warmed serving bowls and serve immediately, garnished with scallion strips.

thai-style seafood soup

serves four

5 cups fish stock

1 lemongrass stem,
   split lengthwise

pared rind of ½ lime or 1 fresh
   kaffir lime leaf

1-inch/2.5-cm piece fresh
   gingerroot, sliced

¼ tsp chili paste, or to taste

4–6 scallions

7 oz/200 g large or medium raw
   shrimp, shelled

salt

9 oz/250 g scallops (16–20)

2 tbsp cilantro leaves

finely chopped red bell pepper or
   fresh red chili rings, to garnish

1 Place the stock in a pan with the lemongrass, lime rind, ginger, and chili paste. Bring just to a boil, then reduce the heat and simmer, covered, for 10–15 minutes.

2 Cut the scallions in half lengthwise, then slice crosswise very thinly. Cut the shrimp almost in half lengthwise, keeping the tails intact. Devein if necessary.

3 Pour the stock through a strainer, then return to the pan and bring to a simmer, with bubbles rising at the edges and the surface trembling. Add the scallions and cook for 2–3 minutes. Taste and season with salt, if needed. Stir in a little more chili paste if wished.

4 Add the scallops and shrimp a poach for 1 minute, or until th turn opaque and the shrimp curl.

5 Drop in the cilantro leaves, the ladle the soup into warmed serving bowls, dividing the shellfish evenly, and garnish with bell peppe or chili rings.

VARIATION

If you have light chicken stock but no fish stock, it will make a equally tasty though different version of this soup.

ot & sour soup

serves four

oz/350 g raw or cooked shrimp
n shells
sp vegetable oil
mongrass stem,
coarsely chopped
esh kaffir lime leaves, shredded
esh green chili, seeded
nd chopped
ups chicken or fish stock
ne
sp Thai fish sauce
and pepper
esh red Thai chili, seeded and
hinly sliced
allion, thinly sliced
sp finely chopped cilantro,
o garnish

COOK'S TIP

devein the shrimp, remove the
ells. Cut a slit along the back
each shrimp and remove the
ne black vein that runs along
length of the back. Wipe with
paper towels.

1 Peel the shrimp and reserve the
shells. Devein the shrimp (see
Cook's Tip), then cover with plastic
wrap and let chill in the refrigerator.

2 Heat the oil in a large, heavy-
bottom pan. Add the shrimp
shells and stir-fry for 3–4 minutes,
or until they turn pink. Add the
lemongrass, lime leaves, chili, and
stock. Pare a thin strip of rind from
the lime and grate the rest. Add the
grated rind to the pan.

3 Bring to a boil, then reduce the
heat and let simmer, covered, for
20 minutes.

4 Strain the liquid and pour it back
into the pan. Squeeze the juice
from the lime and add to the pan with
the fish sauce and salt and pepper
to taste.

5 Bring to a boil, then reduce the
heat and add the shrimp. Simmer
for 2–3 minutes.

6 Add the thinly sliced chili and
scallion. Sprinkle with the
chopped cilantro and serve.

chicken noodle soup

serves four–six

1 sheet dried egg noodles from a
   9 oz/250 g package

1 tbsp corn oil

4 skinless, boneless chicken
   thighs, diced

1 bunch of scallions, sliced

2 garlic cloves, chopped

¾-inch/2-cm piece fresh gingerroot,
   finely chopped

3¾ cups chicken stock

generous ¾ cup coconut milk

3 tsp Thai red curry paste

3 tbsp peanut butter

2 tbsp light soy sauce

salt and pepper

1 small red bell pepper, seeded
   and chopped

½ cup frozen peas

VARIATION

You can use other types
of noodles in this soup, such
as rice or cellophane noodles.
Prepare according to the
package directions.

1 Place the noodles in a shallow heatproof dish and let soak in boiling water according to the package directions.

2 Heat the oil in a large, heavy-bottom pan or preheated wok. Add the chicken and stir-fry for 5 minutes, or until lightly browned. Add the white part of the scallions, the garlic, and ginger and stir-fry for 2 minutes.

3 Add the stock, coconut milk, curry paste, peanut butter, and soy sauce. Season to taste with salt and pepper. Bring to a boil, stirring constantly, then simmer for 8 minutes, stirring occasionally. Add the bell pepper, peas, and green scallion tops and cook for an additional 2 minutes.

4 Add the drained noodles and heat through. Spoon into warmed serving bowls and serve immediately.

chicken & coconut milk soup

serves four

1¾ cups canned coconut milk

generous 2 cups chicken stock

6 thin slices fresh galangal

2 lemongrass stems, bruised

4 fresh kaffir lime leaves

8 oz/225 g chicken breast fillets

4 scallions

2 fresh red chilies, seeded and
   finely sliced

4 tbsp Thai fish sauce

2 tbsp lime juice

2 tbsp chopped cilantro

1 Place the coconut milk, stock, galangal, lemongrass, and lime leaves in a large pan and bring to a boil.

2 Cut the chicken into strips and add to the pan. Reduce the heat and simmer for 10 minutes, or until the chicken is cooked.

3 Slice the scallions and add to the pan with the chilies. Simmer for an additional 3 minutes. Stir in the fish sauce, lime juice, and cilantro and serve in warmed bowls.

picy thai soup with shrimp

serves four

bsp tamarind paste

resh red Thai chilies,
very finely chopped

arlic cloves, crushed

nch/2.5-cm piece fresh galangal,
very finely chopped

bsp Thai fish sauce

bsp palm sugar or
superfine sugar

resh kaffir lime leaves,
coarsely torn

ups fish stock

up very thinly sliced carrots

ups diced sweet potato

oz/100 g baby corn cobs,
halved

bsp cilantro, coarsely chopped

oz/100 g cherry tomatoes,
halved

z/225 g cooked fantail shrimp

1 Place the tamarind paste, chilies, garlic, galangal, fish sauce, sugar, lime leaves, and stock in a large, preheated wok. Bring to a boil, stirring constantly.

2 Reduce the heat and add the carrots, sweet potato, and baby corn cobs to the mixture in the wok.

COOK'S TIP

Galangal or Thai ginger is a member of the ginger family, but it is yellow in color with pink sprouts. The flavor is aromatic and less pungent than ginger.

3 Let the soup simmer, uncovered, for 10 minutes, or until the vegetables are just tender.

4 Stir the cilantro, cherry tomatoes, and shrimp into the soup and heat through for 5 minutes.

5 Transfer the soup to warmed serving bowls and serve hot.

mushroom & tofu broth

serves four

4 dried shiitake mushrooms

⅔ cup boiling water

1 tbsp corn oil

1 tsp sesame oil

1 garlic clove, crushed

1 fresh green chili, seeded and
    finely chopped

6 scallions, sliced

1½ cups sliced oyster mushrooms

2 fresh kaffir lime leaves,
    finely shredded

4 cups rich brown stock

2 tbsp lime juice

1 tbsp rice vinegar or white
    wine vinegar

1 tbsp Thai fish sauce

3 oz/85 g firm tofu (drained weight),
    diced

salt and pepper

1 Place the dried shiitake mushrooms in a heatproof bowl and pour over the boiling water. Let soak for 30 minutes. Drain, reserving the liquid, then coarsely chop the black mushrooms.

2 Heat the oils in a large pan or preheated wok over high heat. Add the garlic, chili, and scallions and stir-fry for 1 minute, or until softened but not browned.

3 Add all of the mushrooms, lime leaves, stock, and reserved mushroom liquid. Bring to a boil.

COOK'S TIP

Use a clear, richly colored homemade beef stock, or a Japanese dashi, to make an attractive clear broth. Bouillon cubes generally make a cloudy stock. To make a vegetarian version of the broth, use a well-flavored vegetable stock and replace the fish sauce with light soy sauce.

4 Stir in the lime juice, rice vine and fish sauce, then reduce the heat and let simmer gently for 3–4 minutes.

5 Add the diced tofu and seaso taste with salt and pepper. He gently until boiling, then ladle into warmed serving bowls and serve.

romatic chicken & vegetable soup

serves four

lime

ndful of cilantro

:ups chicken stock

emongrass stem, bruised

small fresh red chili

t and pepper

oz/225 g chicken breast fillet

:arrot

:up snow peas, cut into thin

diagonal strips

> oz/100 g baby corn cobs,

thinly sliced

scallions, thinly sliced

1 Grate the lime. Strip the cilantro leaves from the stems. Reserve the leaves and place the stems in a pan with the stock, lemongrass, chili, and lime rind. Bring to a boil, then cover and simmer for 15 minutes.

2 Strain the stock into a separate pan. Squeeze in the lime juice and add salt and pepper to taste.

3 Dice the chicken and add to the stock. Bring to a boil, then simmer for 5 minutes. Cut the carrot into ribbons and add to the pan with the snow peas and corn. Simmer for 2 minutes, or until the vegetables are tender and the chicken is cooked.

4 Coarsely chop the cilantro leaves and stir into the soup with the scallions. Serve immediately.

chilled avocado, lime & cilantro soup

serves four

2 ripe avocados

1 small mild onion, chopped

1 garlic clove, crushed

2 tbsp chopped cilantro

1 tbsp chopped fresh mint

2 tbsp lime juice

3 cups vegetable stock

1 tbsp rice vinegar or white
     wine vinegar

1 tbsp light soy sauce

salt and pepper

TO GARNISH

2 tbsp sour cream

1 tbsp finely chopped cilantro

2 tsp lime juice

finely shredded lime rind

1 Halve and pit the avocados, then scoop out the flesh. Place in a food processor or blender with the onion, garlic, cilantro, mint, lime juice, and about half the stock and process until completely smooth.

2 Add the remaining stock, rice vinegar, and soy sauce and process again to mix well. Taste and adjust the seasoning if necessary, or add a little extra lime juice if required. Cover and let chill in the refrigerator.

3 To make the lime and cilantro cream garnish, mix the sour cream, cilantro, and lime juice toge in a small bowl. Spoon into the sou just before serving and sprinkle wit shredded lime rind.

creamy corn soup with egg

serves four

1 tbsp vegetable oil

3 garlic cloves, crushed

1 tsp grated fresh gingerroot

3 cups chicken stock

13 oz/375 g canned creamed corn

1 tbsp Thai fish sauce

6 oz/175 g canned white
    crabmeat, drained

salt and pepper

1 egg

TO GARNISH

shredded cilantro

paprika

1 Heat the oil in a large, heavy-bottom pan. Add the garlic and cook for 1 minute, stirring constantly.

2 Add the ginger to the pan, then stir in the stock and creamed corn. Bring to a boil.

3 Stir in the fish sauce, crabmeat, and salt and pepper to taste. Return the soup to a boil.

4 Beat the egg in a small bowl, then stir lightly into the soup so that it sets into long strands. Simmer gently for 30 seconds, or until just set.

5 Ladle the soup into serving bowls and serve hot, garnished with shredded cilantro and paprika sprinkled over the surface.

VARIATION

To give the soup an extra rich flavor kick for a special occasion, stir in 1 tablespoon of rice wine or dry sherry just before you ladle it into bowls.

umpkin & coconut soup

serves six

4 oz/1 kg pumpkin
bsp peanut oil
sp yellow mustard seeds
arlic clove, crushed
arge onion, chopped
elery stalk, chopped
mall fresh red chili, chopped
cups chicken stock
osp dried shrimp
osp coconut cream
and pepper

Using a sharp knife, halve the
pumpkin and remove the seeds.
way the skin and dice the flesh.

Heat the oil in a large, flameproof
casserole. Add the mustard seeds
cook until they begin to pop. Stir
e garlic, onion, celery, and chili
stir-fry for 1–2 minutes.

3 Add the pumpkin with the stock
and dried shrimp to the casserole
and bring to a boil. Reduce the heat,
then cover and simmer for 30 minutes,
or until the ingredients are very tender.

4 Transfer the mixture to a food
processor or blender and process
until smooth. Return to the casserole
and stir in the coconut cream.

5 Season to taste with salt and
pepper and serve hot.

COOK'S TIP

For an extra touch, swirl a
spoonful of thick coconut milk
into each bowl before serving.

281

spinach & ginger soup

serves four

2 tbsp corn oil

1 onion, chopped

2 garlic cloves, finely chopped

1-inch/2.5-cm piece fresh
   gingerroot, finely chopped

3 cups fresh young
   spinach leaves

1 small lemongrass stem,
   finely chopped

4 cups chicken or
   vegetable stock

1 small potato, chopped

1 tbsp rice wine or dry sherry

salt and pepper

1 tsp sesame oil

VARIATION

To make a creamy-textured
spinach and coconut soup, stir in
4 tablespoons of creamed
coconut, or alternatively replace
1¼ cups of the stock with
coconut milk. Serve the soup
with shavings of fresh coconut
sprinkled over the surface.

1 Heat the corn oil in a large pan.
Add the onion, garlic, and ginger
and stir-fry gently for 3–4 minutes, or
until softened but not browned.

2 Reserve 2–3 small spinach leaves.
Add the remaining leaves and
lemongrass to the pan, stirring until the
spinach is wilted. Add the stock and
potato to the pan and bring to a boil.
Reduce the heat, then cover and
simmer for 10 minutes.

3 Transfer the soup to a food
processor or blender and process
until completely smooth.

4 Return the soup to the pan an
add the rice wine, then adjust
seasoning to taste with salt and
pepper. Heat until just about to boi

5 Finely shred the reserved spin
leaves and sprinkle some ove
top. Drizzle with a few drops of
sesame oil and serve hot, garnishe
with the remaining finely shredded
spinach leaves.

Snacks & Appetizers

The structure of a Thai meal is more flexible than in the West, with no first courses and entrées as such; instead, snacks or appetizers  may be served in the afternoon or offered to guests before they sit down to eat a formal meal.

Many of the recipes in this section are savory snacks that are eaten at all times of the day as well as at parties and celebrations. The Thais eat when they are hungry, and street vendors cater for this need with a huge and tempting array of wares from their stalls and bicycles—each street vendor has his own specialty of fast food, from crab cakes to spare ribs, and from steamed mussels to rice soup.

jumbo shrimp rolls with sweet soy sauce

serves four

DIP

1 small fresh red Thai chili, seeded

1 tsp clear honey

4 tbsp soy sauce

SHRIMP ROLLS

2 tbsp cilantro leaves

1 garlic clove

1½ tsp Thai red curry paste

16 won ton skins

1 egg white, lightly beaten

16 raw jumbo shrimp, shelled and
    tails left intact

corn oil, for deep-frying

1 To make the dip, finely chop the chili and place in a small bowl. Add the honey and soy sauce and stir well. Reserve until required.

2 To make the shrimp rolls, finely chop the cilantro and garlic and place in a bowl. Add the curry paste and mix well.

3 Brush each won ton skin with egg white and place a small dab of the cilantro mixture in the center. Place a shrimp on top.

4 Fold the won ton skin over, enclosing the shrimp and leaving the tail exposed. Repeat with the other shrimp.

5 Heat the oil for deep-frying in a large, heavy-bottom pan to 350°–375°F/180°–190°C, or until cube of bread browns in 30 secon Deep-fry the shrimp in small batch for 1–2 minutes each, or until gold brown and crisp. Drain on paper towels and serve with the dip.

fish cakes with hot peanut dip

serves four–five

12 oz/350 g skinless white fish fillet,
    such as cod or haddock

1 tbsp Thai fish sauce

2 tsp Thai red curry paste

1 tbsp lime juice

1 garlic clove, crushed

4 dried kaffir lime leaves, crumbled

1 egg white

3 tbsp chopped cilantro

vegetable oil, for pan-frying

salad greens, to serve

PEANUT DIP

1 small fresh red chili

1 tbsp light soy sauce

1 tbsp lime juice

1 tbsp brown sugar

3 tbsp chunky peanut butter

4 tbsp coconut milk

salt and pepper

snipped fresh chives, to garnish

1 Place the fish fillet in a food processor with the fish sauce, curry paste, lime juice, garlic, lime leaves, and egg white and process to a smooth paste.

2 Stir in the cilantro and quickly process again until mixed. Divide the mixture into 8–10 pieces and roll into balls, then flatten to make round patties. Reserve.

3 To make the dip, halve and se the chili, then chop finely. Pla in a small pan with the remaining ingredients and heat gently, stirring constantly, until well blended. Adju the seasoning to taste, if necessary and transfer to a small bowl. Garni with snipped chives and reserve until required.

4 Heat the oil for pan-frying in a wide skillet until very hot. Pan-fry the fish cakes in batches fo 3–4 minutes on each side, or until golden brown. Drain on paper tow and serve them hot on a bed of sal greens with the peanut dip.

1rimp & chicken sesame toasts

kes seventy-two pieces

kinless, boneless
chicken thighs

oz/100 g cooked,
shelled shrimp

mall egg, beaten

callions, finely chopped

arlic cloves, crushed

osp chopped cilantro

*sp Thai fish sauce

sp pepper

sp salt

slices white bread,
crusts removed

up sesame seeds

n oil, for pan-frying

edded scallion curls,
o garnish (see page 468)

1 Place the chicken and shrimp in a food processor and process until very finely chopped. Add the egg, scallions, garlic, cilantro, fish sauce, pepper, and salt and pulse for a few seconds to mix well. Transfer the mixture to a large bowl.

2 Spread the mixture evenly over the slices of bread, right to the edges. Sprinkle the sesame seeds over a plate and press the spread side of each slice of bread into them to coat evenly.

3 Using a sharp knife, cut the bread into small rectangles, making 6 per slice.

4 Heat a 1-cm/½-inch depth of oil in a wide skillet until very hot. Pan-fry the bread rectangles quickly in batches for 2–3 minutes, or until golden brown, turning them over once.

5 Drain the toasts well on paper towels, then transfer to a serving dish and garnish with shredded scallion curls. Serve hot.

289

jumbo shrimp skewers

serves two as an entrée or four as an appetizer

12 raw jumbo shrimp in shells

3 oranges

MARINADE

1-inch/2.5-cm piece fresh gingerroot

3 garlic cloves, crushed

2 shallots, finely chopped

1 lemongrass stem, finely chopped

1 fresh red chili, finely chopped

pinch of salt

1 tbsp lime juice

1 tbsp soy sauce

2 tbsp rice wine or dry sherry

TO GARNISH

cilantro sprigs

lime wedges

1 To make the marinade, grate the ginger and place in a food processor with the garlic, shallots, lemongrass, chili, salt, lime juice, soy sauce, and rice wine. Process until smooth, then transfer the mixture to a shallow bowl.

2 Using a small knife or scissors, split the shrimp shells down the back, but leave attached. Devein if necessary. Add to the marinade. Cover with plastic wrap and let marinate in the refrigerator for at least 30 minutes and up to 1 hour.

3 Preheat the broiler to medium. Thread each shrimp on to a presoaked bamboo skewer (see Cook's Tip, page 82), inserting the skewer at the tail and coming out at the head end until the pointed end extends at least 3 inches/7.5 cm beyond the shrimp.

4 Broil for 2 minutes on each side, or until the shrimp are pink and cooked through. Insert the skewers in the oranges, then transfer to a plate and garnish with the cilantro sprigs and lime wedges. Serve.

open crabmeat sandwich

serves two

2 tbsp lime juice

¾-inch/2-cm piece fresh gingerroot, grated

¾-inch/2-cm piece lemongrass, finely chopped

5 tbsp mayonnaise

2 large slices crusty bread

1 ripe avocado

5½ oz/150 g cooked crabmeat

pepper

cilantro sprigs, to garnish

lime wedges, to serve

1 Mix 1 tablespoon of the lime juice, the ginger, and lemongrass together in a small bowl. Add the mayonnaise and mix well.

2 Spread 1 tablespoon of the mayonnaise smoothly over each slice of bread.

3 Halve the avocado and remove the pit. Peel and slice the flesh thinly, then arrange the slices on the bread. Sprinkle with a little of the remaining lime juice.

COOK'S TIP

To make homemade lime- and ginger-flavored mayonnaise, place 2 egg yolks, 1 tablespoon lime juice, and ½ teaspoon grated fresh gingerroot in a food processor or blender and blend briefly. With the motor running, gradually add 1¼ cups olive oil, drop by drop, until the mixture is thick and smooth. Season to taste with salt and pepper.

4 Spoon the crabmeat over the avocado, then add the remain[ing] lime juice. Spoon over the remainin[g] mayonnaise, then season with pep[per] to taste and top with a cilantro spri[g]. Serve immediately with lime wedge[s].

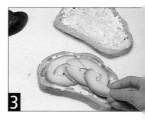

ab omelet

serves four

oz/225 g cooked fresh white
crabmeat, or thawed if frozen
scallions, finely chopped
bsp chopped cilantro
bsp snipped fresh chives
nch of cayenne pepper
bsp vegetable oil
garlic cloves, crushed
sp grated fresh gingerroot
resh red chili, seeded and
finely chopped
bsp lime juice
resh kaffir lime leaves, shredded
sp sugar
sp Thai fish sauce
eggs
bsp coconut cream
sp salt
allion strips, to garnish

COOK'S TIP

You can also serve this omelet
warm. After adding the crab
ixture, cook for 3–4 minutes to
let the mixture heat through,
then serve immediately.

1 Place the crabmeat in a bowl and check for any small pieces of shell. Add the scallions, cilantro, chives, and cayenne and reserve.

2 Heat half the oil in a skillet or preheated wok. Add the garlic, ginger, and chili and stir-fry for 30 seconds. Add the lime juice, lime leaves, sugar, and fish sauce. Simmer for 3–4 minutes, or until reduced. Remove from the heat and let cool. Add to the crab mixture and reserve.

3 Lightly beat the eggs with the coconut cream and salt. Heat the remaining oil in a skillet over medium heat. Add the egg mixture and, as it sets on the bottom, carefully pull the edges in toward the center, letting the unset egg run underneath.

4 When the egg is nearly set, spoon the crab mixture down the center and fold the sides over. Cook for an additional 1–2 minutes to finish cooking the egg, then turn the omelet out of the skillet on to a serving dish. Let cool, then chill for 2–3 hours or overnight. Cut into 4 pieces, then garnish with scallion strips and serve.

steamed crab cakes

serves four

1–2 banana leaves

2 garlic cloves, crushed

1 tsp finely chopped lemongrass

½ tsp pepper

2 tbsp chopped cilantro

3 tbsp creamed coconut

1 tbsp lime juice

7 oz/200 g cooked crabmeat, flaked

1 tbsp Thai fish sauce

2 egg whites

1 egg yolk

8 cilantro leaves

corn oil, for deep-frying

chili dipping sauce, to serve

1 Use the banana leaves to line 8 x ½-cup ramekin dishes or foil containers.

2 Mix the garlic, lemongrass, pepper, and cilantro together in a bowl. Place the creamed coconut and lime juice in a separate bowl and mash until smooth. Stir the 2 mixtures together and add the crabmeat and fish sauce.

3 Whisk the egg whites in a clean, greasefree bowl until stiff, then lightly and evenly fold them into the crab mixture.

4 Spoon the mixture into the prepared ramekin dishes or fo containers and press down lightly. Brush the tops with egg yolk and to each with a cilantro leaf.

5 Place in a steamer half filled w boiling water, then cover with lid and steam for 15 minutes, or un firm to the touch. Pour off the exces liquid and remove from the ramekir dishes or foil containers.

6 Heat the oil for deep-frying in a large, heavy-bottom pan to 350–375°F/180–190°C, or until a cube of bread browns in 30 second Add the crab cakes and deep-fry fo 1 minute, turning them over once, until golden brown. Serve hot with chili dipping sauce.

otato crab cakes

serves four

b/450 g mealy potatoes, diced

oz/175 g cooked white crabmeat,
  drained if canned

scallions, chopped

sp light soy sauce

tsp sesame oil

sp chopped lemongrass

sp lime juice

bsp all-purpose flour, plus extra
  for dusting

t and pepper

bsp vegetable oil

UCE

bsp finely chopped cucumber

bsp clear honey

bsp garlic wine vinegar

tsp light soy sauce

fresh red chili, chopped

GARNISH

fresh red chili, sliced

cumber slices

COOK'S TIP

o not make the cucumber sauce
too far in advance because
the water from the cucumber
will make the sauce runny and
dilute the flavor.

1 Cook the diced potatoes in a large pan of boiling water for 10 minutes, or until cooked through. Drain well and mash.

2 Mix the crabmeat into the potato with the scallions, soy sauce, sesame oil, lemongrass, lime juice, and flour. Season to taste with salt and pepper.

3 Divide the potato mixture into 8 equal-size portions and shape them into small patties, using floured hands.

4 Heat the vegetable oil in a preheated wok or skillet. Add the crab cakes, 4 at a time, and cook for 5–7 minutes, turning once. Keep warm and repeat with the remaining cakes.

5 Meanwhile, make the sauce. Mix the cucumber, honey, vinegar, soy sauce, and chopped chili together in a small serving bowl.

6 Garnish the crab cakes with the sliced chili and cucumber slices and serve with the sauce.

2

3

5

mussels in spiced batter

serves four

40 large live mussels in shells

2 tbsp all-purpose flour

2 tbsp rice flour

½ tsp salt

1 tbsp dry unsweetened coconut

1 egg white

1 tbsp rice wine or dry sherry

2 tbsp water

1 small fresh red Thai chili, seeded and chopped

1 tbsp chopped cilantro

corn oil, for deep-frying

lime wedges, to serve

1 Clean the mussels by scrubbing or scraping the shells and pulling out any beards that are attached to them. Discard any with broken shells or any that refuse to close when tapped.

2 Place the mussels in a large pan with just the water that clings to their shells and cook, covered, over high heat for 3–4 minutes, shaking the pan occasionally, until they have opened. Drain well, let cool slightly, then remove from the shells. Discard any mussels that remain closed.

3 To make the batter, sift the all-purpose flour, rice flour, and salt into a large bowl. Add the coconut, egg white, rice wine, and water and beat until well mixed and a batter forms. Stir the chili and cilantro into the batter.

4 Heat a 2-inch/5-cm depth of oil for deep-frying in a large, heavy-bottom pan to 350–375°F/180–190°C, or until a cube of bread browns in 30 seconds. Holding the mussels with a fork, dip them quickly into the batter, then drop into the hot oil and deep-fry for 1–2 minutes, or until crisp and golden brown.

5 Drain the mussels on paper towels and serve hot with lime wedges to squeeze over.

COOK'S TIP

If you reserve the mussel shell the cooked mussels can be replaced in them to serve.

ragrant mussels

erves two as an entrée
r four as an appetizer

b 4 oz/1 kg live mussels in shells
resh or dried kaffir lime leaves
bsp water
emongrass stem, bruised
garlic cloves, crushed
nerous ¾ cup coconut cream
bsp chopped cilantro
lt and pepper
armed crusty bread,
to serve

Clean the mussels by scrubbing
or scraping the shells and pulling
any beards that are attached.
ard any with broken shells or any
 refuse to close when tapped.

Chop the lime leaves and place
in a large pan with the water,
ongrass, and garlic. Heat until
ing. Add the mussels, then cover
 cook for 3–4 minutes, or until they
e opened. Discard any mussels that
ain closed. Transfer to a serving
, cover, and place in a low oven.

3 Boil the cooking liquid hard until
reduced by half, then stir in the
coconut cream. Boil to reduce and
thicken slightly. Stir in the cilantro and
add salt and pepper to taste.

4 Pour over the mussels and serve
with warmed crusty bread.

297

steamed mussels with lemongrass & basil

2 lb 4 oz/1 kg live mussels in shells

2 shallots, finely chopped

1 lemongrass stem, finely sliced

1 garlic clove, finely chopped

3 tbsp rice wine or dry sherry

2 tbsp lime juice

1 tbsp Thai fish sauce

4 tbsp chopped fresh basil

salt and pepper

2 tbsp butter

fresh basil leaves, to garnish

crusty bread, to serve

COOK'S TIP

Fresh clams in shells are also
very good when cooked
by this method.

1 Clean the mussels by scrubbing or scraping the shells and pulling out any beards that are attached to them. Discard any with broken shells or any that refuse to close when tapped.

2 Place the shallots, lemongrass, garlic, rice wine, lime juice, and fish sauce in a large, heavy-bottom pan and place over high heat.

3 Add the mussels, then cover and steam for 3–4 minutes, shaking the pan occasionally, until the mussels have opened.

4 Discard any mussels that remain closed, then stir in the chopped basil and season to taste with salt and pepper.

5 Scoop out the mussels with a slotted spoon and divide between 4 deep bowls. Quickly whisk the butter into the pan juices, then pour the juices over the mussels.

6 Garnish each bowl with fresh basil leaves and serve with pl of crusty bread to mop up the juice

roasted spare ribs with honey & soy

serves four

2 lb 4 oz/1 kg Chinese-style
    spare ribs

½ lemon

½ small orange

1-inch/2.5-cm piece fresh
    gingerroot

2 garlic cloves

1 small onion, chopped

2 tbsp soy sauce

2 tbsp rice wine or dry sherry

½ tsp Thai seven-spice powder

2 tbsp clear honey

1 tbsp sesame oil

lemon twists, to garnish

orange wedges, to serve

1 Preheat the oven to 350°F/180°C. Place the spare ribs in a wide roasting pan, then cover loosely with foil and cook for 30 minutes.

2 Meanwhile, remove any seeds from the lemon and orange and place them in a food processor with the ginger, garlic, onion, soy sauce, rice wine, seven-spice powder, honey, and oil. Process until smooth.

3 Increase the oven temperature to 400°F/200°C. Pour off any fat from the spare ribs, then spoon the puréed mixture over the spare ribs and toss to coat evenly.

4 Return the ribs to the oven and roast for 40 minutes, turning a basting them occasionally, until gol brown. Garnish with lemon twists a serve hot with orange wedges.

rispy pork & peanut baskets

serves four

heets phyllo pastry, about 16½ x
11 inches/42 x 28 cm each

bsp vegetable oil, plus extra
for brushing

arlic clove, crushed

erous 1 cup ground pork

sp Thai red curry paste

callions, finely chopped

bsp chunky peanut butter

bsp light soy sauce

bsp chopped cilantro

t and pepper

ntro sprigs, to garnish

Preheat the oven to 400°F/200°C.
Cut each sheet of phyllo pastry
24 x 2¾-inch/7-cm squares, to
e a total of 48 squares. Brush each
re lightly with oil and arrange the
res in stacks of 4 in 12 small patty
s, pointing outward. Press the
ry down into the pans.

Bake the pastry shells in the
preheated oven for 6–8 minutes,
ntil golden brown.

3 Meanwhile, heat 1 tablespoon of oil in a heavy-bottom skillet. Add the garlic and cook for 30 seconds, then stir in the pork and stir-fry over high heat for 4–5 minutes, or until the meat is golden brown.

4 Add the curry paste and scallions and continue to stir-fry for an additional 1 minute, then stir in the peanut butter, soy sauce, and cilantro. Season to taste with salt and pepper.

5 Spoon the pork mixture into the phyllo baskets, then garnish with cilantro sprigs and serve hot.

COOK'S TIP

When using phyllo pastry, remember that it dries out very quickly and becomes brittle and difficult to handle. Work quickly and cover any sheets of pastry you're not using with plastic wrap and a dampened cloth.

lemongrass chicken skewers

serves four

2 long or 4 short lemongrass stems

2 large skinless, boneless chicken
   breasts, about 14 oz/400 g
   in total

1 small egg white

1 carrot, finely grated

1 small fresh red chili, seeded
   and chopped

2 tbsp snipped fresh garlic chives

2 tbsp chopped cilantro

salt and pepper

1 tbsp corn oil

TO GARNISH

cilantro sprigs

lime slices

mixed salad greens, to serve

1 If the lemongrass stems are long, cut them in half across the center to make 4 short lengths. Cut each stem in half lengthwise, so that you have 8 sticks.

2 Coarsely chop the chicken pieces and place them in a food processor with the egg white. Process to a smooth paste, then add the carrot, chili, chives, cilantro, and salt and pepper to taste. Process for a few seconds to mix well. Transfer the mixture to a large bowl. Cover and chill in the refrigerator for 15 minutes.

3 Preheat the broiler to medium. Divide the mixture into 8 equal-size portions and use your hands to shape the mixture around the lemongrass "skewers."

VARIATION

If you can't find whole
lemongrass stems, use presoaked
wooden skewers instead
(see Cook's Tip, page 338), and
add ½ teaspoon ground
lemongrass to the mixture with
the other flavorings.

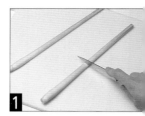

4 Brush the skewers with oil and cook under the hot broiler for 4–6 minutes, turning them occasionally, until golden brown and thoroughly cooked. Alternatively, g over medium–hot coals.

5 Transfer to serving plates. Gar with cilantro sprigs and lime s and serve hot with salad greens.

eamed won ton bundles

serves four

erous 1 cup ground pork

>sp dried shrimp, finely chopped

esh green chili, finely chopped

hallots, finely chopped

p cornstarch

mall egg, beaten

p dark soy sauce

p rice wine or dry sherry

and pepper

won ton skins

p sesame oil

i dipping sauce, to serve

Mix the pork, dried shrimp, chili,
and shallots together in a bowl.
the cornstarch with half the egg
stir into the pork mixture with the
auce and rice wine. Season to
with salt and pepper.

2 Arrange the won ton skins flat on a clean counter and place 1 tablespoon of the pork mixture on to the center of each skin.

3 Brush the skins with the remaining egg and carefully pull up the edges, pinching together lightly at the top and leaving a small gap so that the filling can just be seen.

4 Place enough water in the bottom of a steamer and bring to a boil. Brush the inside of the top part of the steamer with the oil.

5 Arrange the won tons in the top, then cover and steam for 15–20 minutes. Serve hot with a chili dipping sauce.

stuffed chicken wings

serves four

8 chicken wings

3 tbsp dried shrimp

3 tbsp hot water

1¾ cups ground pork

1 garlic clove, crushed

1 tbsp Thai fish sauce

½ tsp salt

½ tsp pepper

2 scallions, finely chopped

¼ tsp ground turmeric

1 small egg, beaten

2 tbsp rice flour

corn oil, for deep-frying

fresh red chilies, to garnish

TO SERVE

cucumber slices

chili dipping sauce

1 Using a small, sharp knife, cut around the end of the bone at the cut end of each wing, then loosen the flesh away from around the bone, scraping it downward with the knife and pulling back the skin as you go. When you reach the next joint, grasp the end of the bone and twist sharply to break it at the joint. Remove the bone and turn back the flesh.

2 Continue to scrape the meat away down the length of the next long bone, exposing the joint. Twist to break the bone at the joint and remove, leaving just the wing tip in place.

3 Meanwhile, soak the dried shrimp in the hot water for 10–15 minutes. Drain, then chop. Place the pork, shrimp, garlic, fish sauce, salt, and pepper in a food processor and process to a smooth paste. Transfer to a bowl and add scallions. Stir well. Use the mixture stuff the chicken wings, pressing it down inside with your finger.

4 Beat the turmeric into the bea egg and reserve until require Dip each wing into the rice flour, shaking off the excess.

5 Heat a 2-inch/5-cm depth of in a large, heavy-bottom pan 350–375°F/180–190°C, or until a cube of bread browns in 30 secon Dip the floured chicken wings quic into the beaten egg, then drop car into the hot oil and deep-fry in sm batches for 8–10 minutes, turning them over once. Drain the chicken wings on paper towels. Garnish w chilies and serve with cucumber sl and a chili dipping sauce.

chicken satay

serves eight

2 lb/900 g chicken breast meat,
cut into ¼-inch/5-mm thick,
1-inch/2.5-cm wide strips

MARINADE

1 lemongrass stem (tender inner
part only)

2 tbsp vegetable oil

2 tbsp soy sauce

2 tsp tamarind paste

2 garlic cloves, crushed

1 tsp ground cumin

1 tsp ground coriander

1 tbsp lime juice

1 tsp brown sugar

PEANUT SAUCE

2 tbsp smooth peanut butter

generous ¾ cup coconut cream

2 tsp Thai red curry paste

1 tbsp fish sauce

1 tbsp brown sugar

1 Thread the chicken on to presoaked bamboo skewers (see Cook's Tip, page 82).

2 To make the marinade, chop the lemongrass and place in a food processor with the oil, soy sauce, tamarind paste, garlic, cumin, coriander, lime juice, and sugar. Process to a paste. Transfer to a bowl.

3 Add the chicken to the marina and toss to coat. Cover with plastic wrap and let marinate in the refrigerator for at least 1 hour.

4 Preheat the broiler to medium Place the peanut butter, coco cream, red curry paste, fish sauce, sugar in a pan. Heat gently, stirring constantly, to form a smooth sauce

5 Cook the chicken under the h broiler for 3–5 minutes on ea side, or until the chicken is cooked through. Alternatively, grill over medium–hot coals. Reheat the sau adding a little hot water if necessar and serve with the chicken satay.

ot chili relish with crudités

serves four

ISH

arlic cloves

0 large fresh red chilies, seeded
and finely chopped

up water

sp salt

p sugar

e of 1 lime

sp Thai fish sauce

sp vegetable oil

JDITES

ot sticks

shes

umber batons

y corn cobs

1 Finely chop the garlic and place in a preheated wok with the remaining relish ingredients. Bring to a boil, then cover and simmer for 10 minutes.

2 Transfer the mixture to a food processor and blend until smooth.

3 Prepare the vegetable crudités. Transfer the relish to a bowl and serve with the crudités.

sticky ginger chicken wings

serves four

2 garlic cloves, coarsely chopped

1 piece preserved ginger in syrup,
  coarsely chopped

1 tsp coriander seeds

2 tbsp preserved ginger syrup

2 tbsp dark soy sauce

1 tbsp lime juice

1 tsp sesame oil

12 chicken wings

TO GARNISH

lime wedges

cilantro leaves

1 Place the garlic, preserved ginger, and coriander seeds in a mortar and, using a pestle, grind to a paste, gradually working in the ginger syrup, soy sauce, lime juice, and oil.

2 Tuck the pointed tip of each chicken wing underneath the thicker end of the wing to make a neat triangular shape. Place in a large bowl.

3 Add the garlic and ginger paste to the bowl and toss the chicken wings in the mixture to coat evenly. Cover with plastic wrap and let marinate in the refrigerator for several hours or overnight.

4 Preheat the broiler to medium. Arrange the chicken wings in a single layer on a foil-lined broiler pan and cook under the hot broiler for 12–15 minutes, turning them occasionally, until golden brown and thoroughly cooked.

5 Alternatively, cook on a lightly oiled grill rack over medium–hot coals. Transfer to individual serving plates and garnish with lime wedges and cilantro leaves, then serve immediately.

chicken fried in banana leaves

serves four–six

arlic clove, chopped

sp finely chopped fresh
gingerroot

sp pepper

ilantro sprigs

osp Thai fish sauce

osp whiskey

kinless, boneless chicken breasts

3 banana leaves, cut into 3-inch/
7.5-cm squares

n oil, for pan-frying

i dipping sauce, to serve

COOK'S TIP

To make a sweet chili dipping
auce to serve with the chicken
pieces, mix equal amounts of
hili sauce and tomato ketchup
ogether, then stir in a dash of
rice wine to taste.

1 Place the garlic, ginger, pepper, cilantro sprigs, fish sauce, and whiskey in a mortar and, using a pestle, grind to a smooth paste.

2 Cut the chicken into 1-inch/ 2.5-cm chunks and toss in the paste to coat evenly. Cover and let marinate in the refrigerator for 1 hour.

3 Place a piece of chicken on a square of banana leaf and wrap it up like a package to enclose the chicken completely. Secure with wooden toothpicks or tie with a piece of string.

4 Heat an 1/8-inch/3-mm depth of oil for pan-frying in a large, heavy-bottom skillet until hot.

5 Pan-fry the packages for 8–10 minutes, turning them over occasionally, until golden brown and the chicken is thoroughly cooked. Serve with a chili dipping sauce.

chicken balls with dipping sauce

serves four–six

2 large skinless, boneless
   chicken breasts
3 tbsp vegetable oil
2 shallots, finely chopped
½ celery stalk, finely chopped
1 garlic clove, crushed
2 tbsp light soy sauce
1 small egg, lightly beaten
salt and pepper
1 bunch of scallions
DIPPING SAUCE
3 tbsp dark soy sauce
1 tbsp rice wine or dry sherry
1 tsp sesame seeds
scallion tassels, to garnish
   (see Cook's Tip, page 356)

1 Cut the chicken into ¾-inch/2-cm pieces. Heat half the oil in a large skillet. Add the chicken and stir-fry over high heat for 2–3 minutes, or until golden. Remove the chicken with a slotted spoon and reserve until required.

2 Add the shallots, celery, and garlic to the skillet and stir-fry for 1–2 minutes, or until softened but not browned.

3 Place the reserved chicken, shallots, celery, and garlic in a food processor and process until finely ground. Add 1 tablespoon of the light soy sauce, just enough egg to make a fairly firm mixture, and salt and pepper to taste.

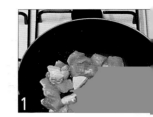

4 Trim the scallions and cut into 2-inch/5-cm lengths. Reserve until required. Make the dipping sauce by mixing the dark soy sauce, rice wine, and sesame seeds together in a small bowl. Reserve.

5 Form the chicken mixture into 16–18 walnut-size balls between the palms of your hands. Heat the remaining oil in the skillet and then stir-fry the balls in small batches for 4–5 minutes, or until golden brown. As each batch is cooked, drain on paper towels and keep hot.

6 Stir-fry the reserved scallions for 1–2 minutes, or until they begin to soften, then stir in the remaining light soy sauce. Serve with the chicken balls and dipping sauce, garnished with scallion tassels.

›ring rolls

makes thirty

bsp vegetable oil

cups lean ground pork

jarlic clove, crushed

resh red chili, seeded and
finely chopped

oz/115 g cooked, shelled shrimp

callions, finely chopped

nch/2.5-cm piece fresh
gingerroot, finely grated

bsp chopped cilantro

sp Thai fish sauce

spring roll wrappers

n oil, for deep-frying

eet chili dipping sauce, to serve

1 Heat the vegetable oil in a skillet. Add the pork, garlic, and chili and cook, stirring, until the pork is browned.

2 Chop the shrimp, then add to the skillet with the scallions, ginger, cilantro, and fish sauce. Cook, stirring, until heated through. Remove the skillet from the heat and let cool.

3 Prepare the spring roll wrappers according to the package directions.

4 Place a spoonful of the pork mixture down the center of each spring roll wrapper, leaving a space at the top and bottom and down the side. Brush the edges with water. Fold the top and bottom over and then fold in the sides to form a sealed roll.

5 Just before serving, heat the oil for deep-frying in a large pan or wok until nearly smoking. Deep-fry the rolls in batches for 2–3 minutes, or until golden brown. Drain on paper towels and keep warm while cooking the remainder. Serve with a sweet chili dipping sauce.

stuffed eggs with pork & crabmeat

serves four

4 large eggs

scant 1 cup ground pork

6 oz/175 g canned white
    crabmeat, drained

1 garlic clove, crushed

1 tsp Thai fish sauce

½ tsp ground lemongrass

1 tbsp chopped cilantro

1 tbsp dry unsweetened coconut

salt and pepper

⅔ cup all-purpose flour

about ⅔ cup coconut milk

corn oil, for deep-frying

cucumber flowers, to garnish

green salad, to serve

1 Place the eggs in a pan of simmering water and bring to a boil, then let simmer for 10 minutes. Drain the eggs, then crack the shells and cool under cold running water. Peel off the shells.

2 Cut the eggs lengthwise down the center and scoop out the yolks. Place the yolks in a bowl with the pork, crabmeat, garlic, fish sauce, lemongrass, cilantro, and coconut. Season to taste with salt and pepper and mix well.

3 Divide the mixture into 8 equal-size portions, then fill each of the egg whites with the mixture, pressing together with your hands to form the shape of a whole egg.

4 Whisk the flour and enough coconut milk together to form thick batter. Season to taste.

5 Heat a 2-inch/5-cm depth of c in a large, heavy-bottom pan 350–375°F/180–190°C, or until a cube of bread browns in 30 second Dip each egg into the coconut batt then shake off the excess.

6 Deep-fry the eggs in batches f 5 minutes, turning occasionall until golden brown. Remove with a slotted spoon and drain on paper towels. Transfer to plates, then garr with cucumber flowers and serve w a green salad.

ork appetizer in lettuce cups

serves six

resh red chilies

garlic cloves, finely chopped

bsp chopped cilantro root

bsp grated fresh gingerroot

bsp vegetable oil

bsp hot water

b 2 oz/500 g ground lean pork

resh kaffir lime leaves,
finely shredded

osp Thai fish sauce

sp brown sugar

osp coarsely chopped cilantro

leaves romaine lettuce or similar

firm lettuce leaves (see Cook's
Tip, page 450)

GARNISH

ntro leaves

n strips of fresh red chili

1 Seed and finely chop the chilies, then place in a food processor with the garlic, cilantro root, ginger, oil, and water. Process until smooth.

2 Transfer to a preheated wok or large skillet.

3 Stir-fry the paste for 4 minutes over medium heat, then increase the heat and add the pork. Stir-fry for 3 minutes, or until colored.

4 Add the lime leaves, fish sauce, sugar, and chopped cilantro. Continue to stir-fry until the pork is dry.

5 Arrange the pork in lettuce cups, then garnish with cilantro leaves and strips of chili and serve.

313

pork-stuffed omelet

serves four

2 garlic cloves, chopped

4 black peppercorns

4 cilantro sprigs

2 tbsp vegetable oil

1¾ cups ground pork

2 scallions, chopped

1 large firm tomato, chopped

6 large eggs

1 tbsp Thai fish sauce

¼ tsp ground turmeric

mixed salad greens, tossed, to serve

1 Place the garlic, peppercorns, and cilantro in a mortar and, using a pestle, grind to a smooth paste.

2 Heat 1 tablespoon of the oil in a large skillet. Add the paste and stir-fry for 1–2 minutes, or until it just changes color.

3 Stir in the pork and stir-fry until it is lightly browned. Add the scallions and tomato, and stir-fry for an additional 1 minute, then remove the skillet from the heat.

4 Heat the remaining oil in a small, heavy-bottom skillet. Beat the eggs with the fish sauce and turmeric, then pour one-fourth of the egg mixture into the skillet. As the mixture begins to set, stir lightly to ensure that all the liquid egg is set.

5 Spoon one-fourth of the pork mixture down the center of the omelet, then fold the sides inward toward the center, enclosing the filling. Transfer to a heatproof plate and keep warm. Make 3 more omelets with the remaining egg and fill with the remaining pork mixture.

6 Slide the omelets on to serving plates and serve with salad.

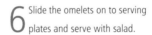

egetarian spring rolls

serves four

- oz/25 g fine cellophane noodles
- bsp peanut oil, plus extra for deep-frying
- garlic cloves, crushed
- tsp grated fresh gingerroot
- cup thinly sliced oyster mushrooms
- scallions, finely chopped
- cup fresh bean sprouts
- small carrot, finely shredded
- tsp sesame oil
- bsp light soy sauce
- bsp rice wine or dry sherry
- tsp pepper
- bsp chopped cilantro
- bsp chopped fresh mint
- spring roll wrappers
- tsp cornstarch
- resh mint sprig, to garnish
- li dipping sauce, to serve

1 Place the noodles in a heatproof bowl, then pour over enough boiling water to cover and let stand for 4 minutes. Drain and rinse in cold water, then drain again. Use a sharp knife to cut into 2-inch/5-cm lengths.

2 Heat the peanut oil in a preheated wok or wide skillet. Add the garlic, ginger, mushrooms, scallions, bean sprouts, and carrot and stir-fry for 1 minute, or until soft.

3 Stir in the sesame oil, soy sauce, rice wine, pepper, cilantro, and mint, then remove the wok from the heat. Stir in the noodles.

4 Arrange the spring roll wrappers on a counter, pointing diagonally. Mix the cornstarch with a little water and use to brush the edges of a wrapper. Spoon some filling on to the pointed side of the same wrapper.

5 Roll the point of the wrapper over the filling, then fold the side points inward over the filling. Continue to roll up the wrapper away from you, moistening the tip with more cornstarch mixture to secure the roll. Make up all the spring rolls in the same way.

6 Heat the oil for deep-frying in a wok or deep skillet to 350–375°F/180–190°C, or until a cube of bread browns in 30 seconds. Deep-fry the rolls in batches for 2–3 minutes each, or until golden brown and crisp. Drain and transfer to a plate. Garnish with a mint sprig and serve with a chili dipping sauce.

tuna & tomato salad with ginger dressing

serves four

½ cup shredded Napa cabbage

3 tbsp rice wine or dry sherry

2 tbsp Thai fish sauce

1 tbsp finely shredded fresh
   gingerroot

1 garlic clove, finely chopped

½ small fresh red Thai chili,
   finely chopped

2 tsp brown sugar

2 tbsp lime juice

14 oz/400 g fresh tuna steak

corn oil, for brushing

4½ oz/125 g cherry tomatoes

fresh mint leaves and mint sprigs,
   coarsely chopped, to garnish

COOK'S TIP

The dressing can be made in
advance and spooned over the
dish just before serving.

1 Place a small pile of shredded Napa cabbage on a large serving plate. Place the rice wine, fish sauce, ginger, garlic, chili, sugar, and 1 tablespoon of lime juice in a screw-top jar and shake well to combine.

2 Using a sharp knife, cut the tuna into strips of an even thickness. Sprinkle with the remaining lime juice.

3 Brush a wide skillet or ridged grill pan with oil and heat until very hot. Arrange the tuna strips in the skillet and cook until just firm and light golden, turning them over once. Remove the tuna strips from the skillet and reserve.

4 Add the tomatoes to the skillet and cook over high heat until lightly browned. Spoon the tuna and tomatoes over the Napa cabbage, spoon over the dressing. Garnish with fresh mint and serve warm.

sweet & sour seafood salad

serves six

18 live mussels in shells

6 large scallops, shelled

7 oz/200 g baby squid, cleaned

2 shallots, finely chopped

6 raw jumbo shrimp, shelled
    and deveined

¼ cucumber

1 carrot

¼ head Napa cabbage, shredded

DRESSING

4 tbsp lime juice

2 garlic cloves, finely chopped

2 tbsp Thai fish sauce

1 tsp sesame oil

1 tbsp brown sugar

2 tbsp chopped fresh mint

½ tsp pepper

salt

1 Clean the mussels by scrubbing or scraping the shells and pulling out any beards that are attached to them. Discard any with broken shells or any that refuse to close when tapped. Place the mussels in a large pan with just the water that clings to their shells and cook, covered, over high heat for 3–4 minutes, shaking the pan occasionally, until they have opened. Remove the mussels with a slotted spoon, reserving the liquid in the pan. Discard any mussels that remain closed.

2 Using a sharp knife, separate the corals from the scallops, then cut the white parts in half horizontally. Cut the tentacles from the squid and slice the body cavities into rings.

3 Add the shallots to the liquid i the pan and simmer over high heat until the liquid is reduced to 3 tablespoons. Add the scallops, squid, and jumbo shrimp and stir fo 2–3 minutes, or until cooked. Rem the pan from the heat and transfer the mixture to a wide bowl. Add the mussels.

4 Cut the cucumber and carrot i half lengthwise, then slice thi on a diagonal angle to make long, pointed slices. Toss with the Napa cabbage. To make the dressing, pla all the ingredients in a screw-top ja and shake well until evenly combir Season to taste with salt.

5 Add the vegetables to the seafood in the bowl and toss together. Spoon the dressing over serve immediately.

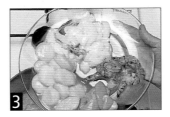

Fish & Seafood

The Thais are primarily a fish-eating nation, with meat often being reserved for special celebrations. The waterways of Thailand are teeming with many types of fish—even in the channels between the paddy fields—and the warm seas bring an abundance of fish and shellfish.

Even in the heart of Bangkok city, the markets are packed with fresh fish and seafood of all kinds. In Thai coastal towns, rows of thatch-roofed beach kiosks sell every type of fresh seafood from the warm Gulf waters—from grilled or sautéed fish with ginger, to shrimp in coconut milk and cilantro—to locals and visitors alike.

steamed yellow fish fillets

serves four

1 lb 2 oz/500 g firm fish fillets, such
   as red snapper, sole, or angler fish

1 red bird chili

1 small onion, chopped

3 garlic cloves, chopped

2 cilantro sprigs

1 tsp coriander seeds

½ tsp ground turmeric

½ tsp pepper

1 tbsp Thai fish sauce

2 tbsp coconut milk

1 small egg, beaten

2 tbsp rice flour

fresh red and green chili strips,
   to garnish

stir-fried vegetables, to serve

1 Using a sharp knife, remove any skin from the fish and cut the fillets diagonally into ¾-inch/2-cm wide strips.

2 Place the bird chili, onion, garlic, cilantro, and coriander seeds in a mortar and, using a pestle, grind to a smooth paste.

3 Transfer the paste to a bowl a add the turmeric, pepper, fish sauce, coconut milk, and beaten e stirring to mix evenly. Spread the ri flour out on a large plate. Dip the f strips into the paste mixture, then the rice flour to coat lightly.

4 Bring the water in the bottom a steamer to a boil, then arra the fish strips in the top of the stea Cover and steam for 12–15 minute or until the fish is just firm.

5 Garnish the fish with the chili strips and serve immediately stir-fried vegetables.

sh curry

serves four

hallots, coarsely chopped

nch/5-cm piece fresh gingerroot,
finely sliced

nch/5-cm piece lemongrass,
outer leaves discarded

nch/5-cm piece fresh galangal,
finely chopped

esh red chilies, seeded and
coarsely chopped

osp ground almonds

sp ground turmeric

sp salt

cups coconut cream

sh steaks, such as cod, turbot,
or halibut

GARNISH

esh red chili, cut into thin strips

sp toasted slivered almonds

d, to serve

1 Coarsely chop the shallots and place in a food processor with the ginger, lemongrass, galangal, chilies, ground almonds, turmeric, and salt. Add 6 tablespoons of the coconut cream and process to a smooth paste.

2 Pour the paste into a large pan. Bring to a boil and cook, stirring constantly, for 4 minutes. Add the remaining coconut cream and return to a boil.

3 Place the fish steaks in the pan and let simmer for 10 minutes, turning once, until the fish is cooked and flakes easily when tested with a fork. If the sauce is too thin, transfer the fish to a warmed serving dish and boil the sauce to reduce to the desired consistency. Garnish with chili strips and toasted slivered almonds and serve with a salad of your choice.

baked fish with bell pepper, chilies & bas

serves four

handful of fresh basil leaves

1 lb 10 oz/750 g whole red
   snapper, sea bass, or tilapia,
   cleaned

2 tbsp peanut oil

2 tbsp Thai fish sauce

2 garlic cloves, crushed

1 tsp finely grated fresh gingerroot
   or galangal

2 large fresh red chilies,
   diagonally sliced

1 yellow bell pepper, seeded
   and diced

1 tbsp palm sugar

1 tbsp rice vinegar or white
   wine vinegar

2 tbsp water or fish stock

2 tomatoes, seeded and sliced into
   thin wedges

mixed salad, to serve

COOK'S TIP

Almost any whole fish can be
cooked by this method, but
snapper, sea bass, or tilapia are
particularly good with the
Thai flavors.

1 Preheat the oven to 375°F/190°C.
Reserve a few basil leaves for the
garnish and tuck the rest inside the
body cavity of the fish.

2 Heat 1 tablespoon of the oil in a
wide skillet. Add the fish and
cook quickly to brown, turning once.
Place the fish on a large piece of foil in
a roasting pan and spoon over the fish
sauce. Wrap the foil over the fish
loosely and bake in the preheated
oven for 25–30 minutes, or until just
cooked through.

3 Meanwhile, heat the remaining
oil in a clean skillet. Add the
garlic, ginger, and chilies and cook for
30 seconds. Add the bell pepper and
stir-fry for an additional 2–3 minutes
to soften.

4 Stir in the sugar, rice vinegar,
water, then add the tomatoes
bring to a boil. Remove the skillet
the heat.

5 Remove the fish from the oven
and transfer to a warmed serv
plate. Add the fish juices to the skill
then spoon the sauce over the fish.
Sprinkle with the reserved basil lea
and serve immediately with a salad

curried mussel soup

serves four

1 tsp coriander seeds

1 tsp cumin seeds

2 lb/900 g live mussels in shells

scant ½ cup white wine

scant ¼ cup butter

1 onion, finely chopped

1 garlic clove, finely chopped

1 tsp grated fresh gingerroot

1 tsp ground turmeric

pinch of cayenne pepper

2½ cups fish stock

4 tbsp heavy cream

2 tbsp all-purpose flour

2 tbsp chopped cilantro,
   to garnish

1 Cook the coriander and cumin seeds in a dry skillet until they begin to smell aromatic and start to pop. Transfer to a mortar and, using a pestle, grind to a powder. Reserve.

2 Clean the mussels by scrubbing or scraping the shells and pulling out any beards that are attached to them. Discard any with broken shells or any that refuse to close when tapped. Place the mussels in a large pan with the wine and cook, covered, over high heat for 3–4 minutes, shaking the pan occasionally, until the mussels have opened. Discard any mussels that remain closed. Drain, reserving the cooking liquid, and let the mussels stand until cool enough to handle. Remove two-thirds of the mussels from their shells and set them all aside. Pour the mussel cooking liquid through a strainer and reserve.

3 Heat half the butter in a large Add the onion and cook gentl 4–5 minutes, or until softened but colored. Add the garlic and ginger a cook for an additional 1 minute bef adding the roasted and ground spic the turmeric, and cayenne. Cook fo 1 minute before adding the stock, reserved mussel cooking liquid, anc cream. Simmer for 10 minutes.

4 Cream the remaining butter a flour together to a thick paste Add the paste to the simmering sou and stir until dissolved and the sou has thickened slightly. Add the mus and heat gently for 2 minutes. Garr with cilantro and serve.

sh cakes with sweet & sour dip

serves four

b/450 g firm white fish, skinned
and coarsely chopped

bsp Thai fish sauce

bsp Thai red curry paste

fresh kaffir lime leaf, shredded

bsp chopped cilantro

egg

tsp brown sugar

ge pinch of salt

cup green beans, thinly sliced
crosswise

getable oil, for pan-frying

VEET & SOUR DIP

tbsp sugar

tbsp cold water

tbsp white rice vinegar

small fresh chilies, finely chopped

tbsp Thai fish sauce

GARNISH

allion tassels (see page 356)

esh red chili flowers
(see page 416)

1 To make the fish cakes, place the
fish, fish sauce, curry paste, lime
leaf, cilantro, egg, brown sugar, and
salt in a food processor and process
until smooth. Scrape into a bowl and
stir in the green beans. Reserve.

2 To make the dipping sauce, place
the sugar, water, and rice vinegar
in a small pan and heat gently until the
sugar has dissolved. Bring to a boil,
then reduce the heat and simmer for
2 minutes. Remove the pan from the
heat and stir in the chilies and fish
sauce. Let cool until required.

3 Heat a skillet with enough oil to
cover the bottom generously.
Divide the fish mixture into 16 balls.
Flatten the balls into patties and cook
in the oil for 1–2 minutes on each side
until golden. Drain on paper towels.
Garnish with scallion tassels and chili
flowers and serve with the dip.

whole fried fish with soy & ginger

serves four–six

6 dried shiitake mushrooms

3 tbsp rice vinegar

2 tbsp brown sugar

3 tbsp dark soy sauce

3-inch/7.5-cm piece fresh
    gingerroot, finely chopped

4 scallions, diagonally sliced

2 tsp cornstarch

2 tbsp lime juice

1 sea bass, about 2 lb 4 oz/
    1 kg, cleaned

salt and pepper

4 tbsp all-purpose flour

corn oil, for frying

1 radish, sliced but left whole,
    to garnish

TO SERVE

shredded Napa cabbage

radish slices

COOK'S TIP

Buy a very fresh whole fish on
the day you plan to cook it, and
ask your fish dealer to clean it,
preferably leaving the head on.

1 Place the dried mushrooms in a bowl, then cover with hot water and let soak for 10 minutes. Drain well, reserving a scant ½ cup of the liquid. Using a sharp knife, cut the mushrooms into thin slices.

2 Mix the reserved mushroom liquid with the rice vinegar, sugar, and soy sauce. Place in a pan with the mushrooms and bring to a boil. Reduce the heat and simmer for 3–4 minutes.

3 Add the ginger and scallions and simmer for 1 minute. Blend the cornstarch and lime juice together, then add to the pan and stir for 1–2 minutes, or until the sauce thickens and clears. Reserve until required.

4 Season the fish inside and out, then dust lightly with flour, carefully shaking off the excess.

5 Heat a 1-inch/2.5-cm depth of in a wide skillet to 350–375°F 180–190°C, or until a cube of brea browns in 30 seconds. Lower the fi into the oil and cook on one side fo 3–4 minutes, or until golden. Use 2 metal spatulas to turn the fish an cook on the other side for an additi 3–4 minutes, or until golden brown

6 Lift the fish out of the skillet, draining off the excess oil, and place on a serving plate. Heat the reserved sauce until boiling, then sp it over the fish. Serve immediately w Napa cabbage and radish slices, garnished with the sliced radish.

baked cod with a curry crust

serves four

½ tsp sesame oil

4 cod fillet pieces, about

    5½ oz/150 g each

1½ cups fresh white bread crumbs

2 tbsp blanched almonds, chopped

2 tsp Thai green curry paste

finely grated rind of ½ lime, plus

    extra thinly pared rind to garnish

salt and pepper

lime slices, to garnish

TO SERVE

boiled new potatoes

mixed salad greens

1 Preheat the oven to 400°F/200°C. Brush the oil over the bottom of a wide, shallow ovenproof dish or pan, then arrange the cod pieces in a single layer.

2 Mix the bread crumbs, almonds, curry paste, and grated lime rind together in a bowl, stirring well to blend thoroughly and evenly. Season to taste with salt and pepper.

3 Carefully spoon the crumb mixture over the fish pieces, pressing lightly with your hand to hold it in place.

4 Bake the dish, uncovered, in the preheated oven for 35–40 minutes, or until the fish is cooked through and the crumb topping is golden brown.

5 Serve the dish hot, garnished with lime slices and rind and accompanied by boiled new potatoes and mixed salad greens.

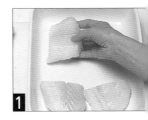

COOK'S TIP

To test whether the fish is cook
through, use a fork to pierce it
the thickest part—if the flesh
white all the way through an
flakes apart easily, it is
cooked sufficiently.

ɔicy thai seafood stew

serves four

z/200 g squid, cleaned and
tentacles discarded

ɔ 2 oz/500 g firm white fish fillet,
preferably angler fish or halibut

ɔsp corn oil

hallots, finely chopped

arlic cloves, finely chopped

ɔsp Thai green curry paste

mall lemongrass stems,
finely chopped

ɔp shrimp paste

erous 2 cups coconut milk

z/200 g raw jumbo shrimp,
shelled and deveined

live clams in shells, cleaned

esh basil leaves, finely shredded

h basil leaves, to garnish

hly cooked rice, to serve

1 Using a sharp knife, cut the squid
body cavities into thick rings and
the white fish into bite-size chunks.

2 Heat the oil in a large skillet or
preheated wok. Add the shallots,
garlic, and curry paste and stir-fry for
1–2 minutes. Add the lemongrass and
shrimp paste, then stir in the coconut
milk and bring to a boil.

3 Reduce the heat until the liquid is
simmering gently, then add the
white fish, squid, and shrimp to the
skillet and simmer for 2 minutes.

4 Add the clams and simmer for an
additional 1 minute, or until the
clams have opened. Discard any clams
that remain closed.

5 Sprinkle the shredded basil leaves
over the stew. Transfer to serving
plates, then garnish with whole basil
leaves and serve immediately with rice.

VARIATION

If you prefer, live mussels in
shells can be used instead of
clams—add them after the
shrimp and continue as
in the recipe.

spiced steamed fish

serves four–six

1-inch/2.5-cm piece fresh
   gingerroot, finely grated

1 lemongrass stem (base only),
   thinly sliced

6 fresh red chilies, seeded and
   coarsely chopped

1 small red onion, finely chopped

1 tbsp Thai fish sauce

2 lb/900 g whole fish, cleaned

2 fresh kaffir lime leaves,
   thinly sliced

2 fresh basil sprigs

TO SERVE

freshly cooked rice

cucumber, cut into thin sticks

1 Place the ginger, lemongrass, chilies, onion, and fish sauce in a food processor. Process to a coarse paste, adding a little water, if needed.

2 Cut 3–4 deep slits crosswise on each side of the fish. Spread over the spice paste, rubbing it well into the slits. Place the fish in a dish deep enough to hold the liquid that collects during steaming. Sprinkle over the lime leaves and basil.

3 Set up a steamer or place a rack into a wok or deep pan. Bring about 2 inches/5 cm of water to a boil in the steamer or wok.

4 Place the dish of fish into the steamer or on to the rack. Reduce the heat to a simmer, then cover tightly and steam the fish for 15–20 minutes, or until the fish is cooked through. Serve with freshly cooked rice and cucumber sticks.

COOK'S TIP

You can use any whole fish in this recipe, such as sea bass, r snapper, trout, or tilapia.

pan-fried spiced salmon

serves four

1-inch/2.5-cm piece fresh
   gingerroot, grated
1 tsp coriander seeds, crushed
¼ tsp chili powder
1 tbsp lime juice
1 tsp sesame oil
4 salmon fillet pieces with skin,
   about 5½ oz/150 g each
2 tbsp vegetable oil
cilantro leaves, to garnish
TO SERVE
freshly cooked rice
stir-fried vegetables

1 Mix the ginger, crushed coriander, chili powder, lime juice, and sesame oil together in a bowl.

2 Place the salmon on a wide, nonmetallic plate or dish and spoon the mixture over the flesh side of the fillets, spreading it to coat each piece of salmon evenly.

3 Cover the dish with plastic wrap and let chill in the refrigerator for 30 minutes.

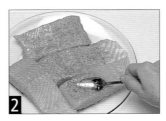

4 Heat a wide, heavy-bottom skillet or ridged grill pan with the vegetable oil over high heat. Place the salmon in the hot skillet, skin-side down, and cook for 4–5 minutes, without turning, until the salmon is crusty underneath and the flesh flakes easily.

5 Serve the salmon immediately with freshly cooked rice, garnished with cilantro leaves, and fried vegetables.

COOK'S TIP

Use a heavy-bottom skillet or solid grill pan to ensure that the fish cooks evenly throughout without sticking. If the fish is very thick, you may prefer to turn it over to cook on the other side for 2–3 minutes.

iced tuna in sweet & sour sauce

serves four

esh tuna steaks, about 1 lb 2 oz/
500 g in total

sp pepper

osp peanut oil

nion, diced

mall red bell pepper, seeded and
cut into short thin sticks

arlic clove, crushed

cucumber, seeded and cut
into short thin sticks

ineapple slices, diced

sp finely chopped fresh
gingerroot

osp brown sugar

osp cornstarch

tbsp lime juice

osp Thai fish sauce

up fish stock

GARNISH

e slices

cumber slices

COOK'S TIP
Tuna can be served quite
lightly cooked. It can be dry
if overcooked.

1 Sprinkle the tuna steaks with pepper on both sides. Heat a heavy-bottom skillet or ridged grill pan and brush with a little of the oil. Arrange the tuna steaks in the skillet and cook for 8 minutes, turning them over once.

2 Meanwhile, heat the remaining oil in a separate skillet. Add the onion, bell pepper, and garlic and cook gently for 3–4 minutes to soften.

3 Remove the skillet from the heat and stir in the cucumber, pineapple, ginger, and sugar.

4 Blend the cornstarch with the lime juice and fish sauce, then stir into the stock and add to the skillet. Stir over medium heat until boiling, then cook for 1–2 minutes, or until thickened and clear.

5 Spoon the sauce over the tuna and serve immediately, garnished with slices of lime and cucumber.

salmon with red curry in banana leaves

serves four

4 salmon steaks, about
6 oz/175 g each
2 banana leaves, halved
1 garlic clove, crushed
1 tsp grated fresh gingerroot
1 tbsp Thai red curry paste
1 tsp brown sugar
1 tbsp Thai fish sauce
2 tbsp lime juice
TO GARNISH
lime wedges
whole fresh red chilies
finely chopped fresh red chili

1 Preheat the oven to 425°F/220°C. Place a salmon steak in the center of each half banana leaf.

2 Mix the garlic, ginger, curry paste, sugar, and fish sauce together, then spread over the surface of the fish. Sprinkle with lime juice.

3 Carefully wrap the banana leaves around the fish, tucking in the sides as you go to make neat, compact pockets.

4 Place the pockets seam-side down on a baking sheet. Bak the preheated oven for 15–20 min or until the fish is cooked and the banana leaves are beginning to br Serve garnished with lime wedges whole chilies, and finely chopped

COOK'S TIP
Fresh banana leaves are ofte sold in packages containing several leaves, but if you buy more than you need, they wil store in the refrigerator for about a week.

ꜱconut shrimp

.up dry unsweetened coconut

ꜰup fresh white bread crumbs

ꜱp Chinese five-spice powder

ꜱp salt

ely grated rind of 1 lime

ꜰgg white

ꜱ/450 g raw fantail shrimp

ꜰn oil, for frying

ꜰon wedges, to garnish

Mix the dry unsweetened
coconut, bread crumbs, Chinese
ꜱspice powder, salt, and lime rind
ꜰther in a bowl.

Lightly whisk the egg white in a
separate bowl.

Rinse the shrimp under cold
running water and pat dry with
ꜰr towels.

Dip the shrimp into the egg
white, then into the coconut
ꜱb mixture, so that they are
ꜰly coated.

5 Heat about 2 inches/5 cm of oil in a large, preheated wok.

6 Add the shrimp to the wok and stir-fry for 5 minutes, or until golden and crispy.

7 Remove the shrimp with a slotted spoon, then transfer to paper towels and let drain thoroughly.

8 Transfer the coconut shrimp to warmed serving dishes and garnish with lemon wedges. Serve immediately.

shrimp skewers with tamarind glaze

1 garlic clove, chopped

1 fresh red Thai chili, seeded
  and chopped

1 tbsp tamarind paste

1 tbsp sesame oil

1 tbsp dark soy sauce

2 tbsp lime juice

1 tbsp brown sugar

16 large raw jumbo shrimp in shells

lime wedges, to garnish

TO SERVE

crusty bread

salad greens

COOK'S TIP

Before using wooden or bamboo
skewers, soak them in water for
at least 30 minutes to prevent
them burning under the broiler.

1 Place the garlic, chili, tamarind
paste, sesame oil, soy sauce,
lime juice, and sugar in a small pan.
Stir constantly over low heat until the
sugar is dissolved, then remove the
pan from the heat and let cool
completely.

2 Rinse the shrimp under cold
running water and pat dry with
paper towels. Arrange in a single layer
in a wide, nonmetallic dish. Spoon the
marinade over the shrimp and turn to
coat evenly. Cover and let marinate in
the refrigerator for at least 2 hours or
preferably overnight.

3 Preheat the broiler to medium.
Thread 4 shrimp on to each
presoaked skewer and cook under
preheated broiler for 5–6 minutes,
turning them over once, until they
pink and begin to brown. Alternat
grill over hot coals.

4 Thread a wedge of lime on to
end of each skewer and serv
with crusty bread and salad green

stir-fried squid with hot black bean sauce

serves four

1 lb 10 oz/750 g squid, cleaned and
   tentacles discarded

1 large red bell pepper, seeded

scant 1 cup snow peas

1 head bok choy

3 tbsp black bean sauce

1 tbsp Thai fish sauce

1 tbsp rice wine or dry sherry

1 tbsp dark soy sauce

1 tsp brown sugar

1 tsp cornstarch

1 tbsp water

1 tbsp corn oil

1 tsp sesame oil

1 small fresh red Thai chili,
   chopped

1 garlic clove, finely chopped

1 tsp grated fresh gingerroot

2 scallions, chopped

COOK'S TIP

Quick stir-frying is an ideal
cooking method for squid,
because if overcooked it can
be tough. It also seals in the
colors, flavors, and nutritional
value of fresh vegetables.

1 Cut the squid body cavities into
fourths lengthwise. Use the tip of
a small, sharp knife to score a diamond
pattern into the flesh, without cutting
all the way through. Pat dry with
paper towels.

2 Cut the bell pepper into long, thin
slices. Cut the snow peas in half
diagonally. Coarsely shred the bok choy.

3 Mix the black bean sauce, fish
sauce, rice wine, soy sauce, and
sugar together in a bowl. Blend the
cornstarch with the water and stir into
the other sauce ingredients. Reserve
until required.

4 Heat the oils in a preheated
Add the chili, garlic, ginger, a
scallions and stir-fry for 1 minute.
the bell pepper slices and stir-fry f
2 minutes.

5 Add the squid and stir-fry ove
high heat for an additional
1 minute. Stir in the snow peas ar
bok choy and stir for an additional
1 minute, or until wilted.

6 Stir in the sauce ingredients a
cook, stirring constantly, for
2 minutes, or until the sauce thick
and clears. Serve immediately.

spicy scallops with lime & chili

serves four

16 large scallops, shelled

1 tbsp butter

1 tbsp vegetable oil

1 tsp crushed garlic

1 tsp grated fresh gingerroot

1 bunch of scallions,
  finely sliced

finely grated rind of 1 lime

1 small fresh red chili, seeded and
  very finely chopped

3 tbsp lime juice

lime wedges, to garnish

freshly cooked rice, to serve

1 Using a sharp knife, trim the scallops to remove any black intestine, then wash and pat dry with paper towels. Separate the corals from the white parts, then slice each white part in half horizontally, making 2 circles.

2 Heat the butter and oil in a skillet or preheated wok. Add the garlic and ginger and stir-fry for 1 minute without browning. Add the scallions and stir-fry for an additional 1 minute.

3 Add the scallops and continu stir-frying over high heat for 4–5 minutes. Stir in the lime rind, chili, and lime juice and cook for a additional 1 minute.

4 Transfer the scallops to servir plates, then spoon over the p juices and garnish with lime wedg Serve hot with freshly cooked rice.

hrimp & pineapple curry

serves four

resh pineapple

cups coconut cream

bsp Thai red curry paste

osp fish sauce

sp sugar

oz/350 g raw jumbo shrimp

bsp chopped cilantro

amed jasmine rice, to serve

VARIATION

For an extra touch, shred scallions and sprinkle over just before serving.

1 Peel the pineapple and chop the flesh. Heat the coconut cream, pineapple, curry paste, fish sauce, and sugar until almost boiling.

2 Shell and devein the shrimp. Add the shrimp and cilantro to the pan and simmer for 3 minutes, or until the shrimp are cooked.

3 Serve the shrimp with steamed jasmine rice.

Meat & Poultry

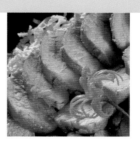

Because of the Thai Buddhist religion, which forbids the killing of animals, most butchers are immigrant workers in Thailand. Religion does not forbid eating meat, though it is often regarded as a special treat. Chicken is much more common than beef, and it's not unusual to see chicken, or sometimes pork, combined with seafood such as shrimp or crabmeat—a combination which works surprisingly well. Duck, another Thai favorite, is frequently grill-roasted with warm spices and soy or sweet glazes, much as in the customary Chinese style.

beef & bell peppers with lemongrass

serves four

1 lb 2 oz/500 g lean beef fillet

2 tbsp vegetable oil

1 garlic clove, finely chopped

1 lemongrass stem, finely shredded

1-inch/2.5-cm piece fresh
   gingerroot, finely chopped

1 red bell pepper, seeded and
   thickly sliced

1 green bell pepper, seeded and
   thickly sliced

1 onion, thickly sliced

2 tbsp lime juice

salt and pepper

freshly cooked noodles or rice,
   to serve

3 Add the beef and stir-fry for an additional 2–3 minutes, or until lightly colored. Stir in the lemongrass and ginger and remove the skillet from the heat.

1 Cut the beef into long, thin strips, cutting across the grain.

2 Heat the oil in a large skillet or preheated wok over high heat. Add the garlic and stir-fry for 1 minute.

4 Remove the beef from the skillet and reserve to one side. Add the bell peppers and onion to the skillet and stir-fry over high heat for 2–3 minutes, or until the onions are just turning golden brown and slightly softened.

5 Return the beef to the skillet, then stir in the lime juice and season to taste with salt and pepper. Serve with freshly cooked noodles or rice.

eef & coconut curry

serves four

b 12 oz/800 g braising steak

bsp vegetable oil

onions, thinly sliced

bsp Thai red curry paste

bsp tamarind paste or lime juice

bsp Thai fish sauce

 cups coconut milk

sp sugar

cardamom pods, crushed

small pineapple, peeled

and chopped

SERVE

shly cooked rice

imp chips

3 Stir in the tamarind paste, fish sauce, coconut milk, and sugar. Bring to a boil, then reduce the heat and return the beef and onions to the casserole with the cardamom.

4 Simmer gently, uncovered, for 1–1½ hours, or until the beef is tender. Stir from time to time, and if it is becoming dry, cover with a lid.

5 Add the pineapple and cook for an additional 5 minutes. The curry should be quite dry, but add a little water if necessary.

6 Serve immediately with rice and shrimp chips.

Cut the beef into cubes. Heat the oil in a flameproof casserole. vn the beef in batches and reserve.

Add the onions to the oil and cook for 5 minutes, then reserve the beef. Add the curry paste cook gently for 1 minute, ng constantly.

stir-fried beef with bean sprouts

serves four

1 bunch of scallions

2 tbsp corn oil

1 garlic clove, crushed

1 tsp finely chopped fresh
   gingerroot

1 lb 2 oz/500 g lean beef fillet, cut
   into thin strips

1 large red bell pepper, seeded
   and sliced

1 small fresh red chili, seeded
   and chopped

3 cups fresh bean sprouts

1 small lemongrass stem,
   finely chopped

2 tbsp smooth peanut butter

4 tbsp coconut milk

1 tbsp rice vinegar or white
   wine vinegar

1 tbsp soy sauce

1 tsp brown sugar

9 oz/250 g medium egg noodles

salt and pepper

1 Thinly slice the scallions, reserving some slices to use as a garnish.

2 Heat the oil in a skillet or preheated wok over high heat. Add the scallions, garlic, and ginger and stir-fry for 2–3 minutes to soften. Add the beef and continue stir-frying for 4–5 minutes, or until evenly browned.

COOK'S TIP

When preparing lemongrass, take care to remove the outer layers, which can be tough and fibrous. Use only the tender part at the center, which has the finest flavor.

3 Add the bell pepper and stir-fry an additional 3–4 minutes. Add the chili and bean sprouts and stir-fry for 2 minutes. Mix the lemongrass, peanut butter, coconut milk, rice vinegar, soy sauce, and sugar together in a bowl, then stir into the skillet.

4 Meanwhile, cook the egg noodles in boiling salted water for 4 minutes, or according to the package directions. Drain and stir into the skillet, tossing to mix evenly.

5 Season to taste with salt and pepper. Sprinkle with the reserved scallions and serve hot.

red-hot beef with cashew nuts

serves four

1 lb 2 oz/500 g lean boneless
   beef sirloin
1 tsp vegetable oil
MARINADE
1 tbsp sesame seeds
1 garlic clove, chopped
1 tbsp finely chopped fresh
   gingerroot
1 fresh red Thai chili, chopped
2 tbsp dark soy sauce
1 tsp Thai red curry paste
TO FINISH
1 tsp sesame oil
4 tbsp unsalted cashew nuts
1 scallion, thickly
   sliced diagonally
cucumber slices, to garnish

1 Using a sharp knife, cut the beef into ½-inch/1-cm wide strips. Place them in a large, nonmetallic bowl.

2 To make the marinade, toast the sesame seeds in a heavy-bottom skillet over medium heat for 2–3 minutes, or until golden brown, shaking the skillet occasionally.

3 Place the seeds in a mortar with the garlic, ginger, and chili and, using a pestle, grind to a smooth paste. Add the soy sauce and curry paste and mix well.

4 Spoon the paste over the beef strips and toss to coat the meat evenly. Cover and let marinate in the refrigerator for at least 2–3 hours or overnight.

5 Heat a heavy-bottom skillet or ridged grill pan until very hot brush with vegetable oil. Place the strips in the skillet and cook quickly turning frequently, until lightly browned. Remove the skillet from heat and spoon the beef into a pile a hot serving dish.

6 Heat the sesame oil in a small skillet. Add the cashew nuts a quickly cook until golden. Add the scallion and stir-fry for 30 seconds. Sprinkle the mixture on top of the strips, then garnish with cucumber slices and serve immediately.

beef satay with peanut sauce

1 lb 2 oz/500 g lean beef fillet

2 garlic cloves, crushed

¾-inch/2-cm piece fresh gingerroot,
    finely grated

1 tbsp brown sugar

1 tbsp dark soy sauce

1 tbsp lime juice

2 tsp sesame oil

1 tsp ground coriander

1 tsp ground turmeric

½ tsp chili powder

PEANUT SAUCE

1¼ cups coconut milk

8 tbsp chunky peanut butter

½ small onion, grated

2 tsp brown sugar

½ tsp chili powder

1 tbsp dark soy sauce

TO GARNISH

chopped cucumber

red bell pepper pieces

1 Cut the beef into ½-inch/1-cm cubes and place in a large bowl.

2 Add the garlic, ginger, sugar, soy sauce, lime juice, sesame oil, coriander, turmeric, and chili powder. Mix well to coat the pieces of meat evenly. Cover and let marinate in the refrigerator for at least 2 hours or overnight.

3 Preheat the broiler to high. To make the peanut sauce, place the ingredients in a small pan and over medium heat until boiling. Remove the pan from the heat an keep warm.

4 Thread the beef cubes on to presoaked bamboo skewers. Cook the skewers under the hot b for 3–5 minutes, turning frequentl until golden. Alternatively, grill ove coals. Transfer to a large serving p then garnish with chopped cucum and red bell pepper pieces and se with the peanut sauce.

hot beef & coconut curry

serves four

1¾ cups coconut milk

2 tbsp Thai red curry paste

2 garlic cloves, crushed

1 lb 2 oz/500 g braising steak

2 fresh kaffir lime leaves, shredded

3 tbsp lime juice

2 tbsp Thai fish sauce

1 large fresh red chili, seeded
   and sliced

½ tsp ground turmeric

salt and pepper

2 tbsp chopped fresh basil leaves

2 tbsp chopped cilantro leaves

shredded coconut, to garnish

freshly cooked rice, to serve

COOK'S TIP

This recipe uses one of the larg
milder red chili peppers—
either fresno or Dutch—simp
because they give more color
the dish. If you prefer to use
small Thai chilies, you'll nee
only one because they are
much hotter. For an elegant
presentation, garnish the
rice with a few strips of
fresh red chili.

1 Place the coconut milk in a large pan and bring to a boil. Reduce the heat and simmer gently for 10 minutes, or until it has thickened. Stir in the curry paste and garlic and simmer for an additional 5 minutes.

2 Cut the beef into ¾-inch/ 2-cm chunks. Add to the pan and bring to a boil, stirring constantly. Reduce the heat and add the kaffir lime leaves, lime juice, fish sauce, sliced chili, turmeric, and ½ teaspoon of salt.

3 Cover the pan and continue simmering for 20–25 minutes, or until the meat is tender, adding a little water if the sauce looks too dry.

4 Stir in the basil and cilantro a season to taste with salt and pepper. Sprinkle with shredded co and serve with freshly cooked rice

spicy fried ground pork

serves four

2 garlic cloves

3 shallots

1-inch/2.5-cm piece fresh
   gingerroot

2 tbsp corn oil

1 lb 2 oz/500 g ground lean pork

2 tbsp Thai fish sauce

1 tbsp dark soy sauce

1 tbsp Thai red curry paste

4 dried kaffir lime leaves, crumbled

4 plum tomatoes, chopped

3 tbsp chopped cilantro

salt and pepper

TO GARNISH

cilantro sprigs

scallion tassels (see Cook's Tip)

freshly cooked fine egg noodles,
   to serve

1 Finely chop the garlic, shallots, and ginger. Heat the oil in a large skillet or preheated wok over medium heat. Add the garlic, shallots, and ginger and stir-fry for 2 minutes. Stir in the pork and continue stir-frying until golden brown.

2 Stir in the fish sauce, soy sauce, curry paste, and lime leaves and stir-fry for an additional 1–2 minutes over high heat.

3 Add the chopped tomatoes and cook for an additional 5–6 minutes, stirring occasionally. Stir in the chopped cilantro and season to taste with salt and pepper.

4 Serve hot, spooned onto freshly cooked fine egg noodles, garnished with cilantro sprigs and scallion tassels.

COOK'S TIP

To make the scallion tassels make a few cuts lengthwise down the stem of each scallion. Place in a bowl of ice-cold water and let stand until the tassels open out. Drain well before using.

roasted red pork

serves four

1 lb 5 oz/600 g pork fillets

Napa cabbage, shredded

1 fresh red chili flower (see page 416), to garnish

MARINADE

2 garlic cloves, crushed

1 tbsp grated fresh gingerroot

1 tbsp light soy sauce

1 tbsp Thai fish sauce

1 tbsp rice wine or dry sherry

1 tbsp hoisin sauce

1 tbsp sesame oil

1 tbsp palm sugar or brown sugar

½ tsp Chinese five-spice powder

few drops of red food coloring (optional)

1 Mix all the ingredients for the marinade together in a small bowl, then spread over the pork, turning to coat evenly. Place in a large, nonmetallic dish, then cover and let marinate in the refrigerator overnight.

2 Preheat the oven to 425°F/220°C. Place a rack in a roasting pan, then half fill the pan with boiling water. Lift the pork from the marinade and place on the rack. Reserve the marinade.

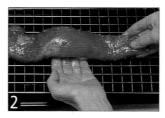

1 fresh red chili flower (see page 416), to garnish

3 Roast in the preheated oven 20 minutes. Baste with the marinade, then reduce the heat to 350°F/180°C and continue roastin an additional 35–40 minutes, bast occasionally with the marinade, un the pork is a rich, reddish brown a thoroughly cooked.

4 Cut the pork into slices and arrange on a bed of shredded Napa cabbage. Garnish with a red chili flower and serve.

ork steaks with lemongrass

serves four

emongrass stems, outer
leaves removed

garlic cloves, crushed

tsp pepper

bsp sugar

bsp Thai fish sauce

bsp soy sauce

bsp sesame oil

bsp lime juice

scallions, finely chopped

bsp coconut milk

pork steaks

e wedges, to garnish

VARIATION

The pork steaks are perfect for
ooking over medium–hot coals
on the grill.

1 Finely chop the lemongrass and
place in a bowl with the garlic,
pepper, sugar, fish sauce, soy sauce,
oil, lime juice, scallions, and coconut
milk. Mix well to combine.

2 Place the pork steaks in a large,
shallow, nonmetallic dish. Pour
over the marinade and turn the steaks
until coated. Cover the dish with plastic
wrap and let marinate in the
refrigerator for 1 hour.

3 Preheat the broiler to medium.
Cook the pork steaks under the
hot broiler for 5 minutes on each side,
or until cooked through. Garnish with
lime wedges and serve immediately.

stir-fried pork & corn

2 tbsp vegetable oil

1 lb 2 oz/500 g lean boneless pork, cut into thin strips

1 garlic clove, chopped

3 cups fresh corn kernels

1⅓ cups green beans, cut into short lengths

2 scallions, chopped

1 small fresh red chili, chopped

1 tsp sugar

1 tbsp light soy sauce

3 tbsp chopped cilantro

freshly cooked egg noodles or rice, to serve

1 Heat the oil in a large skillet or preheated wok. Add the pork and stir-fry quickly over high heat until lightly browned.

2 Stir in the garlic, corn, beans, scallions, and chili and continue stir-frying over high heat for 2–3 minutes, or until the vegetables are heated through and almost tender.

3 Stir in the sugar and soy sauce and stir-fry for an additional 30 seconds over high heat.

4 Sprinkle with the cilantro and serve immediately with freshly cooked egg noodles or rice.

COOK'S TIP

In Thailand, long beans would be used for dishes such as this, but you can substitute green beans, which are more easily available. Look out for long beans in Asian food stores—they are like long string beans and have a similar flavor, but their texture is crisp, and they cook more quickly.

ork with soy & sesame glaze

serves four

pork fillets, about
  9½ oz/275 g each

tbsp dark soy sauce

tbsp clear honey

garlic cloves, crushed

tbsp sesame seeds

onion, thinly sliced into rings

tbsp all-purpose flour, seasoned

rn oil, for frying

isp salad greens, to serve

Preheat the oven to 400°F/200°C. Trim the pork fillets and place in a
le, nonmetallic dish.

Mix the soy sauce, honey, and garlic together in a small bowl, n spread over the pork, turning to t evenly.

3 Lift the pork fillets into a roasting pan or shallow, ovenproof dish and sprinkle evenly with sesame seeds.

4 Roast the pork in the preheated oven for 20 minutes, spooning over any juices. Cover loosely with foil to prevent overbrowning and roast for an additional 10–15 minutes, or until the meat is thoroughly cooked.

5 Meanwhile, dip the onion slices in the seasoned flour and shake off the excess. Heat the oil in a small skillet. Add the onion rings and cook until golden and crisp, turning occasionally. Serve the pork in slices with the fried onions on a bed of crisp salad greens.

tamarind pork

serves four

2 tbsp vegetable oil

1 lb 5 oz/600 g lean boneless pork,
   cut into thin strips

generous 2¼ cups canned bamboo
   shoots, drained

freshly cooked noodles, to serve

SPICE PASTE

1-inch/2.5-cm piece fresh
   gingerroot

4 shallots, finely chopped

2 garlic cloves, finely chopped

1 tsp ground coriander

2 fresh red chilies, seeded and
   finely chopped

½ tsp ground turmeric

6 blanched almonds, finely chopped

2 tbsp tamarind paste

2 tbsp hot water

1 To make the spice paste, peel the ginger and finely chop. Place the shallots, garlic, ginger, coriander, chilies, turmeric, almonds, tamarind paste, and water in a food processor and process until smooth.

2 Heat the oil in a preheated wok or skillet over high heat. Add the pork and cook for 3 minutes, or until the meat is colored. Add the spice paste and continue to cook for an additional 2–3 minutes.

3 Add the bamboo shoots and cook for an additional 2 minutes, or until the pork is cooked through. Serve with freshly cooked noodles.

VARIATION

If you cannot find shallots,
replace them with
ordinary small onions.

spiced pork sausages

serves four

3½ cups ground lean pork

scant ¾ cup cooked rice

1 garlic clove, crushed

1 tsp Thai red curry paste

1 tsp pepper

1 tsp ground coriander

½ tsp salt

3 tbsp lime juice

2 tbsp chopped cilantro

3 tbsp peanut oil

TO GARNISH

cucumber slices

fresh red chili strips

Chili & Coconut Sambal (see page
432) or soy sauce, to serve

3 Heat the oil in a large skillet over medium heat. Add the sausages, in batches if necessary, and cook for 8–10 minutes, turning them over occasionally, until they are evenly golden brown and cooked through. Transfer to a serving plate, then garnish with cucumber slices and a few strips of red chili and serve hot with Chili & Coconut Sambal or soy sauce.

COOK'S TIP

These sausages can also be served as an appetizer—shape the mixture slightly smaller to make 16 bite-size sausages. Serve with a soy dipping sauce.

1 Place the pork, rice, garlic, curry paste, pepper, coriander, salt, lime juice, and chopped cilantro in a bowl and knead together with your hands to mix evenly.

2 Use your hands to form the mixture into 12 small sausage shapes. Using sausage casings, if available, will help to keep the sausages together when cooked.

hai-style burgers

small lemongrass stem

small fresh red chili, seeded

garlic cloves

scallions

oz/200 g closed-cup mushrooms

½ cups ground lean pork

tbsp Thai fish sauce

tbsp chopped cilantro

lt and pepper

-purpose flour, for dusting

rn oil, for pan-frying

tbsp mayonnaise

tbsp lime juice

SERVE

sesame hamburger buns

redded Napa cabbage

COOK'S TIP

You can add a spoonful of your
favorite relish to each burger,
or add a few Crisp Pickled
Vegetables (see page 422) for
a change of texture.

3 Heat the oil in a skillet over
medium heat. Add the burgers
and cook for 6–8 minutes, until cooked.

4 Meanwhile, mix the mayonnaise
with the lime juice in a small
bowl. Split the hamburger buns and
spread the lime-flavored mayonnaise
on the cut surfaces. Add shredded
Napa cabbage, then top with a burger
and sandwich together. Serve.

Place the lemongrass, chili, garlic,
and scallions in a food processor
process to a smooth paste. Add
mushrooms and process until very
y chopped.

Add the pork, fish sauce, and
cilantro. Season well with salt
pepper, then divide the mixture
4 equal portions and form into
ourger shapes with lightly
red hands.

lamb with lime leaves

serves four

2 fresh red Thai chilies

2 tbsp peanut oil

2 garlic cloves, crushed

4 shallots, chopped

2 lemongrass stems, sliced

6 fresh kaffir lime leaves

1 tbsp tamarind paste

2 tbsp palm sugar

1 lb/450 g lean boneless lamb

    (leg or loin fillet)

2½ cups coconut milk

6 oz/175 g cherry tomatoes, halved

1 tbsp chopped cilantro

freshly cooked Thai fragrant rice,

    to serve

1 Using a sharp knife, seed and very finely chop the chilies. Reserve until required.

2 Heat the oil in a large, preheated wok. Add the garlic, shallots, lemongrass, lime leaves, tamarind paste, sugar, and chilies to the wok and stir-fry for 2 minutes.

3 Using a sharp knife, cut the lamb into thin strips or cubes.

4 Add the lamb to the wok and stir-fry for 5 minutes, tossing well so that the lamb is evenly coated in the spice mixture.

5 Pour the coconut milk into the wok and bring to a boil. Reduce the heat and let simmer for 20 minutes.

6 Add the cherry tomatoes and chopped cilantro to the wok and simmer for 5 minutes. Transfer to serving plates and serve hot with fragrant rice.

COOK'S TIP

Peanut oil is used here for flavor—it is a common oil used for stir-frying.

red lamb curry

1 lb 2 oz/500 g lean boneless
    leg of lamb

2 tbsp vegetable oil

1 large onion, sliced

2 garlic cloves, crushed

2 tbsp Thai red curry paste

⅔ cup coconut milk

1 tbsp brown sugar

1 large red bell pepper, seeded and
    thickly sliced

½ cup lamb or beef stock

1 tbsp Thai fish sauce

2 tbsp lime juice

generous 1 cup canned
    water chestnuts, drained

2 tbsp chopped cilantro

2 tbsp chopped fresh basil

salt and pepper

fresh basil leaves, to garnish

freshly cooked jasmine rice, to serve

VARIATION

This curry can also be made with other lean red meats. Try replacing the lamb with trimmed duck breasts or pieces of lean braising beef. This richly spiced curry uses the typically red-hot chili flavor of Thai red curry paste, made with dried red chilies, to give it a warm, russet-red color.

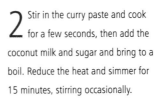

1 Trim the meat and cut it into 1¼-inch/3-cm cubes. Heat the oil in a large skillet or preheated wok over high heat. Add the onion and garlic and stir-fry for 2–3 minutes to soften. Add the meat and stir-fry the mixture quickly until lightly browned.

2 Stir in the curry paste and cook for a few seconds, then add the coconut milk and sugar and bring to a boil. Reduce the heat and simmer for 15 minutes, stirring occasionally.

3 Stir in the bell pepper, stock, fish sauce, and lime juice, then cover and simmer for an additional 15 minutes, or until the meat is tender.

4 Add the water chestnuts, cilantro, and basil and season to taste with salt and pepper. Transfer to serving plates, then garnish with basil leaves and serve with jasmine rice.

stir-fried lamb with mint

serves four

generous ⅓ cup fresh mint leaves

2 tbsp vegetable oil

2 garlic cloves, finely sliced

2 fresh red chilies, seeded and
cut into thin strips

1 onion, thinly sliced

1½ tbsp Madras curry paste

1 lb 2 oz/500 g lamb fillet, cut
into thin strips

8 oz/225 g canned baby
corn cobs, drained

4 scallions, finely chopped

1 tbsp Thai fish sauce

freshly cooked rice, to serve

VARIATION

You can use fresh baby corn
cobs, halved, instead of
canned ones, if you prefer.

---

1 Coarsely shred the mint leaves
and reserve until required. Heat
half the oil in a preheated wok or large
skillet. Add the garlic and chilies and
cook until soft. Remove and reserve.
Add the onion and cook for 5 minutes,
or until soft. Remove and reserve.

2 Heat the remaining oil in the wok.
Add the curry paste and cook for
1 minute. Add the lamb, in batches if
necessary, and cook for 5–8 minutes,
or until cooked through and tender.

3 Return the onion to the wok with
the baby corn cobs, scallions,
mint, and fish sauce. Cook until heated
through. Sprinkle the garlic and chilies
over and serve with rice.

roast chicken with ginger & lime

serves four

1¼-inch/3-cm piece fresh
  gingerroot, finely chopped

2 garlic cloves, finely chopped

1 small onion, finely chopped

1 lemongrass stem, finely chopped

½ tsp salt

1 tsp black peppercorns

3 lb 5 oz/1.5 kg roasting chicken

1 tbsp coconut cream

2 tbsp lime juice

2 tbsp clear honey

1 tsp cornstarch

2 tsp water

stir-fried vegetables, to serve

1 Place the ginger, garlic, onion, lemongrass, salt, and peppercorns in a mortar and, using a pestle, grind to a smooth paste.

2 Using poultry shears or strong kitchen scissors, cut the chicken in half lengthwise. Spread the paste all over the chicken, both inside and out, and spread it on to the flesh under the breast skin. Cover and let chill in the refrigerator for at least several hours or overnight.

3 Preheat the oven to 350°F/180°C. Heat the coconut crea[m] lime juice, and honey together in a small pan, stirring until smooth. Brush a little of the mixture evenly over the chicken.

4 Place the chicken halves on a baking sheet over a roasting [pan] half filled with boiling water. Roast [in] the preheated oven for 1 hour, or u[ntil] the chicken is a rich golden brown color, basting occasionally with the lime and honey mixture.

5 When the chicken is cooked, [boil] the water from the roasting p[an] to reduce it to a scant ½ cup. Blen[d] cornstarch and water together and [stir] into the reduced liquid. Bring gent[ly] to a boil, then stir until slightly thickened and clear. Serve the chick[en] with the sauce and freshly cooked [stir]-fried vegetables.

ed chicken with cherry tomatoes

serves four

bsp corn oil

b/450 g skinless,

 boneless chicken

garlic cloves, crushed

bsp Thai red curry paste

bsp grated fresh galangal or

 gingerroot

bsp tamarind paste

resh kaffir lime leaves

oz/225 g sweet potato

 cups coconut milk

oz/225 g cherry tomatoes, halved

bsp chopped cilantro

shly cooked jasmine or Thai

 fragrant rice, to serve

Heat the oil in a large,
preheated wok.

Using a sharp knife, thinly slice
the chicken. Add the chicken to
wok and stir-fry for 5 minutes.

Add the garlic, curry paste,
galangal, tamarind paste, and
leaves to the wok and stir-fry for
inute.

4 Using a sharp knife, peel and dice
the sweet potato.

5 Add the coconut milk and sweet
potato to the mixture in the wok
and bring to a boil. Let bubble over
medium heat for 20 minutes, or until
the juices begin to thicken and reduce.

6 Add the cherry tomatoes and
cilantro to the curry and cook for
an additional 5 minutes, stirring
occasionally. Transfer to serving plates
and serve hot with jasmine or Thai
fragrant rice.

green chicken curry

serves four

6 skinless, boneless chicken thighs

1¾ cups coconut milk

2 garlic cloves, crushed

2 tbsp Thai fish sauce

2 tbsp Thai green curry paste

12 baby eggplants

3 fresh green chilies, finely chopped

3 fresh kaffir lime leaves, shredded,
    plus extra to garnish (optional)

salt and pepper

4 tbsp chopped cilantro

freshly cooked rice, to serve

1 Cut the chicken into bite-size pieces. Pour the coconut milk into a preheated wok or large skillet over high heat and bring to a boil.

2 Add the chicken, garlic, and fish sauce to the wok and return to a boil. Reduce the heat and simmer gently for 30 minutes, or until the chicken is just tender.

3 Remove the chicken from the wok with a slotted spoon. Keep warm.

4 Stir the curry paste into the wok. Add the eggplants, chilies, and lime leaves and simmer for 5 minutes.

5 Return the chicken to the wok and bring to a boil. Season to taste with salt and pepper, then stir in the cilantro. Transfer to serving plates and garnish with lime leaves, if using. Serve immediately with freshly cooked rice.

COOK'S TIP

Baby eggplants, or "Asian eggplants" as they are also known, are traditionally used i this curry, but they are not always available. If you can't fi them in an Asian food store, u chopped ordinary eggplant, c substitute a few green peas.

chicken & mango stir-fry

6 skinless, boneless chicken thighs

1-inch/2.5-cm piece fresh
   gingerroot, grated

1 garlic clove, crushed

1 small fresh red chili, seeded
   and chopped

1 large red bell pepper, seeded

4 scallions

2 cups snow peas

3½ oz/100 g baby corn cobs

1 large firm ripe mango

2 tbsp corn oil

1 tbsp light soy sauce

3 tbsp rice wine or dry sherry

1 tsp sesame oil

salt and pepper

snipped fresh chives, to garnish

1 Cut the chicken into long, thin strips and place in a bowl. Mix the ginger, garlic, and chili together in a separate bowl, then stir into the chicken strips to coat them evenly.

2 Slice the bell pepper thinly, cutting diagonally. Diagonally slice the scallions. Cut the snow peas and baby corn cobs in half diagonally. Peel the mango, then remove the pit and slice the flesh thinly.

3 Heat the corn oil in a large skillet or preheated wok over high heat.

4 Add the chicken and stir-fry for 4–5 minutes, until just turning golden brown. Add the bell pepper and stir-fry over medium heat for 4–5 minutes, or until soft.

5 Add the scallions, snow peas, and baby corn cobs and stir-fry for an additional 1 minute.

6 Mix the soy sauce, rice wine, and sesame oil together in a small bowl and stir it into the skillet. Add the mango and stir gently for 1 minute to heat thoroughly. Season to taste with salt and pepper and serve immediately, garnished with snipped chives.

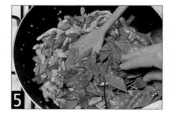

stir-fried chicken with thai basil

serves four

1 lb 5 oz/600 g skinless, boneless
   chicken breast fillets
2 tbsp vegetable oil
4 garlic cloves, crushed
4 scallions, finely chopped
4 fresh green chilies, seeded and
   finely chopped
1 green bell pepper, seeded and
   thinly sliced
generous ½ cup fresh Thai basil
   leaves, coarsely chopped
2 tbsp Thai fish sauce
fresh basil leaves, to garnish
freshly cooked rice, to serve

1 Using a sharp knife, cut the
chicken into thin strips.

2 Heat the oil in a preheated wok.
Add the garlic and scallions and
cook for 2 minutes. Add the chilies and
bell pepper and cook for an additional
2 minutes.

3 Add the chicken and cook until
browned. Stir in the basil and fish
sauce and stir-fry until the chicken is
cooked through. Garnish with basil
leaves and serve with rice.

COOK'S TIP
Thai basil is available in Asian
food stores. If you cannot find i
omit it from the recipe.

hicken with lemongrass & chili

serves four

fresh red chilies

tbsp vegetable oil

garlic cloves, thinly sliced

onion, thinly sliced

lemongrass stems, outer part
removed, very finely chopped

chicken thighs with bones
and skin

tbsp Thai fish sauce

tbsp brown sugar

cup chicken stock

COOK'S TIP

If the chicken mixture becomes
too dry during cooking, add a
little water.

1 Using a small knife, seed and
finely chop the chilies. Heat the
oil in a large skillet. Add the garlic
and onion and cook gently for
5–10 minutes, or until soft.

2 Add the lemongrass and chilies
and cook for 2 minutes. Add the
chicken and cook for 5 minutes, or
until browned all over.

3 Add the fish sauce, sugar, and
stock. Bring to a boil, then reduce
the heat and simmer, covered, for
30 minutes, or until the chicken is
cooked through. Serve immediately.

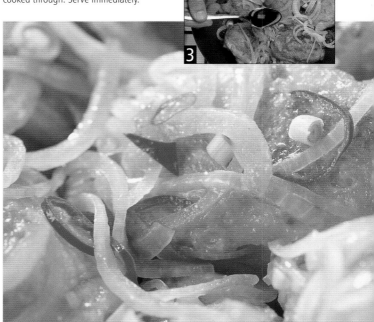

spiced cilantro chicken

4 skinless, boneless chicken breasts

2 garlic cloves

1 fresh green chili, seeded

¾-inch/2-cm piece fresh gingerroot

4 tbsp chopped cilantro

finely grated rind of 1 lime

3 tbsp lime juice

2 tbsp light soy sauce

1 tbsp superfine sugar

¼ cup coconut milk

TO GARNISH

finely chopped cilantro

cucumber slices

radish slices

½ fresh red chili, seeded and sliced
   into rings

freshly cooked rice, to serve

1 Using a sharp knife, cut 3 deep slashes into the skinned side of each chicken breast. Place the breasts in a single layer in a nonmetallic dish.

2 Place the garlic, chili, ginger, cilantro, lime rind and juice, soy sauce, sugar, and coconut milk in a food processor and process to a smooth paste.

3 Spread the paste over both sides of the chicken breasts, coating them evenly. Cover with plastic wrap and let marinate in the refrigerator for 1 hour.

4 Preheat the broiler to medium the chicken from the marinade then drain off the excess and place a broiler pan. Cook under the hot broiler for 12–15 minutes, or until thoroughly and evenly cooked.

5 Meanwhile, place the remaini marinade in a pan and bring t boil. Reduce the heat and simmer fe several minutes. Transfer the chicke breasts to serving plates. Garnish w chopped cilantro, cucumber slices, radish slices, and chili rings and ser with rice.

quick green chicken curry

serves four

6 scallions

1 tbsp vegetable oil

1 lb 5oz/600 g skinless, boneless
   chicken breast, cut into cubes

generous ¾ cup coconut cream

3 tbsp Thai green curry paste

3 tbsp chopped cilantro

freshly cooked noodles, to serve

COOK'S TIP

Store scallions in the salad
compartment of the refrigerator.
They will keep for up to 3 days.

1 Using a small knife, slice the
scallions. Heat the oil in a large
skillet. Add the scallions and the
chicken and cook, stirring constantly,
for 3–4 minutes, or until the chicken
is browned.

2 Stir in the coconut cream and
curry paste and cook for an
additional 5 minutes, or until the
chicken is cooked through. Add a little
water or stock if the sauce becomes
too thick.

3 Stir in the chopped cilantro
and serve immediately with
freshly cooked noodles.

braised chicken with garlic & spices

serves four

4 garlic cloves, chopped

4 shallots, chopped

2 small fresh red chilies, seeded and
   chopped

1 lemongrass stem, finely chopped

1 tbsp chopped cilantro

1 tsp shrimp paste

½ tsp ground cinnamon

1 tbsp tamarind paste

2 tbsp vegetable oil

8 small chicken joints, such as
   drumsticks or thighs

1¼ cups chicken stock

1 tbsp Thai fish sauce

1 tbsp smooth peanut butter

salt and pepper

4 tbsp toasted peanuts, chopped

TO SERVE

stir-fried vegetables

freshly cooked noodles

1 Place the garlic, shallots, chilies,
lemongrass, cilantro, and shrimp
paste in a mortar and, using a pestle,
grind to an almost smooth paste. Add
the cinnamon and tamarind paste to
the mixture.

2 Heat the oil in a wide skillet or
preheated wok. Add the chicken
joints, turning frequently, until golden
brown on all sides. Remove the
chicken from the skillet and keep hot.
Tip away any excess fat.

3 Add the spice paste to the skillet
and stir over medium heat until
lightly browned. Stir in the stock, then
return the chicken joints to the skillet.

4 Bring to a boil, then cover tight
and reduce the heat. Let simm
for 25–30 minutes, stirring
occasionally, until the chicken is ter
and thoroughly cooked. Stir in the f
sauce and peanut butter and simm
for an additional 10 minutes.

5 Season to taste with salt and
pepper and sprinkle the toaste
peanuts over the chicken. Serve ho
with stir-fried vegetables and nood

peanut-crusted chicken

serves six

2 garlic cloves, crushed

1-inch/2.5-cm piece fresh
gingerroot, finely grated

1 lemongrass stem, outer leaves
removed, finely chopped

2 tbsp chopped cilantro leaves

scant 1¼ cups salted peanuts

¾ cup all-purpose flour

2 eggs

4 tbsp milk

12 chicken drumsticks, skin removed

vegetable oil, for oiling

DIPPING SAUCE

1 fresh red chili, seeded and
finely chopped

2 garlic cloves, crushed

½ cup white wine vinegar

2 tbsp brown sugar

1 Preheat the oven to 425°F/220°C. Place the garlic, ginger, lemongrass, cilantro leaves, peanuts, and 2 tablespoons of the flour in a food processor and process until finely ground. Transfer to a shallow dish.

2 Beat the eggs and milk together in a bowl. Spread the remaining flour on a plate. Dip the drumsticks into the flour, then into the egg mixture, and finally into the peanut mixture. Arrange them in an oiled roasting pan.

3 Bake in the preheated oven for 15 minutes, then turn them and cook for an additional 15 minutes. Pour off any excess oil and cook the drumsticks for 5 minutes, or until crisp.

4 To make the sauce, place the ● and garlic in a mortar and, us● a pestle, grind to a paste. Place the● vinegar and sugar in a pan and hea● gently until the sugar dissolves. Bri● to a boil and simmer for 2 minutes ● in the chili-garlic paste. Transfer to ● bowl. Drain the drumsticks on pap● towels and serve with the sauce.

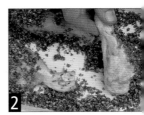

uck breasts with chili & lime

serves four

ooneless duck breasts

garlic cloves, crushed

sp brown sugar

bsp lime juice

bsp soy sauce

sp chili sauce

sp vegetable oil

bsp plum jelly

:up chicken stock

t and pepper

SERVE

;hly cooked rice

p salad greens

1 Using a small, sharp knife, cut deep slashes in the skin of the duck to make a diamond pattern. Place the duck breasts in a wide, nonmetallic dish.

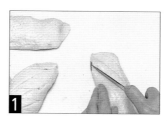

2 Mix the garlic, sugar, lime juice, soy sauce, and chili sauce together in a bowl, then spoon over the duck breasts, turning well to coat evenly. Cover and let marinate in the refrigerator for at least 3 hours or overnight.

3 Drain the duck, reserving the marinade. Heat a large, heavy-bottom skillet until very hot and brush with the oil. Add the duck breasts, skin-side down, and cook for 5 minutes, or until the skin is browned and crisp. Tip away the excess fat. Turn the duck breasts over.

4 Continue cooking on the other side for 2–3 minutes to brown. Add the reserved marinade, plum jelly, and stock and simmer for 2 minutes. Season to taste with salt and pepper. Transfer to individual serving plates, then spoon over the pan juices and serve hot with freshly cooked rice and crisp salad greens.

roasted duckling with pineapple & coconu

serves four

3 lb 8 oz/1.6 kg duckling

salt and pepper

2 tbsp peanut oil

1 small pineapple

1 large onion, chopped

1 garlic clove, finely chopped

1 tsp finely chopped fresh
    gingerroot

½ tsp ground coriander

1 tbsp Thai green curry paste

1 tsp brown sugar

1¾ cup coconut milk

cilantro, chopped

fresh red and green chili flowers,
    to garnish (see page 416)

freshly cooked jasmine rice, to serve

1 Preheat the broiler to medium. Using a large knife or poultry shears, cut the duckling in half lengthwise, cutting through the line of the breastbone. Wipe inside and out with paper towels. Sprinkle with salt and pepper to taste, then prick the skin with a fork and brush with oil.

2 Place the duckling, cut-side down, on a broiler pan and cook under the broiler for 25–30 minutes, turning occasionally, until golden brown. Tip away any fat that builds up in the broiler pan, as it may burn.

3 Let the duck cool, then cut ea half into 2 portions. Peel and the pineapple, then cut the flesh in dice shapes. Reserve.

4 Heat the remaining oil in a la skillet. Add the onion and gar and cook for 3–4 minutes, or until softened. Stir in the ginger, coriand curry paste, and sugar and stir-fry 1 minute.

5 Stir in the coconut milk and b to a boil. Add the duckling portions and the pineapple. Reduc heat and simmer for 5 minutes. Sprinkle with cilantro and garnish red and green chili flowers. Serve freshly cooked jasmine rice.

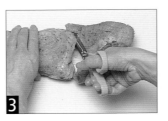

Rice & Noodles

With its monsoon climate and abundant rainfall, Thailand has the ideal conditions for rice growing and has become one of the major rice producers in the world. It is thought that rice grew there as far back as 3500 B.C., so it's not surprising that rice is the staple food of Thailand.

Two main varieties of rice are used in Thai cooking—long-grain and short-grain. The long-grain is Thai fragrant rice, a good quality, white, fluffy rice with delicately scented, separate grains. Glutinous or "sticky" rice is a short-grain rice with a high starch content that causes the grains to stick together.

Noodles also play a vital part in Thai meals, and street vendors serve them as a snack at all times of the day. Rice noodles in flat ribbons (sticks) or thin vermicelli are the most common. Cellophane (mung bean) noodles are also locally made, but egg noodles are often imported from China.

crispy rice noodles

serves four

vegetable oil, for deep-frying,
    plus 1½ tbsp
7 oz/200 g rice vermicelli noodles
1 onion, finely chopped
4 garlic cloves, finely chopped
1 skinless, boneless chicken breast,
    finely chopped
2 fresh red Thai chilies,
    seeded and sliced
4 tbsp dried shiitake mushrooms,
    soaked and thinly sliced
3 tbsp dried shrimp
4 scallions, sliced
3 tbsp lime juice
2 tbsp soy sauce
2 tbsp Thai fish sauce
2 tbsp rice vinegar or white
    wine vinegar
2 tbsp brown sugar
2 eggs, beaten
3 tbsp chopped cilantro
scallion curls, to garnish
    (see page 468)

1 Heat the oil for deep-frying in a large skillet or preheated wok until very hot. Add the rice noodles and deep-fry quickly, occasionally turning them, until puffed up, crisp, and pale golden brown. Lift on to paper towels and drain well.

2 Heat 1 tablespoon of the remaining oil in a separate skillet. Add the onion and garlic and cook for 1 minute. Add the chicken and stir-fry for 3 minutes. Finally, add the chilies, mushrooms, dried shrimp, and scallions.

3 Mix the lime juice, soy sauce, fish sauce, rice vinegar, and sugar together in a bowl, then stir into the skillet and cook for an additional 1 minute. Remove the skillet from the heat.

4 Heat the remaining oil in a wide skillet. Pour in the eggs to coat the bottom of the skillet evenly, making a thin omelet. Cook until set and golden, then turn it over and cook the other side. Turn out and roll up, then slice into long ribbon strips.

5 Toss the fried noodles, stir-fried ingredients, cilantro, and omelet strips together. Garnish with scallion curls and serve.

rice noodles with mushrooms & tofu

serves four

8 oz/225 g rice stick noodles

2 tbsp vegetable oil

1 garlic clove, finely chopped

¾-inch/2-cm piece fresh gingerroot, finely chopped

4 shallots, thinly sliced

1¼ cups sliced shiitake mushrooms

3½ oz/100 g firm tofu (drained weight), cut into ⅝-inch/ 1.5-cm dice shapes

2 tbsp light soy sauce

1 tbsp rice wine or dry sherry

1 tbsp Thai fish sauce

1 tbsp smooth peanut butter

1 tsp chili sauce

2 tbsp toasted peanuts, chopped

shredded fresh basil leaves

1 Place the rice noodles in a bowl, then cover with hot water and let soak for 15 minutes, or according to the package directions. Drain well.

2 Heat the oil in a large skillet. Add the garlic, ginger, and shallots and stir-fry for 1–2 minutes, or until softened and lightly browned.

3 Add the mushrooms and stir-fry for an additional 2–3 minutes. Stir in the tofu and toss gently to brown lightly.

4 Mix the soy sauce, rice wine, fi sauce, peanut butter, and chili sauce together in a small bowl, the stir into the skillet.

5 Stir in the rice noodles and tos coat evenly in the sauce. Sprir with peanuts and shredded basil leaves and serve hot.

VARIATION

For an easy pantry dish, repla the shiitake mushrooms with canned Chinese straw mushrooms. Alternatively, us dried shiitake mushrooms, soaked and drained before us

oodles with shrimp & green bell peppers

serves four

oz/250 g rice noodles

tbsp vegetable oil

garlic cloves, crushed

fresh red chili, seeded and
  thinly sliced

green bell pepper, seeded and
  thinly sliced

scallions, coarsely chopped

tsp cornstarch

tbsp oyster sauce

tbsp Thai fish sauce

tsp sugar

cup chicken stock

oz/250 g small cooked
  shrimp, shelled

Prepare the noodles according to
the package directions. Drain, then
e under cold water and drain again.

2 Heat the oil in a preheated wok.
Add the garlic, chili, bell pepper,
and scallions. Cook for 1 minute, then
transfer to a plate and reserve.

3 Blend the cornstarch with a little
water and add to the wok with
the oyster sauce, fish sauce, sugar, and
stock. Stir over medium heat until the
mixture boils and thickens.

4 Return the bell pepper and
scallion mixture to the wok with
the shrimp and noodles. Cook, stirring,
for 2 minutes, or until heated through.
Transfer to a heated serving bowl and
serve immediately.

sesame noodles with shrimp & cilantro

serves four

1 garlic clove, chopped

1 scallion, chopped

1 small fresh red chili, seeded
   and sliced

handful of cilantro

10½ oz/300 g dried fine egg noodles

2 tbsp vegetable oil

2 tsp sesame oil

1 tsp shrimp paste

8 oz/225 g raw shrimp, shelled

2 tbsp lime juice

2 tbsp Thai fish sauce

1 tsp sesame seeds, toasted

COOK'S TIP

The roots of cilantro are widely used in Thai cooking, so if you can buy cilantro with the root attached, the whole plant can be used in this dish for maximum flavor. If not, just use the stems and leaves.

1 Place the garlic, onion, chili, and cilantro in a mortar and, using a pestle, grind to a smooth paste.

2 Drop the noodles into a pan of boiling water and return to a boil, then simmer for 4 minutes, or according to the package directions.

3 Meanwhile, heat the oils in a large skillet or preheated wok. Stir in the shrimp paste and ground cilantro mixture and stir over medium heat for 1 minute.

4 Stir in the shrimp and stir-fry for 2 minutes. Stir in the lime juice and fish sauce and cook for an additional 1 minute.

5 Drain the noodles and toss them into the skillet. Sprinkle with the toasted sesame seeds and serve immediately.

hot & sour noodle salad

serves four

12 oz/350 g rice vermicelli noodles

4 tbsp sesame oil

3 tbsp soy sauce

juice of 2 limes

1 tsp sugar

4 scallions, finely sliced

1–2 tsp hot chili sauce

2 tbsp chopped cilantro

1 Prepare the noodles according to the package directions. Drain, then toss with half the oil.

2 Mix the remaining oil, soy sauce, lime juice, sugar, scallions, and chili sauce together in a bowl. Stir into the noodles.

3 Stir in the chopped cilantro and serve immediately.

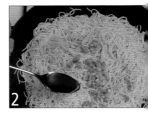

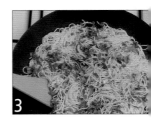

·ied egg noodles

serves four

)z/250 g dried fine egg noodles

tbsp vegetable oil

garlic cloves, crushed

tbsp Thai fish sauce

tbsp lime juice

sp sugar

eggs, lightly beaten

)z/115 g cooked, shelled shrimp

cup fresh bean sprouts

scallions, finely sliced

◦ GARNISH

tbsp finely chopped

roasted peanuts

ndful of cilantro leaves

e slices

Prepare the noodles according to
the package directions. Drain,
rinse and drain again. Reserve.

Heat the oil in a preheated wok.
Add the garlic and cook, stirring,
minute, or until lightly browned
not burned. Stir in the fish sauce,
juice, and sugar and stir until the
r has dissolved.

3 Quickly stir in the eggs and cook
for a few seconds. Stir in the
noodles to coat with the garlic and
eggs. Add the shrimp, bean sprouts,
and half the scallions.

4 When everything is heated
through, transfer the mixture to a
warmed serving dish. Sprinkle the
remaining scallions on top and serve,
garnished with peanuts, cilantro
leaves, and lime slices.

rice noodles with chicken & napa cabbage

serves four

7 oz/200 g rice stick noodles

1 tbsp corn oil

1 garlic clove, finely chopped

¾-inch/2-cm piece fresh gingerroot, finely chopped

4 scallions, chopped

1 fresh red Thai chili, seeded and sliced

10½ oz/300 g skinless, boneless chicken, finely chopped

2 chicken livers, finely chopped

1 celery stalk, thinly sliced

1 carrot, cut into fine short sticks

10½ oz/300 g shredded Napa cabbage

4 tbsp lime juice

2 tbsp Thai fish sauce

1 tbsp soy sauce

2 tbsp shredded fresh mint

slices of pickled garlic

fresh mint sprigs, to garnish

1 Place the rice noodles in a bowl. Cover with hot water and let soak for 15 minutes, or according to the package directions. Drain well.

2 Heat the oil in a large skillet or preheated wok. Add the garlic, ginger, scallions, and chili and stir-fry for 1 minute. Stir in the chicken and chicken livers and stir-fry over high heat for 2–3 minutes, or until beginning to brown.

3 Stir in the celery and carrot and stir-fry for 2 minutes to soften. Add the Napa cabbage, then stir in the lime juice, fish sauce, and soy sauce.

4 Add the noodles and stir to heat thoroughly. Sprinkle with shredded mint and pickled garlic. Serve immediately, garnished with mint sprigs.

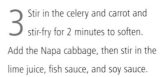

ot & sour noodles

serves four

oz/250 g dried medium
egg noodles
tbsp sesame oil
tbsp chili oil
garlic clove, crushed
scallions, finely chopped
cup sliced white mushrooms
oz/40 g dried shiitake
mushrooms, soaked, drained,
and sliced
bsp lime juice
bsp light soy sauce
sp sugar
SERVE
edded Napa cabbage
bsp shredded cilantro
bsp toasted peanuts,
chopped

1 Cook the noodles in a large pan of boiling water for 3–4 minutes, or according to the package directions. Drain well and return to the pan, then toss with the sesame oil and reserve.

2 Heat the chili oil in a large skillet or preheated wok. Add the garlic, scallions, and white mushrooms and quickly stir-fry to soften them.

COOK'S TIP
Thai chili oil is very hot, so if you want a milder flavor, use vegetable oil for the initial cooking instead, then add a final dribble of chili oil just for seasoning.

3 Add the shiitake mushrooms, lime juice, soy sauce, and sugar and continue stir-frying until boiling. Add the noodles and toss to mix.

4 Arrange the noodles on a bed of Napa cabbage. Sprinkle with cilantro and peanuts and serve.

drunken noodles

serves four

6 oz/175 g rice stick noodles

2 tbsp vegetable oil

1 garlic clove, crushed

2 small fresh green chilies, chopped

1 small onion, thinly sliced

scant 1½ cups ground lean pork
   or chicken

1 small green bell pepper, seeded
   and finely chopped

4 fresh kaffir lime leaves,
   finely shredded

1 tbsp dark soy sauce

1 tbsp light soy sauce

½ tsp sugar

1 tomato, cut into thin wedges

2 tbsp finely sliced fresh
   basil leaves

1 Place the rice noodles in a bowl. Cover with hot water and let soak for 15 minutes, or according to the package directions. Drain well.

2 Heat the oil in a large skillet or preheated wok. Add the garlic, chilies, and onion and stir-fry for 1 minute.

3 Stir in the pork and stir-fry over high heat for an additional 1 minute, then add the bell pepper continue stir-frying for an additiona 2 minutes.

4 Stir in the lime leaves, soy sauc and sugar. Add the noodles an tomato and toss well to heat thoroug Sprinkle with the basil and serve hot.

ad thai noodles

serves four

z/250 g rice stick noodles

sp peanut oil

arlic cloves, finely chopped

oz/125 g pork fillet, chopped

nto ¼-inch/5-mm pieces

z/200 g cooked, shelled shrimp

sp sugar

sp Thai fish sauce

sp tomato ketchup

sp lime juice

ggs, beaten

erous ¾ cup fresh bean sprouts

GARNISH

p dried red chili flakes

allions, thickly sliced

sp chopped cilantro

1 Place the rice noodles in a bowl. Cover with hot water and let soak for 15 minutes, or according to the package directions. Drain well and reserve until required.

2 Heat the oil in a large skillet. Add the garlic and cook over high heat for 30 seconds. Add the pork and stir-fry for 2–3 minutes, or until browned.

3 Stir in the shrimp, then add the sugar, fish sauce, ketchup, and lime juice and continue stir-frying for an additional 30 seconds.

4 Stir in the eggs and stir-fry until lightly set. Stir in the reserved noodles, then add the bean sprouts and stir-fry for an additional 30 seconds.

5 Transfer to a serving dish, sprinkle with chili flakes, scallions, and cilantro, and serve.

thai-style noodle röstis

serves four

4½ oz/125 g rice vermicelli noodles

2 scallions, finely shredded

1 lemongrass stem, finely shredded

3 tbsp finely shredded fresh coconut

vegetable oil, for frying and brushing

TO FINISH

scant ¾ cup fresh bean sprouts

1 small red onion, thinly sliced

1 avocado, thinly sliced

2 tbsp lime juice

2 tbsp rice wine or dry sherry

1 tsp chili sauce

whole fresh red chilies, to garnish

1 Break the rice noodles into short pieces and place in a bowl. Cover with hot water and let soak for 4 minutes, or according to the package directions. Drain thoroughly and pat dry with paper towels. Stir the noodles, scallions, lemongrass, and coconut together.

2 Heat a small amount of oil un very hot in a heavy-bottom sk Brush a 3½-inch/9-cm round cooki cutter with oil and place in the skil Spoon a small amount of noodle mixture into the cutter to just cove bottom of the skillet, then press do with the back of a spoon.

3 Cook for 30 seconds, then car remove the cutter and continu cooking the rösti until golden brov turning it over once. Remove and on paper towels. Repeat with the remaining noodles, to make 12 rös

4 To finish, arrange the noodle röstis in small stacks, with be sprouts, onion, and avocado betw the layers. Mix the lime juice, rice wine, and chili sauce together and spoon over just before serving, garnished with whole red chilies.

rice noodles with spinach

serves four

4 oz/115 g thin rice stick noodles

2 tbsp dried shrimp (optional)

9 oz/250 g fresh young spinach
leaves

1 tbsp peanut oil

2 garlic cloves, finely chopped

2 tsp Thai green curry paste

1 tsp sugar

1 tbsp light soy sauce

COOK'S TIP

It is best to choose young
spinach leaves for this dish
because they are beautifully
tender and cook within a matter
of seconds. If you can only get
older spinach, however, shred
the leaves before adding to the
dish so they cook more quickly.

1 Place the noodles in a bowl, then cover with hot water and let soak for 15 minutes, or according to the package directions. Drain well.

2 Place the shrimp, if using, in a bowl, then cover with hot water and let soak for 10 minutes. Drain well. Wash the spinach thoroughly, then drain well and remove any tough stems.

3 Heat the oil in a large skillet or preheated wok. Add the garlic and stir-fry for 1 minute. Stir in the curry paste and stir-fry for 30 seconds. Stir in the soaked shrimp, if using, and stir-fry for 30 seconds.

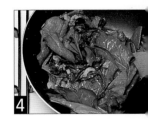

4 Add the spinach and stir-fry for 1–2 minutes, or until the leaves are just wilted.

5 Stir in the sugar and soy sauce, then add the noodles and toss thoroughly to mix evenly. Serve immediately while hot.

crispy duck with noodles & tamarind

serves four

3 duck breasts, about 14 oz/400 g
   in total

2 garlic cloves, crushed

1½ tsp chili paste

1 tbsp clear honey

3 tbsp dark soy sauce

½ tsp Chinese five-spice powder

9 oz/250 g rice stick noodles

1 tsp vegetable oil

1 tsp sesame oil

2 scallions, sliced

1 cup snow peas

2 tbsp tamarind juice

sesame seeds, for sprinkling

1 Prick the duck breast skin all over with a fork and place in a deep dish.

2 Mix the garlic, chili paste, honey, soy sauce, and five-spice powder together, then pour over the duck. Turn the breasts over to coat evenly, then cover and let marinate in the refrigerator for at least 1 hour.

3 Meanwhile, place the rice noodles in a bowl. Cover with hot water and let soak for 15 minutes. Drain well.

4 Preheat the broiler to high. Drain the duck breasts from the marinade, reserving it, and place on a broiler rack. Cook under the preheated broiler for 10 minutes, turning the duck breasts over occasionally, until golden brown. Remove and slice the duck breasts thinly.

5 Heat the oils in a skillet. Add th scallions and snow peas and t for 2 minutes. Stir in the reserved marinade and tamarind juice and br to a boil.

6 Add the sliced duck and noodl and toss to heat thoroughly. Serve immediately, sprinkled with sesame seeds.

spicy fried rice

serves four

1¼ cups long-grain rice

¼ oz/10 g dried mushrooms

2 tbsp vegetable oil

2 eggs, lightly beaten

2 garlic cloves, finely chopped

1 fresh red chili, seeded and
   finely chopped

½-inch/1-cm piece fresh gingerroot,
   finely grated

2 tbsp soy sauce

1 tsp sugar

2 tsp Thai fish sauce

6 scallions, finely chopped

1 lb/450 g cooked, shelled
   small shrimp

14 oz/400 g canned baby corn
   cobs, drained and cut in half

3 tbsp chopped cilantro

1 Place the rice in a strainer and rinse under cold running water. Drain thoroughly. Add the rice to a large pan of boiling salted water, then return to a boil and cook for 10 minutes, or until tender. Drain, then rinse and drain again.

2 Place the mushrooms in a bowl, then cover with warm water and let stand for 20 minutes. Drain and cut into slices.

3 Heat half the oil in a preheated wok. Add the eggs. Stir the uncooked egg to the outside edge of the wok. Cook until firm. Remove the omelet, then roll up and cut into strips.

COOK'S TIP

It is important to rinse the rice under cold running water, because this removes the excess starch. If you have time, wash the rice in several changes of water until the water is clear. Drain well.

4 Heat the remaining oil in the w Add the garlic, chili, and ginge and cook for 1 minute. Add the soy sauce, sugar, fish sauce, and scallio stirring to dissolve the sugar. Stir in reserved rice, shrimp, and corn cob tossing to mix. Cook for 3–4 minut or until the rice is heated through. in the cilantro, then turn into a war serving bowl and serve.

jasmine rice with lemon & basil

serves four

scant 2 cups jasmine rice

3¼ cups water

finely grated rind of ½ lemon

2 tbsp shredded fresh basil

COOK'S TIP

It is important to leave the pan
tightly covered while the rice
cooks and steams inside, so the
grains cook evenly and become
fluffy and separate.

1 Wash the rice in several changes of cold water until the water runs clear. Bring 3¼ cups of water to a boil in a large pan, then add the rice.

2 Return to a rolling boil. Turn the heat to a low simmer, then cover the pan and simmer for an additional 12 minutes.

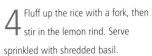

3 Remove the pan from the heat and let stand, covered, for 10 minutes.

4 Fluff up the rice with a fork, then stir in the lemon rind. Serve sprinkled with shredded basil.

gg noodle salad with lime & basil dressing

serves four

oz/225 g dried egg noodles

tsp sesame oil

carrot

cant ⅔ cup fresh bean sprouts

cucumber

scallions, finely shredded

½ oz/150 g cooked turkey breast
  meat, shredded into thin slivers

hopped peanuts, for sprinkling

esh basil leaves, to garnish

RESSING

tbsp coconut milk

tbsp lime juice

tbsp light soy sauce

tsp Thai fish sauce

tsp chili oil

tsp sugar

tbsp chopped cilantro

tbsp chopped fresh basil

Cook the noodles in boiling water
for 4 minutes, or according to the
kage directions. Plunge them into a
vl of cold water to cool, then drain
toss in the sesame oil.

2 Use a vegetable peeler to shave off thin ribbons from the carrot. Blanch the ribbons and bean sprouts in boiling water for 30 seconds, then plunge into cold water for 30 seconds. Drain well. Shave thin ribbons of cucumber with the vegetable peeler.

3 Toss the carrot, bean sprouts, cucumber, and scallions together with the turkey and noodles.

4 Place all the dressing ingredients in a screw-top jar and shake well to mix evenly.

5 Add the dressing to the noodle mixture and toss. Pile on to a serving dish. Sprinkle with peanuts and garnish with basil leaves. Serve cold.

413

coconut rice with pineapple

serves four

1 cup long-grain rice

generous 2 cups coconut milk

2 lemongrass stems

generous ¾ cup water

2 slices fresh pineapple, peeled
and diced

2 tbsp toasted coconut

chili sauce, to serve

VARIATION

A sweet version of this dish
can be made by simply omitting
the lemongrass and stirring
in palm sugar or superfine
sugar to taste during cooking.
Serve as a dessert, with extra
pineapple slices.

---

1 Wash the rice in several changes
of cold water until the water runs
clear. Place in a large pan with the
coconut milk.

2 Place the lemongrass on a
counter and bruise it by hitting
firmly with a rolling pin or mallet.
Add to the pan with the rice and
coconut milk.

3 Add the water and bring to a
boil. Reduce the heat, then cover
the pan tightly and simmer gently for
15 minutes. Remove the pan from the
heat and fluff up the rice with a fork.

4 Remove the lemongrass and stir
in the pineapple. Sprinkle with
toasted coconut and serve immediately
with chili sauce.

stir-fried rice with egg strips

serves four

2 tbsp peanut oil

1 egg, beaten with 1 tsp water

1 garlic clove, finely chopped

1 small onion, finely chopped

1 tbsp Thai red curry paste

1¼ cups long-grain rice, cooked

½ cup cooked peas

1 tbsp Thai fish sauce

2 tbsp tomato ketchup

2 tbsp chopped cilantro

TO GARNISH

fresh red chili flowers

cucumber slices

COOK'S TIP

Many Thai rice dishes are made from leftover rice that has been cooked for an earlier meal. Nothing goes to waste and it's often stir-fried with a few simple ingredients and aromatic flavorings, as in this recipe. If you have any leftover vegetables or meat, this is a good way to use them up.

1 To make chili flowers for the garnish, hold the stem of a fresh red chili with your fingertips and use a small, sharp, pointed knife to cut a slit down the length from near the stem end to the tip. Turn the chili about a quarter turn and make another cut. Repeat to make a total of 4 cuts, then scrape out the seeds. Cut each "petal" again in half, or into fourths, to make 8–16 petals. Place the chili flower in ice water.

2 Heat 1 teaspoon of the oil in a preheated wok or large skillet. Pour in the egg mixture, swirling it to coat the wok evenly and make a thin layer. When set and golden, remove the egg from the wok and roll up. Reserve until required.

3 Add the remaining oil to the w Add the garlic and onion and fry for 1 minute. Add the curry past then stir in the rice and peas.

4 Stir in the fish sauce, ketchup, and cilantro. Remove the wok from the heat and pile the rice on to a serving dish. Slice the egg roll int spiral strips, without unrolling, and to garnish the rice. Add the cucumb slices and chili flowers. Serve hot.

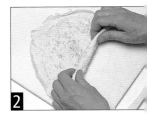

rice with seafood

serves four

12 live mussels in shells

8 cups fish stock

2 tbsp vegetable oil

1 garlic clove, crushed

1 tsp grated fresh gingerroot

1 fresh red Thai chili, chopped

2 scallions, chopped

generous 1 cup long-grain rice

2 small squid, cleaned and sliced

3½ oz/100 g firm white fish fillet,
    such as halibut or angler fish,
    cut into chunks

3½ oz/100 g raw shrimp, shelled

2 tbsp Thai fish sauce

3 tbsp shredded cilantro,
    for sprinkling

1 Clean the mussels thoroughly by scrubbing or scraping the shells and pulling out any beards that are attached to them. Discard any mussels with broken shells or any that refuse to close when firmly tapped. Heat 4 tablespoons of the stock in a large pan. Add the mussels and cook, covered, over a high heat for 3–4 minutes, shaking the pan occasionally, until the mussels have opened. Remove the pan from the heat and discard any mussels that remain closed.

2 Heat the oil in a large skillet or preheated wok. Add the garlic, ginger, chili, and scallions and stir-fry for 30 seconds. Add the remaining stock and bring to a boil.

3 Stir in the rice, then add the squid, white fish, and shrimp. Reduce the heat and simmer gently for 15 minutes, or until the rice is cooked. Add the fish sauce and mussels.

4 Ladle into wide bowls and sprinkle with shredded cilantro before serving.

VARIATION

You could use leftover cooked rice for this dish. Just simmer the seafood gently until cooked, then stir in the rice at the end.

Vegetables & Salads

Many of the vegetables, salad greens, and shoots that Thais use in cooking are native, often growing wild locally. This makes it difficult to produce authentic Thai salads at home.

You may have to substitute a few fresh ingredients with canned ones, but luckily you can now buy a good selection of cultivated Asian vegetables, such as bok choy and Napa cabbage.

A Thai salad can make a stunning centerpiece for any dinner table. Thai cooks usually add strips of finely chopped cooked meat, fish, or shellfish to their salads, or for vegetarian dishes, mushrooms or tofu are added.

Dressings are typically piquant and spicy, with the skillful balance of bitter, salt, sour, hot, and sweet tastes. To finish, a sprinkling of peanuts or dried chilies, chopped cilantro, and a final flourish of chili flowers add color.

crisp pickled vegetables

serves six–eight

½ small cauliflower

½ cucumber

2 carrots

generous 1½ cups green beans

½ small Napa cabbage

generous 2 cups rice vinegar or
   white wine vinegar

1 tbsp superfine sugar

1 tsp salt

3 garlic cloves

3 shallots

3 fresh red Thai chilies, seeded

5 tbsp peanut oil

1 Trim the cauliflower. Peel and seed the cucumber. Peel the carrots. Trim the beans. Trim the cabbage, then cut all the vegetables into bite-size pieces.

2 Place the rice vinegar, sugar, and salt in a large, heavy-bottom pan and bring almost to a boil. Add the vegetables, then reduce the heat and simmer for 3–4 minutes, or until they are just tender but still crisp inside. Remove the pan from the heat and let the vegetables and vinegar cool.

3 Place the garlic, shallots, and chilies in a mortar and, using a pestle, grind to a smooth paste.

4 Heat the oil in a skillet. Add the spice paste and stir-fry gently f 1–2 minutes. Add the vegetables w the vinegar and cook for an additior 2 minutes to reduce the liquid sligh Remove the skillet from the heat an let cool.

5 Serve the pickles cold, or pack into jars and store in the refrigerator for up to 2 weeks.

COOK'S TIP

To make simple carrot flowers, peel the carrot thinly as usual, then use a stripper or small sharp knife to cut narrow "channels" down the length of it at regular intervals. Slice the carrot as usual, and the slices will resemble flowers.

tir-fried green vegetables

serves four

enerous 1 cup snow peas

tbsp vegetable oil

garlic cloves, thinly sliced

-inch/2.5-cm piece fresh
  gingerroot, thinly sliced

oz/175 g fresh young spinach
  leaves, washed and drained

oz/175 g broccoli, cut into
  small florets

cup green beans, halved

epper

tbsp Thai fish sauce

tbsp oyster sauce

tsp sugar

scallions, diagonally chopped

1 Cut the snow peas in half. Heat the oil in a preheated wok. Add the garlic and ginger and cook for 1 minute. Add the spinach, broccoli, and beans and cook for 2 minutes.

2 Add the snow peas to the wok and stir-fry over high heat for 2 minutes.

3 Add pepper to taste, fish sauce, oyster sauce, sugar, and scallions and stir-fry for an additional 2 minutes.

4 Transfer to a warmed serving plate and serve.

spiced cashew nut curry

serves four

1⅔ cups unsalted cashew nuts

1 tsp coriander seeds

1 tsp cumin seeds

2 cardamom pods, crushed

1 tbsp corn oil

1 onion, finely sliced

1 garlic clove, crushed

1 small fresh green chili, seeded
  and chopped

1 cinnamon stick

½ tsp ground turmeric

4 tbsp coconut cream

1¼ cups hot vegetable stock

3 dried kaffir lime leaves,
  crumbled

cilantro leaves, to garnish

freshly cooked jasmine rice, to serve

1 Place the cashew nuts in a bowl, then cover with cold water and let soak overnight. Drain thoroughly. Crush the seeds and cardamom pods in a mortar using a pestle.

2 Heat the oil in a large skillet. Add the onion and garlic and stir-fry for 2–3 minutes to soften but not brown. Add the chili, crushed spices, cinnamon stick, and turmeric and stir-fry for an additional 1 minute.

3 Add the coconut cream and the hot stock to the skillet. Bring to boil, then add the cashew nuts and lime leaves.

4 Cover the skillet, then reduce the heat and simmer for 20 minutes. Serve hot with jasmine rice garnished with cilantro leaves.

COOK'S TIP

All spices give the best flavor when freshly crushed, but if you prefer, you can use ready-ground spices instead of crushing them yourself in a mortar.

ﾏixed vegetables in peanut sauce

serves four

carrots

small cauliflower, trimmed

small heads green bok choy

cup green beans

tbsp vegetable oil

garlic clove, finely chopped

scallions, sliced

tsp chili paste

tbsp soy sauce

tbsp rice wine or dry sherry

tbsp smooth peanut butter

tbsp coconut milk

ﾟ GARNISH

whole fresh red chili

ﾟallion curls (see page 468)

COOK'S TIP

It's important to cut the ﾟvegetables thinly into even-size pieces so they cook quickly and ﾟvenly. Prepare all the vegetables before you begin to cook.

Cut the carrots diagonally into thin slices. Cut the cauliflower ﾟ small florets, then slice the stem ﾟly. Thickly slice the bok choy. Cut beans into 1¼-inch/3-cm lengths.

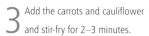

2 Heat the oil in a large skillet or preheated wok. Add the garlic and scallions and stir-fry for 1 minute. Stir in the chili paste and cook for a few seconds.

3 Add the carrots and cauliflower and stir-fry for 2–3 minutes.

4 Add the bok choy and beans and stir-fry for an additional 2 minutes. Stir in the soy sauce and rice wine.

5 Mix the peanut butter with the coconut milk and stir into the skillet, then cook, stirring, for an additional 1 minute. Transfer to a serving dish and garnish with a red chili and scallion curls. Serve hot.

stir-fried ginger mushrooms

serves four

2 tbsp vegetable oil

3 garlic cloves, crushed

1 tbsp Thai red curry paste

½ tsp ground turmeric

15 oz/425 g canned straw
mushrooms, drained and halved

¾-inch/2-cm piece fresh gingerroot,
finely shredded

scant ½ cup coconut milk

1½ oz/40 g dried shiitake
mushrooms, soaked, drained,
and sliced

1 tbsp lemon juice

1 tbsp light soy sauce

2 tsp sugar

½ tsp salt

8 cherry tomatoes, halved

7 oz/200 g firm tofu (drained
weight), diced cilantro leaves,
for sprinkling

scallion curls, to garnish (see
page 468)

freshly cooked Thai fragrant rice,
to serve

1 Heat the oil in a preheated wok
or large skillet. Add the garlic and
cook for 1 minute, stirring. Stir in the
curry paste and turmeric and cook for
an additional 30 seconds.

2 Stir in the straw mushrooms and
ginger and stir-fry for 2 minutes.
Stir in the coconut milk and bring to
a boil.

3 Stir in the shiitake mushrooms,
lemon juice, soy sauce, sugar,
and salt and heat thoroughly. Add the
tomatoes and tofu and toss gently to
heat through.

4 Sprinkle the cilantro over the
mixture and serve hot with freshly
cooked fragrant rice garnished with
scallion curls.

VARIATION

You can vary the mushrooms
depending on your own taste—
try a mixture of oyster with the
shiitake for a change. Even just
ordinary cultivated white
mushrooms are delicious cooked
in this way.

spiced mushrooms

serves four

8 large flat mushrooms

3 tbsp corn oil

2 tbsp light soy sauce

1 garlic clove, crushed

¾-inch/2-cm piece fresh galangal or gingerroot, grated

1 tbsp Thai green curry paste

8 baby corn cobs, sliced

3 scallions, chopped

generous ¾ cup fresh bean sprouts

3½ oz/100 g firm tofu (drained weight), diced

2 tsp sesame seeds, toasted

TO SERVE

chopped cucumber

sliced red bell pepper

1 Preheat the broiler to high. Remove the stems from the mushrooms and reserve. Place the caps on a baking sheet. Mix 2 tablespoons of the oil with 1 tablespoon of the soy sauce and brush over the mushrooms.

2 Cook the mushroom caps under the hot broiler until golden and tender, turning them over once.

3 Meanwhile, chop the mushroo[m] stems finely. Heat the remainin[g] oil in a large skillet or preheated wo[k]. Add the stems, garlic, and galangal and stir-fry for 1 minute.

4 Stir in the curry paste, baby co[rn] cobs, and scallions and stir-fry 1 minute. Add the bean sprouts and stir for an additional 1 minute.

5 Add the diced tofu and remain[ing] soy sauce, then toss lightly to heat. Spoon the mixture into the mushroom caps.

6 Sprinkle with sesame seeds an[d] serve with chopped cucumber and sliced red bell pepper.

COOK'S TIP

Galangal or ginger can be froze[n] for several weeks, either peeled and finely chopped ready to add to dishes, or in whole pieces. Thaw the piece or grate finely from frozen.

oasted spiced bell peppers

red bell peppers

yellow bell peppers

green bell peppers

fresh red Thai chilies, seeded and
 finely chopped

lemongrass stem, finely shredded

tbsp lime juice

tbsp palm sugar

tbsp Thai fish sauce

COOK'S TIP

he flavors will mingle best if the
bell peppers are still slightly
warm when you spoon the
dressing over. Prepare the
dressing while the bell peppers
re cooking, so it's ready to pour
over when they are cooked.

Preheat the broiler or grill or the
 oven to 350°F/180°C. Roast the
 peppers under the hot broiler, grill
 r hot coals, or roast in the oven,
 ing them over occasionally, until
 skins are charred. Let cool slightly,
 n remove the skins. Cut each in half
 remove the core and seeds.

2 Slice the bell peppers thickly and transfer to a large bowl.

3 Place the chilies, lemongrass, lime juice, sugar, and fish sauce in a screw-top jar and shake well until thoroughly mixed.

4 Pour the dressing evenly over the peppers. Let cool completely, then cover with plastic wrap and let chill in the refrigerator for at least 1 hour before serving. Transfer to a serving dish to serve.

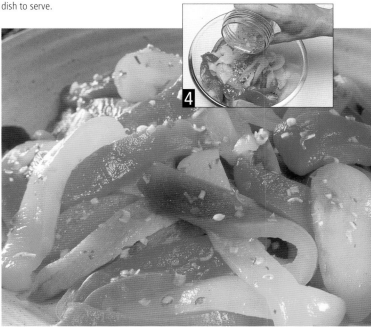

sweet potato cakes with soy-tomato sauc

2 sweet potatoes, 1 lb 2 oz/500 g
   in total

2 garlic cloves, crushed

1 small fresh green chili, chopped

2 cilantro sprigs, chopped

1 tbsp dark soy sauce

all-purpose flour, for dusting

vegetable oil, for pan-frying

sesame seeds, for sprinkling

cilantro sprigs, to garnish

SOY-TOMATO SAUCE

2 tsp vegetable oil

1 garlic clove, finely chopped

¾-inch/2-cm piece fresh gingerroot,
   finely chopped

3 tomatoes, skinned and chopped

2 tbsp dark soy sauce

1 tbsp lime juice

2 tbsp chopped cilantro

1 To make the soy-tomato sauce, heat the oil in a preheated wok. Add the garlic and ginger and stir-fry for 1 minute. Add the tomatoes and stir-fry for an additional 2 minutes. Remove the wok from the heat and stir in the soy sauce, lime juice, and cilantro. Keep warm.

2 Peel the sweet potatoes and grate finely (you can do this quickly in a food processor). Place the garlic, chili, and cilantro in a mortar and, using a pestle, grind to a smooth paste. Stir in the soy sauce and mix with the grated sweet potatoes.

3 Spread the flour out on a plate Divide the mixture into 12 equ portions, then dip into the flour and pat into flat, round patty shapes.

4 Heat a shallow layer of oil in a wide skillet. Cook the sweet potato patties over high heat until golden, turning once.

5 Drain on paper towels and sprinkle with sesame seeds. Transfer to a large serving plate, th garnish with cilantro sprigs and se hot with the soy-tomato sauce.

chili & coconut sambal

1 small coconut

1 slice fresh pineapple, finely diced

1 small onion, finely chopped

2 small fresh green chilies, seeded
    and chopped

2-inch/5-cm piece lemongrass,
    chopped

½ tsp salt

1 tsp shrimp paste

1 tbsp lime juice

2 tbsp chopped cilantro

cilantro sprigs, to garnish

VARIATION

To make a quicker version of this
sambal, stir 1 teaspoon of Thai
green curry paste into freshly
grated coconut and add finely
diced pineapple and lime
juice to taste.

1 Puncture 2 of the coconut "eyes"
with a screwdriver and pour the
milk out from the shell. Crack the
coconut open, then prize away the
flesh and coarsely grate it into a bowl.

2 Mix the coconut with the
pineapple, onion, chilies, and
lemongrass.

3 Blend the salt, shrimp paste, and
lime juice together in a separate
bowl, then stir into the sambal.

4 Stir in the cilantro. Spoon into a
small serving dish and garnish
with cilantro sprigs.

weet & sour potato stir-fry

serves four

waxy potatoes, diced
tbsp vegetable oil
yellow bell pepper, diced
red bell pepper, diced
carrot, cut into short thin sticks
zucchini, cut into short thin sticks
garlic cloves, crushed
fresh red chili, sliced
bunch of scallions,
  halved lengthwise
tbsp coconut milk
sp chopped lemongrass
sp lime juice
ely grated rind of 1 lime
tbsp chopped cilantro

COOK'S TIP

Check that the potatoes are not vercooked in step 1, otherwise the potato pieces will disintegrate when they are stir-fried in the wok.

1 Cook the diced potatoes in a pan of boiling water for 5 minutes. Drain thoroughly.

2 Heat the oil in a preheated wok or large skillet. Add the potatoes, diced bell peppers, carrot, zucchini, garlic, and chili and stir-fry for 2–3 minutes.

3 Stir in the scallions, coconut milk, chopped lemongrass, and lime juice and stir-fry for an additional 5 minutes.

4 Add the lime rind and cilantro and stir-fry for 1 minute. Serve hot.

VARIATION

Almost any combination of vegetables is suitable for this dish; the yellow and red bell peppers, for example, can be replaced with crisp green beans or snow peas.

potatoes in creamed coconut

1 lb 5 oz/600 g potatoes

1 onion, thinly sliced

2 fresh red Thai chilies,
  finely chopped

½ tsp salt

½ tsp pepper

3 oz/85 g creamed coconut

1½ cups vegetable or chicken stock

cilantro or fresh basil, chopped,
  to garnish

1 Peel the potatoes, then using a sharp knife, cut them into ¾-inch/2-cm chunks.

2 Place the potatoes in a pan with the onion, chilies, salt, pepper, and creamed coconut. Stir in the stock.

3 Bring to a boil, stirring constantly. Reduce the heat, then cover and simmer gently, stirring occasionally, until the potatoes are tender.

4 Adjust the seasoning to taste if necessary, then sprinkle with chopped cilantro or basil. Serve hot.

COOK'S TIP

If the potatoes are a thin-skinned, or a new variety, simp wash or scrub to remove any d and cook with the skins on. T adds extra nutrients to the finished dish, and cuts down the preparation time. Baby ne potatoes can be cooked whol

otato & spinach yellow curry

serves four

garlic cloves, finely chopped

¼-inch/3-cm piece fresh galangal, finely chopped

lemongrass stem, finely chopped

tsp coriander seeds

tbsp vegetable oil

tsp Thai red curry paste

tsp ground turmeric

nerous ¾ cup coconut milk

oz/250 g potatoes, cut into ¾-inch/2-cm cubes

ant ½ cup vegetable stock

oz/200 g fresh young spinach leaves

small onion, thinly sliced

Place the garlic, galangal, lemongrass, and coriander seeds mortar and, using a pestle, grind smooth paste.

Heat 2 tablespoons of the oil in a skillet or preheated wok. Stir in garlic paste mixture and stir-fry for seconds. Stir in the curry paste and neric, then add the coconut milk bring to a boil.

3 Add the potatoes and stock. Return to a boil, then reduce the heat and simmer, uncovered, for 10–12 minutes, or until the potatoes are almost tender.

4 Stir in the spinach and simmer until the leaves are wilted.

5 Meanwhile, heat the remaining oil in a separate skillet. Add the onion and cook until crisp and golden brown.

6 Place the fried onions on top of the curry just before serving.

red bean curry

serves four

14 oz/400 g green beans

1 garlic clove, finely sliced

1 fresh red Thai chili, seeded
   and chopped

½ tsp paprika

1 piece lemongrass stem,
   finely chopped

2 tsp Thai fish sauce

½ cup coconut milk

1 tbsp corn oil

2 scallions, sliced

VARIATION

Young string beans can be used
instead of green beans. Remove
any strings from the beans, then
cut at a diagonal angle in short
lengths. Cook as in the recipe
until tender.

---

1 Cut the beans into 2-inch/5-cm
pieces and cook in boiling water
for 2 minutes. Drain well.

2 Place the garlic, chili, paprika,
lemongrass, fish sauce, and
coconut milk in a food processor and
process to a smooth paste.

3 Heat the oil in a large skillet or
preheated wok. Add the scallions
and stir-fry over high heat for 1 minute.
Add the paste and bring the mixture
to a boil.

4 Simmer for 3–4 minutes to reduce
the liquid by about half. Add
the beans and simmer for an additional
1–2 minutes, or until tender. Transfer
to a serving dish and serve hot.

vegetable & coconut curry

serves four

2 lb 4 oz/1 kg mixed vegetables

1 onion, coarsely chopped

3 garlic cloves, thinly sliced

1-inch/2.5-cm piece fresh
  gingerroot, thinly sliced

2 fresh green chilies, seeded
  and finely chopped

1 tbsp vegetable oil

1 tsp ground turmeric

1 tsp ground coriander

1 tsp ground cumin

7 oz/200 g creamed coconut

2½ cups boiling water

salt and pepper

2 tbsp chopped cilantro,
  to garnish

freshly cooked rice, to serve

1 Cut the mixed vegetables into chunks. Place the onion, garlic, ginger, and chilies in a food processor and process until almost smooth.

2 Heat the oil in a large, heavy-bottom skillet. Add the onion mixture and cook for 5 minutes.

3 Add the turmeric, coriander, and cumin and cook for 3–4 minutes, stirring. Add the mixed vegetables and stir to coat in the spice paste.

4 Mix the creamed coconut and boiling water together in a pitcher. Stir until the coconut has dissolved. Add the coconut milk to vegetables, then cover and simmer 30–40 minutes, or until the vegeta are tender.

5 Season to taste with salt and pepper, then garnish with the chopped cilantro and serve with ric

COOK'S TIP

Use whatever vegetables you have to hand, such as cauliflower, zucchini, potatoes carrots, and green beans.

asian vegetables with yellow bean sauce

serves four

1 eggplant

salt

2 tbsp vegetable oil

3 garlic cloves, crushed

4 scallions, chopped

1 small red bell pepper, seeded and
    thinly sliced

4 baby corn cobs, halved
    lengthwise

scant 1 cup snow peas

7 oz/200 g green bok choy,
    coarsely shredded

14½ oz/425 g canned straw
    mushrooms, drained

generous ¾ cup fresh bean sprouts

2 tbsp rice wine or dry sherry

2 tbsp yellow bean sauce

2 tbsp dark soy sauce

1 tsp chili sauce

1 tsp sugar

½ cup chicken or vegetable stock

1 tsp cornstarch

2 tsp water

1 Cut the eggplant into 2-inch/5-cm long thin sticks. Place in a colander, then sprinkle with salt and let stand for 30 minutes. Rinse in cold water and dry with paper towels.

2 Heat the oil in a skillet or preheated wok. Add the garlic, scallions, and bell pepper and stir-fry over high heat for 1 minute. Stir in the eggplant pieces and stir-fry for an additional 1 minute, or until softened.

3 Stir in the corn cobs and snow peas and stir-fry for 1 minute. Add the bok choy, mushrooms, and bean sprouts and stir-fry for 30 seconds.

4 Mix the rice wine, yellow bean sauce, soy sauce, chili sauce, and sugar together in a bowl, then add to the skillet with the stock. Bring to a boil, stirring constantly.

5 Slowly blend the cornstarch with the water to form a smooth paste, then stir quickly into the skillet and cook for an additional 1 minute. Serve immediately.

crispy tofu with chili-soy sauce

serves four

10½ oz/300 g firm tofu
  (drained weight)
2 tbsp vegetable oil
1 garlic clove, sliced
1 carrot, cut into short thin sticks
½ green bell pepper, seeded and cut
  into short thin sticks
1 fresh red Thai chili, seeded and
  finely chopped
2 tbsp soy sauce
1 tbsp lime juice
1 tbsp Thai fish sauce
1 tbsp brown sugar
pickled garlic slices, to serve
  (optional)

1 Drain the tofu and pat dry with paper towels. Cut the tofu into ¾-inch/2-cm cubes.

2 Heat the oil in a preheated wok or large skillet. Add the garlic and stir-fry for 1 minute. Remove the garlic and add the tofu, then cook quickly, turning gently to brown well on all sides.

3 Remove the tofu, then drain well and keep hot. Stir the carrot and bell pepper into the wok and stir-fry for 1 minute.

4 Transfer the carrot and bell pepp to a dish. Pile the tofu on top.

5 Mix the chili, soy sauce, lime juice, fish sauce, and sugar together in a bowl, stirring until the sugar is dissolved.

6 Spoon the sauce over the tofu and serve topped with pickled garlic slices, if using. Serve hot.

tir-fried broccoli in oyster sauce

serves four

4 oz/400 g broccoli

tbsp peanut oil

shallots, finely chopped

garlic clove, finely chopped

tbsp rice wine or dry sherry

tbsp oyster sauce

tsp pepper

tsp chili oil

Cut the broccoli into small florets. Blanch in a pan of boiling water 30 seconds, then drain well.

Heat the oil in a large skillet or preheated wok. Add the shallots d garlic and stir-fry for 1–2 minutes, until golden brown.

Stir in the broccoli and stir-fry for 2 minutes. Add the rice wine and ster sauce and stir for an additional minute.

Stir in the pepper and drizzle with a little chili oil just before serving.

COOK'S TIP

To make chili oil, put fresh red or green chilies into a jar and top up with olive oil or a light vegetable oil. Cover with a lid and let infuse for at least 3 weeks before using.

vegetable fritters with sweet chili dip

serves four

1 cup all-purpose flour

1 tsp ground coriander

1 tsp ground cumin

1 tsp ground turmeric

1 tsp salt

½ tsp pepper

2 garlic cloves, finely chopped

1¼-inch/3-cm piece fresh
   gingerroot, chopped

2 small fresh green chilies,
   finely chopped

1 tbsp chopped cilantro

scant 1 cup cold water

1 onion, chopped

1 potato, coarsely grated

¾ cup canned corn kernels

1 small eggplant, diced

4½ oz/125 g Chinese kale, cut into
   short lengths

coconut oil, for deep-frying

SWEET CHILI DIP

2 fresh red Thai chilies,
   finely chopped

4 tbsp superfine sugar

4 tbsp rice vinegar or white
   wine vinegar

1 tbsp light soy sauce

1 Make the dip by mixing all the ingredients together thoroughly until the sugar is dissolved. Cover and reserve until required.

2 To make the fritters, place the flour in a bowl and stir in the coriander, cumin, turmeric, salt, and pepper. Add the garlic, ginger, green chilies, and cilantro with just enough of the water to form a thick batter.

3 Add the onion, potato, corn kernels, eggplant, and broccoli the batter and stir well to distribute ingredients evenly.

4 Heat the oil in a deep skillet or wok to 350–375°F/180–190°C or until a cube of bread browns in 30 seconds. Drop tablespoons of the batter into the hot oil and cook in batches until golden and crisp, turning once.

5 Drain the fritters well on paper towels and serve hot with the sweet chili dip.

corn fritters

serves four

generous ½ cup all-purpose flour

1 large egg

2 tsp Thai green curry paste

5 tbsp coconut milk

14 oz/400 g canned or frozen
   corn kernels

4 scallions

1 tbsp chopped cilantro

1 tbsp chopped fresh basil

salt and pepper

vegetable oil, for pan-frying

lime wedges, to garnish

chili relish, to serve

1 Place the flour, egg, curry paste, coconut milk, and about half the corn kernels in a food processor and process to a smooth, thick batter.

2 Finely chop the scallions and stir into the batter with the remaining corn, chopped cilantro, and basil. Season well with salt and pepper.

3 Heat a small amount of oil in a wide, heavy-bottom skillet. Drop in tablespoonfuls of the batter and cook for 2–3 minutes, or until golden brown.

4 Turn them over and cook for a additional 2–3 minutes, or unt golden. Cook in batches, making 12–16 fritters, keeping the cooked fritters hot while you cook the remaining batter.

5 Transfer the fritters to a servin plate, then garnish with lime wedges and serve with a chili relish

ok choy with crabmeat

serves four

heads green bok choy, about
9 oz/250 g in total

tbsp vegetable oil

garlic clove, thinly sliced

tbsp oyster sauce

½ oz/100 g cherry
tomatoes, halved

oz/175 g canned white
crabmeat, drained

lt and pepper

VARIATION

For a vegetarian version of this
dish, omit the crabmeat and
replace the oyster sauce with
tablespoons of light soy sauce.

1 Using a sharp knife, cut the bok choy into 1-inch/2.5-cm thick slices.

2 Heat the oil in a large skillet or preheated wok. Add the garlic and stir-fry quickly over high heat for 1 minute.

3 Add the bok choy and stir-fry for 2–3 minutes, or until the leaves wilt but the stems are still crisp.

4 Add the oyster sauce and tomatoes and stir-fry for an additional 1 minute.

5 Add the crabmeat and season well with salt and pepper. Stir to heat thoroughly and break up the crabmeat before serving.

bamboo shoot salad

serves four

2 shallots, unpeeled

2 garlic cloves, unpeeled

2 tbsp Thai fish sauce

3 tbsp lime juice

½ tsp dried chili flakes

1 tsp granulated sugar

1 tbsp round-grain rice

2 tsp sesame seeds

12 oz/350 g canned bamboo
   shoots, drained

2 scallions, chopped

Napa cabbage or lettuce, shredded

fresh mint leaves, to garnish

1 Preheat the broiler to medium. Place the shallots and garlic under the hot broiler and cook until charred on the outside and tender inside. Let cool slightly, then remove the skins and discard. Place the flesh in a mortar and, using a pestle, grind to a smooth paste.

2 Mix the shallot and garlic paste with the fish sauce, lime juice, chili flakes, and sugar in a small bowl.

3 Place the rice and sesame seeds in a heavy-bottom skillet and cook to a rich golden brown color, shaking the skillet to brown evenly. Remove the skillet from the heat and let cool slightly. Crush the toasted rice and sesame seeds lightly in a mortar using a pestle.

4 Use a sharp knife to shred the bamboo shoots into short thin sticks and place in a bowl. Stir in the shallot and garlic dressing, tossing to coat evenly. Stir in the toasted rice and sesame seeds, then the scallion.

5 Pile the salad on to a serving dish and surround with shredded Napa cabbage. Garnish with mint leaves and serve.

asian lettuce cups

serves four

8 leaves romaine lettuce, or similar
  firm lettuce leaves

2 carrots

2 celery stalks

3½ oz/100 g baby corn cobs

2 scallions

⅔ cup fresh bean sprouts

2 tbsp roasted peanuts, chopped

DRESSING

2 tbsp smooth peanut butter

3 tbsp lime juice

3 tbsp coconut milk

2 tsp Thai fish sauce

1 tsp superfine sugar

1 tsp grated fresh gingerroot

¼ tsp Thai red curry paste

1 Wash and trim the lettuce leaves, leaving them whole. Arrange on a serving plate or on individual plates.

2 Trim the carrots and celery and cut into short thin sticks. Trim the corn cobs and scallions and slice both diagonally.

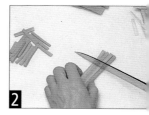

3 Toss all the prepared vegetables together with the bean sprouts. Divide the salad mixture evenly between the individual lettuce cups.

COOK'S TIP

Choose leaves with a deep cup shape to hold the salad neatly. If you prefer, Napa cabbage may be used in place of the romaine lettuce. To remove the leaves from the whole head without tearing them, cut a thick slice from the base end so the leaves are not attached by their stems, then gently ease away the leafy parts.

4 To make the dressing, place all the ingredients in a screw-top j and shake well until thoroughly mixe

5 Spoon the dressing evenly over the salad cups and sprinkle with chopped peanuts. Serve immediately

450

ggplant & mushroom stuffed omelet

serves four

tbsp vegetable oil

garlic clove, finely chopped

small onion, finely chopped

small eggplant, diced

small green bell pepper, seeded
and chopped

large dried shiitake mushroom,
soaked, drained, and sliced

tomato, diced

tbsp light soy sauce

tsp sugar

tsp pepper

large eggs

) GARNISH

lad greens

mato wedges

cumber slices

pping sauce, to serve

COOK'S TIP

f you heat the skillet thoroughly
before adding the oil, and
heat the oil before adding
the ingredients, you should
not have a problem with
the ingredients sticking to
the skillet.

1 Heat half the oil in a large skillet.
Add the garlic and cook over high
heat for 30 seconds. Add the onion
and the eggplant and continue to stir-
fry until golden.

2 Add the bell pepper and stir-fry
for an additional 1 minute to
soften. Stir in the mushroom, tomato,
soy sauce, sugar, and pepper. Remove
from the skillet and keep hot.

3 Beat the eggs together lightly.
Heat the remaining oil in a clean
skillet, swirling to coat a wide area.
Pour in the egg and swirl to set around
the skillet.

4 When the egg is set, spoon the
filling into the center. Fold in
the sides of the omelet to form a
square package.

5 Slide the omelet carefully on to a
warmed dish and garnish with
salad greens, tomato wedges, and
cucumber slices. Serve with a
dipping sauce.

thai green salad

serves four

1 small head romaine lettuce

1 bunch of scallions

½ cucumber

4 tbsp coarsely shredded and
   toasted fresh coconut

DRESSING

4 tbsp lime juice

2 tbsp Thai fish sauce

1 small fresh red Thai chili,
   finely chopped

1 tsp sugar

1 garlic clove, crushed

2 tbsp chopped cilantro

1 tbsp chopped fresh mint

COOK'S TIP

This salad is good for picnics—to
pack it easily, pack the leaves
into a large plastic container or
unbreakable salad bowl, and
nestle the jar of dressing in the
center. Cover with plastic wrap.
Packed this way, the salad stays
crisp, and if the dressing leaks
during transit, there's no mess.

1 Tear or coarsely shred the
lettuce leaves and place in
a large salad bowl.

2 Trim and thinly slice the scallions
diagonally, then add them to the
salad bowl.

3 Use a vegetable peeler to shave
thin slices along the length of the
cucumber and add to the salad bowl.

4 Place all the ingredients for the
dressing in a screw-top jar and
shake well to mix thoroughly.

5 Pour the dressing over the salad
and toss well to coat all the
leaves evenly.

6 Sprinkle the coconut over the
salad and toss in lightly just
before serving.

cucumber salad

1 cucumber

1 tsp salt

1 small red onion

1 garlic clove, crushed

½ tsp chili paste

2 tsp Thai fish sauce

1 tbsp lime juice

1 tsp sesame oil

COOK'S TIP

Once the salad is made, it can be chilled with the dressing for 1–2 hours, but is best eaten on the day of making.

VARIATION

For a change, peel the cucumber and cut it into small dice shapes, then salt and drain as above. Drain and toss with the onions and dressing as before.

---

1 Trim the cucumber and coarsely grate the flesh. Place in a strainer over a large bowl, then sprinkle with the salt and let stand for 20 minutes. Discard the liquid.

2 Chop the onion finely, then toss into the cucumber. Spoon into 4 serving bowls. Alternatively, use a large serving dish.

3 Mix the garlic, chili paste, fish sauce, lime juice, and oil together in a small bowl, then spoon over the salad. Cover with plastic wrap and let chill in the refrigerator before serving.

hai-style caesar salad

serves four

large head romaine lettuce, with
  outer leaves removed, or 2 hearts

egetable oil, for deep-frying

–6 large rice paper wrappers or
  4 oz/115 g rice paper flakes

mall bunch of cilantro, leaves
  stripped from stems

RESSING

• cup rice vinegar

–3 tbsp Thai fish sauce

garlic cloves, coarsely chopped

tbsp sugar

-inch/2.5-cm piece fresh
  gingerroot, coarsely chopped

• cup corn oil

alt and pepper

1 Tear the lettuce leaves into bite-size pieces and place in a large salad bowl.

2 To make the dressing, place the vinegar, fish sauce, garlic, sugar, and ginger in a food processor and process for 15–30 seconds.

3 With the motor running, gradually pour in the corn oil until a creamy liquid forms. Season to taste with salt and pepper. Pour into a pitcher.

4 Heat 3 inches/7.5 cm of vegetable oil in a deep-fat fryer or wok to 350–375°F/180–190°C, or until a cube of bread browns in 30 seconds.

5 Meanwhile, break the rice wrappers into bite-size pieces and dip each into a bowl of water to soften. Lay on a clean dish towel and pat completely dry.

6 Working in batches, add the rice paper pieces to the hot oil and deep-fry for 15 seconds, or until crisp. Using a slotted spoon, transfer to paper towels to drain.

7 Add the cilantro leaves to the lettuce and toss to mix. Add the fried rice paper "chips" and drizzle over the dressing. Toss to coat the leaves and serve immediately.

VARIATION
Substitute 2 tablespoons of the corn oil with sesame oil for a different flavor.

455

green papaya salad

serves four

8 oz/225 g snow peas

2 papayas

DRESSING

2 garlic cloves, crushed

2 fresh red chilies, seeded and
finely chopped

1 tsp sugar

2 tbsp soy sauce

juice of 1 lime

½ head Napa cabbage

TO GARNISH

12 cherry tomatoes

2 tbsp chopped peanuts

VARIATION

Replace the chopped peanuts
with chopped cashew nuts, if
you prefer. For an extra touch,
lightly toast the nuts before
adding to the salad.

1 Place the snow peas in a pan of
boiling salted water. Return to a
boil and cook for 2 minutes. Drain
through a strainer, then refresh under
cold water. Cut into short thin sticks
and place in a bowl.

2 Peel the papayas, then remove
the black seeds and grate the
flesh into the bowl with the snow
peas. Cover and let chill in the
refrigerator until ready to serve.

3 Mix the garlic, chilies, sugar, s
sauce, and lime juice together
a bowl. Pour over the papaya salad
and mix well.

4 Arrange the Napa cabbage in
large serving bowl, then place
salad on top. Cut the cherry tomato
in half. Garnish the salad with
the tomatoes and chopped peanuts
before serving.

pineapple & cucumber salad

serves four

1 cucumber

1 small fresh pineapple

1 red onion, thinly sliced

1 bunch of watercress

DRESSING

3 tbsp lemon juice

2 tbsp soy sauce

1 tsp sugar

1 tsp chili sauce

2 tbsp chopped fresh mint

1 Peel the cucumber and cut into fourths lengthwise. Scoop out the seeds with a teaspoon and cut each quarter into ½-inch/1-cm pieces. Place in a bowl.

2 Peel the pineapple and cut into fourths lengthwise. Remove the core. Cut each fourth in half lengthwise, then cut into ½-inch/1-cm pieces and add to the cucumber. Add the onion and watercress and mix.

3 To make the dressing, place all ingredients in a small bowl and whisk together.

4 Pour the dressing over the salad and toss together. Transfer to a large serving platter and serve.

hai salad with peanut dressing

serves four

oz/250 g white cabbage,
    shredded

carrots, cut into short thin sticks

celery stalks, cut into short
    thin sticks

⅔ cups fresh bean sprouts

½ cucumber, cut into short
    thin sticks

PEANUT SAUCE

tbsp smooth peanut butter

generous ¾ cups coconut cream

tsp Thai red curry paste

tbsp Thai fish sauce

tbsp brown sugar

O GARNISH

ried onions

liced fresh green chilli

1 Set a steamer above a pan of
boiling water. Add the cabbage,
rrots, and celery and steam for
-4 minutes until just tender. Let cool.

2 Arrange the bean sprouts on a
large, shallow serving dish.
rrange the cabbage, carrots, celery,
d cucumber on top.

3 To make the sauce, place all the
ingredients in a pan. Heat gently,
stirring, adding a little hot water, if
necessary, to make a coating sauce.

4 Spoon a little of the sauce over
the vegetables and garnish with
fried onions and sliced chili. Serve the
rest of the sauce separately.

grilled eggplant & sesame salad

serves four

8 baby eggplants

salt

2 tsp chili oil

1 tbsp soy sauce

1 tbsp Thai fish sauce

1 tbsp corn oil

1 garlic clove, thinly sliced

1 fresh red Thai chili, seeded
   and sliced

1 tsp sesame oil

1 tbsp lime juice

1 tsp brown sugar

1 tbsp chopped fresh mint

1 tbsp sesame seeds, toasted

fresh mint leaves, to garnish

1 Cut the eggplants lengthwise into thin slices to within 1 inch/ 2.5 cm of the stem end. Place in a colander, sprinkling with salt between the slices, and let stand for 30 minutes. Rinse in cold water and pat dry with paper towels.

2 Preheat the broiler to medium. Mix the chili oil, soy sauce, and fish sauce together in a bowl, then brush over the eggplants. Cook under the hot broiler, or grill over hot coals, for 6–8 minutes, turning them over occasionally and brushing with more chili oil glaze, until golden brown and softened. Arrange on a serving platter.

3 Heat the corn oil in a large skillet. Add the garlic and chili and cook for 1–2 minutes, until just beginning to brown. Remove the skillet from the heat and add the sesame oil, lime juice, sugar, and any remaining chili oil glaze.

4 Add the chopped mint and spoon the warm dressing over the eggplants. Let marinate for 20 minutes, then sprinkle with the toasted sesame seeds. Serve garnished with mint leaves.

arrot & mango salad

serves four

carrots

small ripe mango

oz/200 g firm tofu
  (drained weight)

tbsp snipped fresh chives

RESSING

tbsp orange juice

tbsp lime juice

tsp clear honey

tsp orange flower water

tsp sesame oil

tsp sesame seeds, toasted

1 Coarsely grate the carrots. Peel, pit, and thinly slice the mango.

2 Cut the tofu into ½-inch/1-cm dice-shaped pieces and toss together with the carrots and mango in a wide salad bowl.

3 To make the dressing, place all the ingredients in a screw-top jar and shake well until thoroughly mixed. Pour the dressing over the salad and toss well to coat the salad evenly.

4 Just before serving, toss the salad lightly and sprinkle with snipped chives. Serve immediately.

COOK'S TIP

A food processor will grate
the carrots in seconds—
especially useful if you're
catering for a crowd.

thai seafood salad

serves four

1 lb/450 g live mussels in shells

8 raw jumbo shrimp

12 oz/350 g squid, cleaned and
  sliced widthwise into rings

4 oz/115 g cooked, shelled shrimp

1 red onion, finely sliced

1 red bell pepper, seeded and
  finely sliced

⅔ cup fresh bean sprouts

4 oz/115 g shredded bok choy

DRESSING

1 garlic clove, crushed

1 tsp grated fresh gingerroot

1 fresh red chili, seeded and
  finely chopped

2 tbsp chopped cilantro

1 tbsp lime juice

1 tsp finely grated lime rind

1 tbsp light soy sauce

5 tbsp corn or peanut oil

2 tsp sesame oil

salt and pepper

4 tbsp cold water

1 Clean the mussels by scrubbing or scraping the shells and pulling out any beards that are attached to them. Discard any with broken shells or any that refuse to close when tapped.

2 Place the mussels in a large pan with just the water that clings to their shells. Cook over high heat for 3–4 minutes, shaking the pan occasionally, until the mussels have opened. Discard any that remain closed. Strain the mussels, reserving the cooking liquid, and refresh under cold water. Drain again and reserve.

3 Bring the reserved cooking liquid to a boil and add the jumbo shrimp. Simmer for 5 minutes. Add the squid and cook for an additional 2 minutes, or until the shrimp and squid are cooked through. Remove with a slotted spoon and plunge into a bowl of cold water. Reserve the cooking liquid. Drain the shrimp and squid.

4 Remove the mussels from their shells and place in a bowl with the jumbo shrimp, squid, and cooked, shelled shrimp. Cover and let chill in the refrigerator for 1 hour.

5 To make the dressing, place all the ingredients, except the oils, in a food processor and process to a smooth paste. Add the oils, reserved cooking liquid, salt and pepper to taste, and water, then process again to mix.

6 Just before serving, mix the onion, bell pepper, bean sprouts and bok choy in a bowl and toss with 2–3 tablespoons of the dressing. Arrange the vegetables on a large serving plate or in a bowl. Toss the remaining dressing with the seafood to coat and add to the vegetables. Serve immediately.

thai noodle salad with shrimp

serves four

3 oz/85 g rice vermicelli noodles or
  rice sticks

1⅔ cups snow peas, cut crosswise
  in half, if large

5 tbsp lime juice

4 tbsp Thai fish sauce

1 tbsp sugar, or to taste

1-inch/2.5-cm piece fresh
  gingerroot, finely chopped

1 fresh red chili, seeded and thinly
  sliced on the diagonal

4 tbsp chopped cilantro, plus extra
  for garnishing

4-inch/10-cm piece cucumber,
  peeled, seeded, and diced

2 scallions, thinly sliced
  on the diagonal

16–20 large cooked, shelled shrimp

2 tbsp chopped unsalted peanuts or
  cashews (optional)

TO GARNISH

4 cooked whole shrimp

lemon slices

VARIATION

Replace the cilantro with the
same amount of mint and the
lemon slices with lime.

1 Place the rice noodles in a large bowl and pour over enough hot water to cover. Let stand for 4 minutes, or until soft. Drain and rinse under cold running water, then drain again and reserve.

2 Bring a pan of water to a boil. Add the snow peas and simmer for 1 minute. Drain and rinse under cold running water until cold, then drain and reserve.

3 Whisk the lime juice, fish sauce, sugar, ginger, chili, and cilantro together in a large bowl. Stir in the cucumber and scallions. Add the drained noodles, snow peas, and the shrimp. Toss the salad gently together.

4 Divide the noodle salad between 4 large plates. Sprinkle with chopped cilantro and the peanuts, if using, then garnish each plate with a whole shrimp and a lemon slice. Serve immediately.

COOK'S TIP

There are many sizes of rice
noodles available—make sure
you use the thin rice noodles,
called rice vermicelli, rice sticks
or *sen mee*, otherwise the salad
will be too heavy.

broiled beef salad

serves four

1¾ oz/50 g dried oyster mushrooms

1 lb 5 oz/600 g rump steak

1 red bell pepper, seeded and
thinly sliced

scant ⅓ cup roasted cashew nuts

red and green lettuce leaves

fresh mint leaves, to garnish

DRESSING

2 tbsp sesame oil

2 tbsp Thai fish sauce

2 tbsp sweet sherry

2 tbsp oyster sauce

1 tbsp lime juice

1 fresh red chili, seeded and
finely chopped

1 Put the mushrooms in a heatproof bowl, cover with boiling water, and let stand for 20 minutes. Drain, then cut into slices.

2 Preheat the broiler to medium or heat a ridged grill pan. To make the dressing, place all the ingredients in a bowl and whisk to combine.

3 Cook the steak under the preheated grill or on the hot g pan, turning once, for 5 minutes, o until browned on both sides but st rare in the center. Cook the steak longer if desired.

4 Slice the steak into thin strips and place in a bowl with the mushrooms, bell pepper, and nuts. Add the dressing and toss together

5 Arrange the lettuce on a large serving platter and place the mixture on top. Garnish with mint leaves. Serve at room temperature.

hot & sour beef salad

serves four

1 tsp black peppercorns

1 tsp coriander seeds

1 red bird chili

¼ tsp Chinese five-spice powder

9 oz/250 g lean beef fillet

1 tbsp dark soy sauce

6 scallions

1 carrot

¼ cucumber

8 radishes

1 red onion

¼ head Napa cabbage

2 tbsp peanut oil

1 garlic clove, crushed

1 tsp finely chopped lemongrass

1 tbsp chopped fresh mint

1 tbsp chopped cilantro

DRESSING

3 tbsp lime juice

1 tbsp light soy sauce

2 tsp brown sugar

1 tsp sesame oil

1 Crush the peppercorns, coriander seeds, and chili in a mortar using a pestle, then mix with the five-spice powder and sprinkle on a plate. Brush the beef all over with soy sauce, then roll it in the spices to coat evenly.

2 Cut the scallions into 2½-inch/ 6-cm lengths, then shred them finely lengthwise. Place in a bowl of ice water and let stand until curled. Drain well.

3 Cut the carrot into very thin diagonal slices. Halve the cucumber lengthwise and scoop out the seeds, then slice thinly. Cut the radishes into flower shapes.

4 Slice the onion thinly, cutting each slice from top to root. Coarsely shred the Napa cabbage. Toss all the vegetables, except the scallion curls, together in a large salad bowl.

5 Heat the peanut oil in a large, heavy-bottom skillet. Add the garlic and lemongrass and cook until just turning golden brown. Add the beef and press down with a spatula to ensure it browns evenly. Cook for 3–4 minutes, turning it over once, depending on the thickness. Remove the skillet from the heat.

6 Slice the beef thinly and toss into the salad with the mint and cilantro. Mix all the ingredients for the dressing together in a bowl and stir into the skillet, then spoon over the salad. Garnish with the scallion curls and serve.

roast duck salad

serves four

2 duck breasts

2 Boston lettuces, shredded

¾ cup fresh bean sprouts

1 yellow bell pepper, seeded and
cut into thin strips

½ cucumber, seeded and cut
into short thin sticks

DRESSING

juice of 2 limes

3 tbsp Thai fish sauce

1 tbsp brown sugar

2 tsp sweet chili sauce

1-inch/2.5-cm piece fresh
gingerroot, finely grated

3 tbsp chopped fresh mint

3 tbsp chopped fresh basil

TO GARNISH

2 tsp shredded lime rind

2 tbsp shredded coconut, toasted

1 Preheat the oven to 400°F/200°C. Place the duck breasts on a rack set over a roasting pan and roast in the oven for 20–30 minutes, or until cooked as desired and the skin is crisp. Remove from the oven and let cool.

2 Mix the lettuce, bean sprouts, bell pepper, and cucumber together in a large bowl. Cut the cooled duck into strips and add to the salad. Mix well.

3 Whisk all the ingredients for the dressing together in a separate bowl. Add the dressing to the salad and toss well.

4 Turn the salad out on to a serving plate and garnish with lime rind and shredded coconut before serving.

Desserts & Drinks

The normal conclusion to a Thai meal is a basket of fruit, often including mangoes, mangosteens, jackfruit, guavas, and litchis. Desserts and sweetmeats are mostly made at home for between-meal treats, or made by experts for special occasions, because their preparation can be time-consuming and often requires skillful blending and shaping.

Rice, usually of the glutinous variety, and tapioca are vital ingredients in many candies and cakes, often molded or colored, soaked in scented syrups.

Many Thai drinks are colorful and exotic in flavor. They use the abundant fruits and coconut milk in long, refreshing drinks, sweetened with palm sugar and often served with a dash of whiskey or other spirit.

thai rice pudding

serves four

scant ½ cup short-grain rice

2 tbsp palm sugar

1 cardamom pod, split

1¼ cups coconut milk

⅔ cup water

3 eggs

generous ¾ cup coconut cream

1½ tbsp superfine sugar

sweetened coconut flakes,
   to decorate

fresh fruits, to serve

COOK'S TIP

Cardamom is quite a powerful
spice, so if you find it too strong,
it can be left out or replaced with
a little ground cinnamon.

1 Preheat the oven to 350°F/180°C. Place the rice and palm sugar in a pan. Remove the seeds from the cardamom pod and place in a mortar. Crush the seeds using a pestle, then add to the pan. Stir in the coconut milk and water.

2 Bring to a boil, stirring to dissolve the sugar. Reduce the heat and let simmer, uncovered, stirring occasionally, for 20 minutes, or until the rice is tender and most of the liquid is absorbed.

3 Spoon the rice into 4 individual ovenproof dishes and spread evenly. Place the dishes in a wide roasting pan and pour in enough wa to come halfway up the sides.

4 Beat the eggs, coconut cream, and superfine sugar together in bowl. Spoon over the rice. Cover wit foil and bake in the preheated oven 45–50 minutes, or until set.

5 Turn out the puddings and decorate with coconut flakes. Serve warm or cold with fresh fruit.

mango with sticky rice

serves four

generous 1 cup glutinous rice, soaked
for 30 minutes in cold water

1 cup coconut milk

2 tbsp superfine sugar

pinch of salt

2 large ripe mangoes

1 Drain the rice and rinse thoroughly. Place in a pan with the coconut milk, sugar, and salt. Bring to a boil and simmer, stirring occasionally, until the rice has absorbed all the coconut milk and is very soft.

2 Transfer the rice to a steamer set over a pan of simmering water. Cover and steam for 15 minutes. Let cool slightly. Press the rice into the bottom of 4 ramekins and turn out on to individual plates to form rice domes. Alternatively, spread the rice out on a baking sheet lined with foil, then roll the rice flat with a wet rolling pin. Cut into diamond shapes.

3 Peel the mangoes and cut the flesh into cubes. Arrange the rice diamonds and mango cubes on individual plates or in ramekin dishes and serve.

xotic fruit salad

serves six

tsp jasmine tea

tsp grated fresh gingerroot

uice of 1 lime plus 1 strip of
  lime rind

½ cup boiling water

tbsp superfine sugar

papaya

mango

½ small pineapple

carambola

passion fruit

COOK'S TIP

Carambola have little flavor
when unripe and green, but once
ripened and yellow, they become
delicately sweet and fragrant.
Usually by this stage, the tips of
the ridges have become brown,
so you will need to remove these
before slicing. The easiest and
quickest method of doing this is
to run a vegetable peeler
along each ridge.

1 Place the tea, ginger, and lime
  rind in a heatproof pitcher and
pour over the boiling water. Let infuse
for 5 minutes, then strain the liquid.

2 Add the sugar to the liquid and
  stir well to dissolve. Let the syrup
stand until it is completely cold.

3 Halve, seed, and peel the papaya.
  Halve the mango, then remove
the pit and peel. Peel and remove the
core from the pineapple. Cut the fruits
into bite-size pieces.

4 Slice the carambola crosswise.
  Place the prepared fruits in a wide
serving bowl and pour over the cooled
syrup. Cover with plastic wrap and let
chill in the refrigerator for 1 hour.

5 Cut the passion fruit in half, then
  scoop out the flesh with a
teaspoon and mix with the lime juice.
Spoon over the salad and serve.

tropical fruit in lemongrass syrup

serves four

1 honeydew melon

1 small pineapple

1 papaya

14 oz/400 g litchis, pitted

3 passion fruit

LEMONGRASS SYRUP

¾ cup superfine sugar

⅔ cup water

2 lemongrass stems, bruised

2 fresh kaffir lime leaves

juice of 1 lime

TO DECORATE

1 tbsp grated lime rind

small handful of fresh mint leaves

VARIATION

If fresh litchis are unavailable, replace them with drained canned ones.

1 To make the syrup, place all the ingredients in a pan. Heat gently until the sugar has dissolved. Bring to a boil and cook, uncovered, for 5 minutes. Let stand overnight.

2 Cut the melon in half, then remove the seeds and scoop out the flesh with a melon baller. Place in a bowl. Peel the pineapple, cut into fourths lengthwise, and remove the core. Cut into cubes and add to the melon. Peel the papaya, then remove the seeds, cut the flesh into cubes, and add to the other fruits.

3 Add the litchis. Cut the passion fruit in half and scoop the pulp and seeds into the bowl of fruits. Stir to mix, then transfer to a serving bowl. Remove the lemongrass and lime leaves from the syrup and pour over the fruits. Decorate with the lime rind and mint leaves and serve.

mango & lime sherbet

serves four

scant ½ cup superfine sugar

scant ½ cup water

finely grated rind of 3 limes

2 tbsp coconut cream

2 large ripe mangoes

scant ⅔ cup lime juice

curls of fresh coconut, toasted,
    to decorate

VARIATION

If you prefer, canned mangoes in
syrup can be used to make the
sherbet. Omit the sugar and
water, and infuse the lime rind in
the canned syrup instead.

1 Place the sugar, water, and lime rind in a small pan and heat gently, stirring constantly, until the sugar dissolves. Boil rapidly for 2 minutes to reduce slightly, then remove the pan from the heat and strain into a heatproof bowl or pitcher. Stir in the coconut cream and let cool.

2 Halve the mangoes, then remove the pits and peel thinly. Chop the flesh coarsely and place in a food processor with the lime juice. Process to a smooth purée and transfer to a small bowl.

3 Pour the cooled syrup into the mango purée, mixing evenly. Tip into a large, freezerproof container and freeze for 1 hour, or until slushy in texture. Alternatively, use an ice cream machine.

4 Remove the container from the freezer and beat with an electr mixer to break up the ice crystals. Refreeze for an additional 1 hour, th remove from the freezer and beat th contents again until smooth.

5 Cover the container, then retur to the freezer and leave until fi To serve, remove from the freezer a let stand at room temperature for 15 minutes before scooping into individual glass dishes. Sprinkle wit toasted coconut to decorate.

rose ice

1 Place the water in a small pan and add the coconut cream. Heat the mixture gently without boiling, stirring.

2 Remove the pan from the heat and let cool. Stir in the condensed milk, rose water, and food coloring, if using.

3 Pour the mixture into a large, freezerproof container and freeze for 1–1½ hours, or until slushy.

4 Remove the container from the freezer and break up the ice crystals with a fork. Return to the freezer and freeze until firm.

5 Spoon the ice roughly into a pile on a serving dish and sprinkle with rose petals to decorate.

COOK'S TIP

To prevent the ice thawing too quickly at the table, nestle the bottom of the serving dish in another dish filled with crushed ice.

asy mango ice cream

makes about 4 cups

/₂ cups ready-made traditional
custard

cup whipping cream, lightly
whipped

ish of 2 ripe mangoes, puréed

infectioners' sugar, to taste

ission fruit pulp, to serve

1 Mix the custard, cream, and mango purée together in a bowl.

2 Taste for sweetness and, if necessary, add confectioners' sugar to taste, remembering that when frozen, the mixture will taste less sweet.

3 Transfer the mixture to a large, freezerproof container. Cover and freeze for 2–3 hours, or until just frozen. Spoon into a bowl and mash with a fork or whisk to break down any ice crystals. Return the mixture to the container and freeze for an additional 2 hours. Mash once more, then freeze for 2–3 hours, or until firm.

4 Transfer the ice cream from the freezer to the refrigerator 20–30 minutes before serving. Serve with the passion fruit pulp.

litchi & ginger sherbet

serves four

1 lb 12 oz/800 g canned litchis
  in syrup

finely grated rind of 1 lime

2 tbsp lime juice

3 tbsp preserved ginger syrup

2 egg whites

TO DECORATE

carambola slices

slivers of preserved ginger

1 Drain the litchis, reserving the syrup. Place the litchis in a food processor or blender with the lime rind, juice, and preserved ginger syrup and process until completely smooth. Transfer to a large bowl.

COOK'S TIP

It is not recommended that raw eggs are served to very young children, pregnant women, the elderly, or anyone weakened by chronic illness. The egg whites may be left out of this recipe, but you will need to whisk the sherbet a second time after an additional 1 hour of freezing to obtain a light texture.

2 Mix the purée thoroughly with the reserved litchi syrup, then pour into a large, freezerproof container and freeze for 1–1½ hours or until slushy in texture. Alternatively use an ice cream machine.

3 Remove from the freezer and whisk to break up the ice crystals. Whisk the egg whites in a clean, dry bowl until stiff, then quickly and lightly fold into the ice mixture.

4 Return to the freezer and leave until firm. Serve the sherbet in scoops, with slices of carambola and preserved ginger to decorate.

oconut & ginger ice cream

makes about
4 cups

¾ cups coconut milk

cup whipping cream

egg yolks

tbsp superfine sugar

tbsp preserved ginger syrup

pieces preserved ginger, finely
  chopped

tbsp lime juice

esh mint sprigs, to decorate

⊃ SERVE

chis

eserved ginger syrup

1 Place the coconut milk and cream
in a pan. Heat gently until just
beginning to simmer. Remove the pan
from the heat.

2 Beat the egg yolks, sugar, and
ginger syrup together in a large
bowl until pale and creamy. Slowly
pour in the hot coconut milk mixture,
stirring. Return to the pan and heat
gently, stirring constantly, until the
mixture thickens and coats the back of
a spoon. Remove the pan from the
heat and let cool. Stir in the ginger and
lime juice.

3 Transfer the mixture to a large,
freezerproof container. Cover and
freeze for 2–3 hours, or until just
frozen. Spoon into a bowl and mash
with a fork or whisk to break down any
ice crystals. Return the mixture to the
container and freeze for an additional
2 hours. Mash once more, then freeze
for 2–3 hours, or until firm.

4 Transfer to the refrigerator
20–30 minutes before serving.
Decorate with mint sprigs and serve
with litchis and a little ginger syrup
drizzled over.

485

pineapple with cardamom & lime

serves four

1 pineapple

2 cardamom pods

thinly pared lime rind

4 tbsp water

1 tbsp brown sugar

3 tbsp lime juice

TO DECORATE

fresh mint sprigs

whipped cream

COOK'S TIP

To remove the "eyes" from pineapple, cut off the peel, then use a small, sharp knife to cut a V-shaped channel down the pineapple, cutting diagonally through the lines of brown "eyes" in the flesh, to make spiraling cuts around the fruit.

1 Cut the top and base from the pineapple, then cut away the peel and remove the "eyes" from the flesh (see Cook's Tip). Cut into fourths and remove the core. Slice the pineapple lengthwise and place in a large serving dish.

2 Crush the cardamom pods in a mortar using a pestle and place in a pan with the lime rind and water. Bring the mixture to a boil, then reduce the heat and simmer for 30 seconds.

3 Remove the pan from the heat and add the sugar, then cover with a lid and let infuse for 5 minutes.

4 Stir in the sugar to dissolve, add the lime juice, then strain the syrup over the pineapple. Cover and let chill in the refrigerator for 30 minutes.

5 When ready to serve, decorate with mint sprigs and a spoonful of whipped cream.

balinese banana crêpes

serves six

scant 1½ cups all-purpose flour

pinch of salt

4 eggs, beaten

2 large ripe bananas, mashed

1¼ cups coconut milk

vegetable oil, for frying

TO DECORATE

sliced bananas

6 tbsp lime juice

confectioners' sugar

coconut cream, to serve

1 Place the flour, salt, eggs, bananas, and coconut milk in a food processor or blender and process to a smooth batter. Alternatively, sift the flour and salt into a bowl and make a well in the center, then add the remaining ingredients and beat well until smooth.

2 Let the batter chill in the refrigerator for 1 hour. Remove the batter from the refrigerator and beat briefly again. Heat a small amount of oil in a small skillet until very hot.

3 Drop tablespoonfuls of the batter into the skillet. Cook until the crêpes are golden underneath.

4 Turn over and cook the other sides until golden brown. Cook in batches until all the batter is used up, making 36 crêpes. Remove and let drain on paper towels.

5 Arrange the crêpes in a stack, layered with sliced bananas, sprinkled with lime juice and sugar. Serve with coconut cream.

aramel apple wedges with sesame seeds

serves four

cup rice flour

egg

½ cup cold water

4 crisp dessert apples

2½ tbsp sesame seeds

1¼ cups superfine sugar

2 tbsp vegetable oil, plus extra for
deep-frying

resh basil sprigs, to decorate

1 Place the flour, egg, and water in a large bowl and whisk well until smooth, thick batter forms.

2 Core the apples and cut each into 8 wedges. Drop into the batter nd stir in the sesame seeds.

3 Place the sugar and the 2 tablespoons of oil in a heavy-ttom skillet and heat, stirring, until e sugar dissolves. Continue until e syrup begins to turn golden. emove the skillet from the heat but ep warm.

COOK'S TIP

Take care not to overheat the sugar syrup, otherwise it will become difficult to handle and burn. If it begins to set before you have finished dipping the apple pieces, warm it slightly until it becomes liquid again.

4 Heat the oil for deep-frying in a deep skillet or wok to 350–375°F/180–190°C, or until a cube of bread browns in 30 seconds. Lift the apple pieces one by one from the batter using tongs, lower into the hot oil, and deep-fry for 2–3 minutes, or until golden brown and crisp.

5 Remove with a slotted spoon and dip very quickly into the sugar mixture. Dip the apple wedges briefly into a bowl of ice water and drain on paper towels. Transfer to a serving plate, then decorate with basil and serve immediately.

banana fritters in coconut batter

serves four

½ cup all-purpose flour

2 tbsp rice flour

1 tbsp superfine sugar

1 egg, separated

⅔ cup coconut milk

corn oil, for deep-frying

4 large bananas

TO DECORATE

1 tsp confectioners' sugar

1 tsp ground cinnamon

lime wedges

COOK'S TIP

If you can buy the baby finger bananas that are popular in this dish in the East, leave them whole for coating and frying.

1 Sift the all-purpose flour, rice flour, and sugar into a bowl and make a well in the center. Add the egg yolk and coconut milk.

2 Beat the mixture until a smooth, thick batter forms. Whisk the egg white in a clean, dry bowl until stiff, then fold it into the batter lightly and evenly.

3 Heat a 2½-inch/6-cm depth of oil in a large skillet to 350–375°F/ 180–190°C, or until a cube of bread browns in 30 seconds. Cut the bananas in half crosswise, then dip them quickly into the batter to coat them.

4 Drop the bananas carefully into the hot oil and cook in batches 2–3 minutes, or until golden brown, turning once.

5 Drain on paper towels. Sprinkle with sugar and cinnamon and decorate with lime wedges.

coconut crêpes

serves four

1 cup rice flour

scant ¼ cup superfine sugar

pinch of salt

2 eggs

2½ cups coconut milk

4 tbsp dry unsweetened coconut

vegetable oil, for frying

2 tbsp palm sugar, for sprinkling

fresh mango or banana, to serve

1 Place the rice flour, superfine sugar, and salt in a bowl and add the eggs and coconut milk, whisking until a smooth batter forms. Alternatively, place all the ingredients in a food processor or blender and process to a smooth batter. Beat in half the coconut.

2 Heat a small amount of oil in a wide, heavy-bottom skillet. Pour in a little batter, swirling the skillet to cover the surface thinly and evenly. Cook until the crêpe is pale golden underneath.

3 Turn the crêpe and cook quickly to brown lightly on the other side.

4 Remove the crêpe from the skillet and keep hot while using the remaining batter to make a total of 8 crêpes.

5 Lightly toast the remaining coconut and reserve. Transfer the crêpes folded or loosely rolled to serving plates. Sprinkle with palm sugar and the toasted coconut and serve with slices of mango or banana.

491

crêpes with papaya & passion fruit

serves four

2 eggs

½ cup coconut milk

¾ cup milk

generous ¾ cup all-purpose flour

pinch of salt

1 tbsp superfine sugar

1 tbsp butter, melted

vegetable oil, for frying

sifted confectioners' sugar, for dusting

FILLING

2 papayas

3 passion fruit

juice of 1 lime

2 tbsp confectioners' sugar

COOK'S TIP

To enjoy these crêpes at their very best, serve this dessert as soon as it has been assembled.

1 Whisk the eggs, coconut milk, and milk together in a bowl. Sift the flour and salt into a separate bowl. Stir in the superfine sugar. Make a well in the center of the flour and gradually beat in the egg mixture to form a smooth batter. Stir in the melted butter.

2 Heat an 8–9-inch/20–23-cm nonstick skillet and brush with oil. Pour in enough batter to coat the bottom. Tip the skillet as you pour it in, so the bottom is evenly coated. Cook until browned on the underside and set on top, then turn the crêpe over and cook the other side. Place on a plate, cover with foil, and keep warm while making the remaining crêpes.

3 Peel the papayas, then cut in half and scoop out the seeds, reservir a few. Cut into chunks and place in a bowl. Cut the passion fruit in half and scoop the seeds and pulp into the bow Stir in the lime juice and confectioners' sugar. Put a little filling on one-fourth c each crêpe. Fold in half and then into fourths. Dust with sifted confectioners' sugar. Sprinkle the reserved papaya seeds over and serve at once.

coconut custard squares

serves four

1 tsp butter, melted

6 eggs

1¾ cups coconut milk

scant 1 cup brown sugar

pinch of salt

TO DECORATE

shreds of coconut

strips of lime rind

fresh fruit slices, to serve

COOK'S TIP

Keep an eye on the custard as it bakes, because if it overcooks, the texture will be spoiled. When the custard comes out of the oven, it should be barely set and still slightly wobbly in the center. It will firm up slightly as it cools.

1 Preheat the oven to 350°F/180°C. Brush the melted butter over the inside of a 7½-inch/19-cm square ovenproof dish, about 1½ inches/ 4 cm in depth.

2 Beat the eggs in a large bowl, then beat in the coconut milk, sugar, and salt.

3 Place the bowl over a pan of gently simmering water and stir with a wooden spoon for 15 minutes, or until it begins to thicken. Pour into the prepared dish.

4 Bake in the preheated oven for 20–25 minutes, or until just set. Remove the dish from the oven and let cool completely.

5 Turn the custard out of the dish and cut into squares. Serve decorated with coconut shreds and lime rind together with slices of fruit.

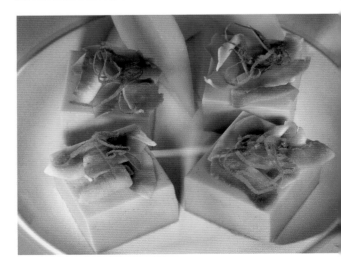

ananas in coconut milk

serves four

4 large bananas

½ cups coconut milk

2 tbsp superfine sugar

pinch of salt

1 tsp orange flower water

1 tbsp shredded fresh mint

2 tbsp cooked mung beans

fresh mint sprigs, to decorate

5 Sprinkle the toasted beans over the bananas and serve warm or cold, decorated with mint sprigs.

1 Peel the bananas and cut them into short chunks. Place in a large pan with the coconut milk, sugar, and salt.

2 Heat gently until boiling and simmer for 1 minute. Remove the pan from the heat.

3 Sprinkle the orange flower water over the banana mixture. Stir in the mint and spoon into a serving dish.

4 Place the mung beans in a heavy-bottom skillet and cook over high heat until they turn crisp and golden, shaking the skillet occasionally. Let the beans cool slightly, then crush lightly in a mortar using a pestle.

sticky rice shapes

serves four

scant 1½ cups glutinous rice

2½ cups granulated sugar

1¼ cups water

few drops of rose water or
   jasmine extract

pink and green food colorings

rose petals or jasmine flowers,
   to decorate

1 Place the rice in a bowl and add enough cold water to cover. Let soak for 3 hours or overnight.

2 Drain the rice and rinse thoroughly in cold water. Line the top part of a steamer with cheesecloth and tip the rice into it. Place over boiling water, then cover and steam for 30 minutes. Remove the rice from the steamer and let cool.

3 Heat the sugar and water gently in a pan until the sugar dissolves. Add the rose water. Bring to a boil and boil for 4–5 minutes to reduce to a thin syrup. Remove the pan from the heat.

4 Divide the rice in half and color one half pale pink, the other half pale green. Form into small balls or shapes using molds (see Cook's Tip).

5 Using 2 forks, dip the rice shapes into the syrup. Drain off the excess syrup and pile on to a dish. Decorate with rose petals or jasmine flowers and serve.

COOK'S TIP

If you prefer, the rice can be shaped in small sweet molds or dariole molds to produce small castle or turret shapes.

coconut cake with lime & ginger syrup

serves four

2 large eggs, separated

pinch of salt

½ cup superfine sugar

5 tbsp butter, melted and
    cooled

5 tbsp coconut milk

1 cup self-rising flour

½ tsp baking powder

3 tbsp dry unsweetened coconut

4 tbsp preserved ginger syrup

3 tbsp lime juice

TO DECORATE

3 pieces preserved ginger

curls of fresh coconut

finely grated lime rind

1 Cut an 11-inch/28-cm circle of parchment paper and press into a 7-inch/18-cm steamer basket to line it.

2 Whisk the egg whites with the salt in a clean, dry bowl until stiff. Gradually whisk in the sugar, 1 tablespoon at a time, whisking hard after each addition until the mixture forms stiff peaks.

3 Whisk in the yolks, then quickly stir in the butter and coconut milk. Sift the flour and baking powder over the mixture, then fold in lightly and evenly with a large metal spoon. Fold in the coconut.

4 Spoon the mixture into the line steamer basket and tuck the sp paper over the top. Place the basket over boiling water, then cover and steam for 30 minutes.

5 Transfer the cake to a plate, remove the paper, and let cool slightly. Mix the ginger syrup and lim juice together and spoon over the cake. Cut into squares and decorate with pieces of preserved ginger, curl of coconut, and lime rind.

melon & ginger crush

serves four

1 melon, about 1 lb 12 oz/800 g

6 tbsp ginger wine

3 tbsp kaffir lime juice or lime juice

crushed ice

1 lime

1 Peel, seed, and coarsely chop the melon. Place the melon in a food processor or blender with the ginger wine and lime juice.

2 Blend together on high speed until the melon mixture is smooth.

3 Place plenty of crushed ice in 4 tall glasses. Pour the melon and ginger crush over the ice.

4 Cut the lime into thin slices, then cut a slit in 4 of the slices and slip one on to the side of each glass. Add the remaining slices of lime to each glass, then serve immediately.

VARIATION

If you prefer a nonalcoholic version of this drink, simply omit the ginger wine, then top up with ginger ale in the glass. For a change of flavor, use a watermelon when they are in season. Ginger wine is available from specialty wine merchants.

ropical fruit punch

serves six

1 small ripe mango

4 tbsp lime juice

1 tsp finely grated fresh gingerroot

1 tbsp brown sugar

1¼ cups orange juice

1¼ cups pineapple juice

1¼ cups rum

crushed ice

TO DECORATE

orange slices

lime slices

pineapple slices

carambola slices

1 Peel and pit the mango and chop the flesh. Place in a food processor or blender with the lime juice, ginger, and sugar and process until smooth.

2 Add the orange and pineapple juices, then add the rum and process again for a few seconds until blended. Divide the crushed ice between 6 glasses and pour the punch over the ice.

3 Add orange and lime slices, then arrange the pineapple and carambola slices on the rim of each glass. Serve immediately.

lime & lemongrass cooler

serves four

egg white

3 tbsp superfine sugar, plus extra
     for frosting

2 limes

1 small lemongrass stem

4 ice cubes

½ cup water

4 lime slices

soda water

1 To frost the rims of the glasses,
pour a little egg white into a
saucer. Spread a small amount of sugar
out on a plate. Dip the rim of each
glass briefly into the egg white, then
into the sugar.

2 Cut each lime into 8 pieces and
coarsely chop the lemongrass.
Place the lime pieces and lemongrass
in a food processor or blender with the
sugar and ice cubes.

3 Add the water and process for a
few seconds. Try not to
overprocess, otherwise the drink will
have a bitter flavor.

4 Strain the mixture into the frosted
glasses. Add a lime slice to each
glass and top up with soda water to
taste. Serve immediately.

mango & coconut smoothie

serves four

2 large ripe mangoes

1 tbsp confectioners' sugar

generous 2 cups coconut milk

5 ice cubes

slivered, toasted coconut, to serve

1 Using a sharp knife, cut the mangoes in half and remove the pit. Peel and coarsely chop the flesh.

2 Place the chopped flesh in a food processor or blender with the sugar and process until completely smooth.

3 Add the coconut milk and ice cubes to the food processor or blender and process until frothy.

4 Pour into 4 tall glasses and sprinkle with slivered, toasted coconut to serve.

VARIATION

If you don't have slivered, toasted coconut, sprinkle with ground ginger, cinnamon, or nutmeg just before serving.

COOK'S TIP

To add a special kick to this drink, add a generous dash of white rum to the food processor or blender with the coconut milk.

thai cocktail sling

serves one

2 tbsp whiskey

1 tbsp cherry brandy

1 tbsp orange-flavored liqueur

1 tbsp lime juice

1 tsp palm sugar

dash of Angostura bitters

2 ice cubes

½ cup pineapple juice

1 small pineapple wedge

1 Place the whiskey, cherry brandy, liqueur, lime juice, sugar, and Angostura bitters in a cocktail shaker. Shake well to mix thoroughly.

2 Place the ice cubes in a large glass. Pour the cocktail mixture over the ice, then top up with the pineapple juice.

3 Cut a slit in the pineapple wedge and arrange on the edge of the glass. Serve immediately.

COOK'S TIP

If the pineapple juice is quite sweet, as Thai pineapple juice is, you may not need to add sugar. So if you're unsure, taste first. Scotch whisky is very highly regarded in Thailand, although a powerful whiskey is distilled locally—if you have the stomach for it!

INDEX